SECURE YOUR FUTURE

Your Personal Companion for Understanding Lifestyle & Financial Aspects of Retirement

Price Waterhouse LLP

IRWIN
Professional Publishing
Chicago • London • Singapore

This publication is designed to provide accurate and
authoritative information in regard to the subject matter
covered. It is sold with the understanding that neither the
author nor the publisher is engaged in rendering legal, accounting,
or other professional service. If legal advice or other expert
assistance is required, the services of a competent professional
person should be sought.

*From a Declaration of Principles jointly adopted by a Committee
of the American Bar Association and a Committee of Publishers.*

Irwin Professional Book Team
Executive editor: *Amy Hollands Gaber*
Senior marketing manager: *Tiffany Chenevert Dykes*
Project editor: *Jane Lightell*
Production supervisor: *Laurie Kersch*
Senior designer: *Heidi J. Baughman*
Assistant manager, desktop services: *Jon Christopher*
Compositor: *Weimer Graphics*
Typeface: *11/13 Times Roman*
Printer: *R. R. Donnelley & Sons Company*

■▼■ **Times Mirror**
Ⓜ **Higher Education Group**

Library of Congress Cataloging-in-Publication Data

Secure your future: your personal companion for understanding
   lifestyle & financial aspects of retirement / Price Waterhouse LLP.
        p.   cm.
   Includes index.
   ISBN 0-7863-0526-6
      1. Retirees—Finance, Personal.   2. Retirement—United States—
   Planning.   3. Retirement income—United States.   4. Estate
   planning—United States.   I. Price Waterhouse (Firm)
   HG179.S378 1996
   332.024'01—dc20   95–36618

FOREWORD

Partner-in-Charge
Retirement and Financial Education
Roger C. Hindman

Several years ago a small group of devoted Price Waterhouse personal financial planning practitioners set out to craft a book on retirement planning. In 1992 we completed our third update to our initial work, *The Price Waterhouse Retirement Planning Adviser.* Reviews of the book over the years have been most gratifying and affirmed our belief that we were on the right track to help people understand and take greater responsibility for their financial futures.

As 1993 and 1994 passed we knew, however, that we wanted to change the fundamental manner in which our audiences approach retirement and increase their understanding of planning issues. We've found that most people center their basic retirement strategy around "how much can I redirect (save) from my current income?" and "what short-term investment strategy will ensure that I don't lose any money?" We have done a major overhaul to our original work to speak more directly to this audience.

Developing life plans for ourselves and our families is not easy, especially in today's ever-changing world and work environment. For many people, daily financial challenges seem daunting enough, so long-term financial issues like retirement don't get attention until today's challenges pass. Knowing what you want for retirement and how to achieve it is often viewed as elusive, complex, and requiring a commitment to saving money that conflicts with daily cash demands.

We believe retirement planning is deceptively simple but should be viewed in the broader context of achieving lifetime personal equilibrium. To regard our retirement—with all of its attendant financial, emotional, physical, and psychological issues—as the responsibility of someone else to plan and fulfill is limiting and can become debilitating. To consider retirement as yet another of life's transitions—a transition full of possibilities, promises, and challenge that is entirely what you plan and make of it—rings a more pleasant, empowering sound for most people.

The goal of this book is to help you understand retirement as a predictable life event. Retirement will happen—the only question is when. Moreover, our goal is to help you understand what you can do today and every day hereafter to accomplish the retirement plans you establish. Implicit in this exercise is knowing the answers to three basic questions: What do you want? What do you have? What can you do to achieve what you want?

Possibility thinking is the context in which you should approach the reading of this book. There are simple choices you can make each day that can have significant effects on the accomplishment of your plan. The important thing is defining what you want. As you work with this book, remember that there is no such thing as a static, single analysis of your retirement situation. Rather, through an evolving, multifaceted process of answering penetrating questions, the type of retirement lifestyle that you want to achieve will become more vivid, realistic, and plausible. Current and future financial, emotional, physical, and mental objectives will become tightly intertwined. To solely focus on one at the expense of another will create conflict at some point.

With the worksheets in the appendix or our interactive software you can experiment with different retirement financial planning scenarios. Don't fall prey to superficial thinking that there's only one way to measure or evaluate your retirement income plan.

This book reflects the contributions and considered thought of many people within Price Waterhouse who seek definition of what they want retirement to be and mean in their own lives. This book is also based on our experiences in working with employees of America's leading companies. Through our telephone counseling, personal meetings, and workshop presentations with thousands of people each year, we have encountered first-hand a wide array of thoughts, ideas, strategies, and perspectives. In many ways, we have tried to represent or respond to these throughout the book.

My personal thanks for making this book all that it is go to Kevin McAuliffe, who made sure that we succinctly articulated essences and who labored over much of the text; Dhiren Rao, who has challenged the team in every way possible on fundamental mathematical realities in retirement planning; Carlos Marin, Freida Kavouras, Dave Voss, Doug Brown, Amie Reed, Jay Rea, Kelly Christensen, Sharon Bargetto, and Susan DeFelice, who provided varied client experiences to consider; Steve Desmond, Mark Ward, Mike Van den Akker, Paul Kiffner, and Larry Brown, who encouraged a perspective of "doing things differently"; Stan Breitbard, Dick Connell, and Jim Swenson, who provided sensitive contexts for many topics through their own transitions to retirement; Amy Hollands Gaber, who regularly encouraged the entire team to feel that we have something of real value that people will repeatedly use; and finally Clare Corbett and Helen Dennis, who have always urged us in these pursuits to connect the financial, emotional, mental, and physical aspects of planning to accomplish a fruitful, satisfying retirement.

As you read this book, keep in mind that we welcome your constructive views on how we can continue to enhance its value for readers of all ages and income levels. You can reach me through my E-mail address, rhindman@notes.pw.com@Internet

AS WE WENT TO PRESS . . .

The House and Senate tax committees were in the midst of producing specific spending cuts and tax reductions that will implement a plan for balancing the budget by 2002. The tax proposals to be considered as part of budget reconciliation consist of significant individual and corporate tax reductions, totaling as much as $245 billion over seven years, as well as sweeping spending cuts for the Medicare and Medicaid systems. Tax simplification is also a focus of the legislation. If enacted, the package will include many new provisions which may affect your tax and financial planning this year and in the future.

The final shape of any legislation is unclear of course, and it also remains an open question whether Congress will be able to agree on a package that President Clinton will sign. That said, here is a summary of the key proposals affecting individuals that lawmakers are now discussing as part of the legislative tax package.

$500 Family Tax Credit.   Individuals with adjusted gross incomes of less than $200,000 would be eligible for a tax credit of $500 for each qualifying child. The credit would be phased out for adjusted gross incomes of between $200,000 and $250,000.

Reduction of Marriage Penalty.   Married couples who file a joint return could receive a credit to reduce the so-called "marriage penalty"—the penalty that results because a married couple's tax liability will often be greater when filing a joint return than if they filed as single individuals.

American Dream Savings Accounts.   This provision would replace the present nondeductible IRAs with new "American Dream" savings accounts to which you could contribute up to $2,000 annually ($4,000 for a married couple). Although contributions would still be non-deductible, distributions would not be taxed if used for a first home, education expenses, long-term care expenses, or retirement after age 59½.

Reduction of Taxable Social Security Benefits.   The 1993 law changes which increased the maximum taxable portion of Social Security benefits to 85 percent could be repealed and replaced with a phase-out provision. This provision would lower the maximum taxable portion of Social Security benefits to 50 percent by the year 2000.

Reduction in Capital Gain Tax Rate.   The maximum tax rate for long-term capital gains would be reduced from its current 28 percent to 19.8 percent through a 50 percent capital gain exclusion. Also, the pre-1986 rules that required two dollars of long-term capital loss to offset one dollar of ordinary income would be reinstated.

Increase to Estate Tax Exemption.   The maximum estate tax exemption would increase from $600,000 per person to $700,000 in 1996, $725,000 in 1997 and $750,000 in 1998. After 1998 this exclusion, as well as the annual gift tax ($10,000) and generation-skipping ($1,000,000) exclusions would be indexed for annual changes in the inflation rate.

Losses on Sale of Personal Residences.   These losses would become deductible as capital losses.

Miscellaneous Tax Credits.   Tax credits are being considered for in-home care of elderly family members and adoption expenses.

Medical Savings Accounts.   These proposals would allow contributions to Medical Savings Accounts for health care costs. While income from the accounts would be taxable, withdrawals would be tax free if used for medical expenses for an individual, his spouse or dependents.

Five-Year Averaging and $5,000 Death Benefit Exclusion.   These provisions would be repealed for distributions in years after 1995, although existing "grandfather" provisions allowing 10- or 5-year averaging and a 20 percent capital gain rate for the pre-1974 portion of lump sum distributions would be retained. (Only persons born before 1936 can use these provisions.)

Tax Simplification and "Taxpayer Rights."   Taxpayers could be affected by several "simplification proposals" and could benefit from an expanded "Taxpayer Bill of Rights."

Some of these proposals, if enacted, would go into effect immediately, or even be retroactive to 1995. Others may not apply until 1996 or future years. Because the fate of these and other tax proposals was uncertain as we went to press, you should consult with your tax adviser to determine how they might affect your tax and retirement planning future.

CONTENTS

Foreword   v

Introduction   1

Section I   **Understanding Retirement   9**

Chapter 1   Preparing Yourself for Retirement   11

Chapter 2   Healthy Behaviors and Aging   21

Chapter 3   Choosing to Work in Retirement   31

Section II   **Retirement Financial Planning   41**

Chapter 4   Retirement Financial Planning—
An Overview   43

Chapter 5   Setting Retirement Goals   57

Chapter 6   Understanding Your Retirement Income
Sources   65

Section III   **Retirement Income Sources   79**

Chapter 7   Adding Up Your Social Security Benefits   81

Chapter 8   Maximizing Your Company Retirement
Benefits   95

Chapter 9   The How's and Why's of Saving for
Retirement   109

Chapter 10 Other Sources of Retirement Income   125

Section IV   **Investing for Retirement   139**

Chapter 11   Sound Investing for Retirement   141

Chapter 12   Investing by Lending—Cash and Fixed-Income Investments   155

Chapter 13   Investing through Ownership—Equities and Hard Assets   173

Chapter 14   The Importance of Asset Allocation   187

Chapter 15   Implementing Your Investment Strategy   197

Section V   **Withdrawing Your Retirement Assets   219**

Chapter 16   Evaluating Early Retirement Offers   221

Chapter 17   How to Evaluate Your Pension Distribution Options   229

Chapter 18   What you Need to Know about Lump Sum Distributions   239

Chapter 19   Managing Your IRA Distributions   249

Section VI   **Medical Issues   261**

Chapter 20   Medical Coverage during Retirement   263

Chapter 21   Long-Term Care and How to Pay for It   273

Section VII   **Estate Planning   283**

Chapter 22   Fundamentals of Estate Planning   285

Chapter 23   Making Sense of Estate Taxes   301

Chapter 24   Understanding Estate Administration and Probate   317

Epilogue   Not All Financial Plans Are Created Equal   323

Appendix   Retirement Planning Worksheets   329

Index   334

INTRODUCTION

What does retirement mean to you? Liberation from work and other burdens? The opportunity to have fewer demands placed on your time? Financial freedom? The years you spend in retirement can be what you want them to be, but only if you understand the emerging realities and changing options and if you can adapt and plan effectively.

There are two ways to plan for retirement. One is to understand what you want and what you have, and then set out to close any gaps between the two. The other is to accept whatever happens when retirement is thrust upon you. While some may claim that the latter is no plan at all, it is in fact a plan—a default plan whose results stem from the conscious actions that you take every day.

This book does not attempt to judge what is right or wrong for retirement. Rather, it is meant to elicit an understanding of what you are doing today and the consequences that those actions will create tomorrow. This book is about effective retirement planning in a changing financial world. And make no mistake—the world *is* changing. Much of our conventional thinking needs to be challenged! What you end up doing, how much money you'll need, and how long you'll have during retirement will have little connection to what earlier generations experienced. So take hold of your retirement vision by forgetting any preconceived notions you've had about those years.

Table I–1	Retirement Planning—The New Order
1940s	**1990s**
Retirement lasted for 5 to 10 years.	Retirement could last 30 years or more.
Pension and Social Security provided for most needs.	Most income will come from savings and investments.
Inflation was not much of a factor since retirement was a short time period.	Increased life expectancy makes long-term inflation much more of a concern.
Retirees could live off of the income from investments.	Many will spend most if not all of their principal.
Retirees passed on their estate to their children.	Retirees could consume the majority of their estate.
Long-term care was not a factor.	The chance of entering a nursing home after 85 is over 30 percent.

THE EMERGING REALITIES

Retirement planning in the 1990s is often plagued by obsolete thinking, much of which we spell out in the pages that follow. Although some assumptions may have once been true, economic, social, and demographic changes have left conventional wisdom outmoded at best and dangerous at worse. And, because of this new order, financial aspects of retirement are certainly not as simple as they used to be, as Table I–1 shows. These days, even if you have a plan in place, failing to reexamine and revise your plan in light of changing circumstances can be worse than having no plan at all. Let's take a closer look at this new order.

Figure I–1

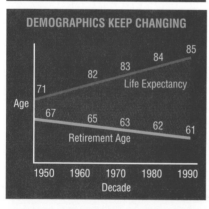

THE OLD AND THE NEW

In the 1940s and 1950s, planning for retirement wasn't a major undertaking. The average life expectancy in the 1940s was roughly age 69. Now the average life span is around 78 years, but that fact can play a statistical trick on your retirement planning because if you make it to 65,

Figure I–2

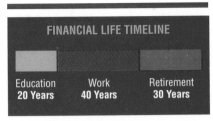

FINANCIAL LIFE TIMELINE

Education	Work	Retirement
20 Years	**40 Years**	**30 Years**

chances are you're going to live past 78. Today men who live to 65 will probably see 80. Women who achieve retirement age will likely live to almost 85.

People need to become comfortable with the notion of retirement as a certain event. Maybe our grandparents and even some of our parents didn't have the opportunity to enjoy a long retirement, but given increasing life expectancies and continuing medical advances, you should be thinking, *"When* I retire," not *"If* I retire." Today's realities mean that you'll probably spend over one-quarter of your life in retirement. Put another way, almost everyone should plan their retirement finances to get themselves through age 90.

THE GOLD WATCH IS COMING SOONER

In the past, no one thought of retiring before age 65. Then two things happened: The era of corporate downsizing came and many baby boomers started asking, **"How can I get more out of life?"** Throughout the late 1980s and early 1990s, more and more companies offered employees incentives to retire early: a boost in their pension payments or a large severance check. We've seen the average retirement age fall to the point that now it's not unusual to hear of retiring at 60 or even 58. For many baby boomers, "55 and fly" has become a personal credo.

With earlier retirement goals and increasing life expectancies, additional savings will be needed to cover basic living expenses, medical costs, and inflation. A monthly pension and Social Security check just won't be the answer for most.

Table I–2	The Pension Funding Challenge	
	Retirement Years	**Amount Needed to Pay a $25,000 Pension***
1940s	5	$110,000
1990s	25	$300,000

*Assumes a 7 percent rate of return.

Why? As Table I–2 shows, it's becoming very costly for companies to pay these pension benefits over long retirement periods. And Social Security is likely to face a significant funding shortfall once all of the baby boomers reach the age at which they can begin to draw Social Security and Medicare benefits. With these new workforce realities, it becomes more important than ever for you to take responsibility for your retirement. It is more critical than ever to understand your retirement goals, where your retirement income will come from, and how much it will be. While pensions and Social Security may provide some retirement income security, they're not likely to provide the total standard of living you want.

WE WANT IT ALL!

The stereotypical retirement picture of a generation gone by was sitting on a porch in a rocking chair. Now it's an airplane headed for Europe, an RV roaming the states, or a round of golf at one of Pete Dye's finest. People used to view retirement as a time when their life slowed down and their spending needs decreased substantially. Now you could be looking at 15 to 20 years during which you'll likely be as active as when you were working, and your need for disposable income may hardly decline at all. Of course, at some point you'll begin to slow down, but then you'll have to prepare for the challenges—and expenses—of aging. Table I–3 compares retirement expenditures in the 1940s and 1990s.

Table I–3	Expenditures During Retirement	
	1940s	**1990s**
Income taxes	Decreased	May increase
Long-term care	Not a consideration	Increased life expectancy requires additional funds
Home mortgage	Paid off	Continuing
Health insurance premiums	Company-paid	Employee-paid or shared with company
Gifts	Level	May increase for estate tax reasons
Travel and entertainment	Level or decreased	Level or increased

ROLL WITH THE PUNCHES

As you progress through your career, chances are you will earn more money as

Figure I–3

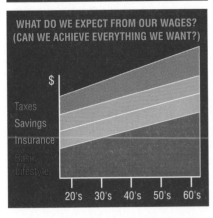

WHAT DO WE EXPECT FROM OUR WAGES?
(CAN WE ACHIEVE EVERYTHING WE WANT?)

$

Taxes

Savings

Insurance

Basic
Lifestyle

20's   30's   40's   50's   60's

you develop additional skills and take on more responsibility. But what do people do with their increased earnings? Of course, Uncle Sam takes his share. But then what? Let's look at the choices.

Your financial planner would hope you would save the money and use it to fund a goal like your children's education or retirement, or to pay off some high-interest debt. But what typically happens? People improve their lifestyle. They buy a bigger home and a nicer car, take better vacations, eat out more often, and upgrade their wardrobe. Often, the urge to get that new set of golf clubs that promises 10 more yards is just too great!

Look at Figure I–3. Notice that as wages increase over time, so do the lifestyle expenses and taxes, yet the amount saved typically remains constant. The sad truth? Accordingly to a Merrill Lynch study, the average American saves about 4.5 percent of his income, or around 35 percent of the estimated amount needed at age 65 to maintain his standard of living. Financial planners say on average Americans will need to save about 13 to 15 percent of their income to achieve their retirement goals. (See Table I–4.)

Table I–4	Retirement Savings Rates Needed by Age Group for Married Couple with Household Income of $75,000 Per Year	
Age	**Rate With Traditional Pension**	**Rate Without Traditional Pension**
25–34	1.2%	4.0%
35–44	8.3	14.1
45–55	20.1	25.1
55–64	19.1	24.2

Source: *The Merrill Lynch Baby Boom Retirement Index*, April 1995 (Prepared by Dr. Douglas Bernheim, Stanford University).

Excuses, Excuses

A recent Towers Perrin survey of 1,000 U.S. employees revealed that 77 percent acknowledge they have "not done enough" or have done "hardly any"

Table I–5	Excuses, Excuses

People in their 20s and 30s

- "I'm too young to worry about retirement."
- "I have more important goals: buying my first home and car, paying off student loans, etc."
- "How can I think of something so far in the future when I can barely even make ends meet!"

People in their 40s and early 50s

- "As soon as my last child graduates . . . "
- "Once I pay off the mortgage . . . "
- "I'm going to stay with this company so I know they will take care of me when I retire."
- "I know if I save really hard those last five years, I'll be just fine."

People over 55

- "I have enough for 10 good years of retirement—that's a lot longer than my parents were retired."
- "I don't need any planning. I'll have my pension and Social Security and that's more than enough."
- "Sixty-five is still a long way off."
- "I'm still too young to think about retirement!"

planning for retirement. As Table I–5 suggests, people have many different reasons why they don't need to plan for their retirement. If any of these sound familiar, we hope you'll cast them aside and open your mind to the new way of thinking this book suggests. A *longer* and *fuller* retirement means you need to save for a bigger nest egg. After all, an active retirement costs more than sitting in a rocking chair. The answer: Get a grip on it and start planning for your retirement today!

MAKE IT YOUR PLAN

With all these myths and new realities, planning for your retirement sounds like a daunting task. Yet it doesn't have to be overwhelming or unpleasant. It doesn't have to take a lot of time and you don't need to be a financial expert. What you do need is some motivation, some basic knowledge, and the good sense to avoid the big mistakes.

What Should *You* Do?

Throughout this book, we will refer to retirement planning as a process, not an event. And that process can be reduced to four basic but very important steps: **analyze, refine, implement, and monitor.**

Analyze.   The first step is to *analyze* your situation. That is, do a *capital sufficiency analysis*—fancy words to describe "running the numbers" to find out what you need to do in the context of your retirement income goals and what resources you have.

Refine.   Like most of us, you probably won't get the perfect answer on the first pass, so you'll need to *refine* your assumptions. Maybe it means saving a little more each year, changing your investment strategy, working part-time during retirement, or retiring later.

Implement.   To achieve your plan you must take action. Otherwise, your plan is just a hollow shell.

Monitor.   The best financial plan is of little use if you don't monitor it, make adjustments where needed, and continue to implement it. In reality, if you are 15 years from retirement, you likely have one plan that will be refined 15 times.

That's where this book comes into your planning. We'll show you how to analyze your situation and to refine your assumptions. We'll explain how it all works: Social Security, company retirement plans, IRAs, investments, estate planning, life insurance, taxes, Medicare, long-term care insurance, and many other topics. And, most importantly, we'll show you how to implement your plan for long-term success.

But you can't stop there! Through the years you'll need to monitor and modify your plan as new tax laws are passed, new investment choices are offered, and your personal situation changes. Remember, retirement planning is an ongoing process that takes time before, during, and after retirement. Sure, there are many steps involved, and the hardest step is often just getting started. But a plan that's not refined and monitored on an ongoing basis is like having no plan at all.

Don't forget, once you get there, retirement means more than just prudently managing your finances. What are you going to do? How are you going to use your time? The relationships with your family, friends, and relatives probably won't be the same. As time passes, health and wellness challenges will grow. While our book is primarily about finances, we'll devote some time to these lifestyle issues, because they're as equally as important as the financial issues over the long run.

We hope you find this book motivating and educational. We hope that it encourages you to think positively about the enormous potential you have **TODAY** to influence the quality of your retirement years. And finally, we hope it encourages you to take flight, to start the journey. Right now you're boarding the flight that will take you to your life's destinations. Read on, and happy flying!

How to Use this Book

Note

This book begins with a discussion of some new ways to think about the nonfinancial aspects of retirement. Chapters 1 through 3 discuss your identity as a retiree, how to make the adjustment from your working years, and whether you might want to consider continuing to work. We also look at the health and wellness aspects of aging. Read it to get some insights on your future as a retiree!

Chapters 4 through 6 are your roadmap for developing your own retirement plan. We outline in detail the process of planning your financial future, how to set retirement goals, and how to tell whether you're on track to reach them. We'll also consider the "levers" that drive your ability to meet your goal, such as investment rate of return, inflation, and your time horizon. We suggest reading these chapters in their entirety to get a complete picture of the retirement planning process.

The next section, Chapters 7 through 10, offers a more detailed look at your retirement income sources, such as Social Security, pensions, and company savings plans. These chapters can be read in conjunction with Chapters 4 through 6 or they can stand alone.

Chapters 11 through 15 discuss how to design and implement an investment program to reach your retirement goals and long-term investment objectives. We'll discuss fundamentals of investing, deal with investment vehicles, and address how to work with investment advisors. Read this for specific information on your long-term investment strategy.

The remainder of our book deals with the more technical side of retirement planning: distributions from retirement plans, income tax issues, risk management and estate planning. These topics may be important today for reasons other than retirement, and they become increasingly more important as you leave the workforce. Here we've tried to be as comprehensive as possible for there are many traps that can snare the unwary, particularly in the income tax treatment of your retirement distributions. Thus, we strongly recommend that you consult with a competent financial advisor as you elect and implement retirement plan distributions.

UNDERSTANDING RETIREMENT

CHAPTER 1   Preparing Yourself for Retirement   11

CHAPTER 2   Healthy Behaviors and Aging   21

CHAPTER 3   Choosing to Work in Retirement   31

These chapters were prepared with the assistance of Helen Dennis, a specialist in aging, employment, and retirement. Her contributions and keen insights on the nonfinancial aspects of retirement are greatly appreciated.

PREPARING YOURSELF FOR RETIREMENT

In this chapter, we answer some basic questions about your new identity as a retiree. Read it to learn more about

- Responding to the psychological changes retirement brings.
- Transitioning from work to retirement.
- Roles and activities that can be important during retirement.
- New approaches to your interpersonal relationships.

By some standards, having enough money is the key to a successful retirement. But bank accounts and investment portfolios are only part of the story. In fact, if you only consider your finances, you may find your retirement experience missing something: a reason to get up in the morning, having something to do, and feeling good about yourself and the world around you.

While this book is primarily about financial planning for retirement, preparing for retirement is not only about numbers. Being rich in worldly possessions and poor in spirit can make for a long, lonely retirement. Coming to grips with the psychological and social changes that you're likely to experience is equally important. Learning about leaving a full-time job, having more time on your hands, and adapting to new aspects of relationships are all notions to ponder as you enter this new phase of life.

Knowing about these changes—and why they occur—can help prepare you to deal with them. Remember, although change is often difficult, it presents opportunities for you to develop into what you want to become.

Perhaps the single most important idea in this chapter is that *you* are in charge. This positive attitude, along with greater self-awareness and knowledge, is a winning combination to create the retirement experience you want. Remember, you have the human capacity to be vital, and this vitality does not have to diminish with years. Vitality has much to do with what choices you make, whether you apply your abilities, and how you respond to change in creating your retirement life.

CHANGE IS PART OF THE RETIREMENT PROCESS

Years ago, many believed that retirement was a period of stability and leisure. Our picture of a retiree was someone passively watching the world go by. Today we know this simply isn't true.

Change is part of every major life phase—retirement is no exception. Noted sociologist Robert Atchley put forth the theory that there are four predictable phases or changes that people go through during retirement. Think of yourself in any one of these phases:

Honeymoon phase. You love the new freedom of retirement. You're doing all the things you never had time to do while working. You're very busy with family, friends, activities, travel, and more. In fact, it's the most exciting time in your life.

Disenchantment. You're in a period of letdown and disappointment. You may have few alternatives because of little money or poor health. If your honeymoon phase was unrealistic, you might come crashing into the disenchantment phase.

Reorientation. You are pulling yourself together, with realistic goals and alternatives that are meaningful and achievable.

Stability. You've mastered the retirement role. You know what's important and how to achieve it and do it. You have learned to manage change and make it work for you.

Actually, you may not experience all of these phases. You may stay in the honeymoon phase for the next 30 years, or you may move from honeymoon to disenchantment, back to honeymoon, and end up in stability. The point is: **RETIREMENT, LIKE ALL OTHER LIFE STAGES BEFORE, IS A DYNAMIC PERIOD OF LIFE WHERE CHANGE IS CERTAIN TO OCCUR.**

THE TRANSITION FROM WORK TO RETIREMENT

Most likely, work currently plays a central role in your life. At a minimum, it provides six major functions:

Financial stability. Work is probably the major source of your income.

Time management. Work provides structure so that your life has some order.

Sense of purpose. Work provides meaning and direction.

Social life. Work brings you in contact with people.

Status. Work often provides status in the community. People may identify who you are by what you do.

Source of power and influence. Work provides the environment for you to create and influence policies, programs, products, and people.

To get a sense of how important work is in your life, see which of the following statements best describes you:

- I place great importance on my work, particularly during the time I spend working.
- I think about my work most of my waking hours, even when I am home.
- I feel I am indispensable to my company.
- I place my work before family, friends, and leisure time.

What Do You Love about Your Job?

Tip

One way to examine the value of your current work experience is to identify the "goodies," that is, what has kept you at your company all these years? Here is a list of what well over 3,000 preretirees said kept them at their jobs. Some motives may be familiar to you.

- Feeling challenged by my work.
- Liking the people I work with.
- The opportunity to learn.
- Traveling for the company.

- Working as a team member.
- Helping the company grow.
- Being part of a respected company.
- The income and benefits.
- Influencing the company's direction and success.

You are in a position to decide which of the "goodies" from work you want to carry over into retirement. Examine the list, decide which of these you will *miss most* when you retire, and begin to think about what you will do to replace them.

If you answered yes to most of these questions, you may have high work identification. In fact, work may be one of your strongest sources of joy and gratification. If work is central to your life, use that information as a planning tool.

You can use your present work values to help identify what you want to do in retirement. Remember, people generally do not go through major personality changes in retirement. In fact, their values remain rather consistent.

But, even with this awareness of the value of work, you may find the transition to retirement difficult. Why? Here are four reasons.

First, retirement is a new experience. As a working adult, the standards and expectations are set for you by your boss, your peers, and your environment. Success is easily measured. You know when you're doing a good job and when you're not. You also know when you're on the right track and what to expect. There are *external factors* that determine your expectations, accomplishments, and effectiveness.

By contrast, the retirement experience is *motivated from within*. You must develop your own mission, goals, and objectives. You develop your own strategies and meaningful activities. You become the judge and the jury. There are few external reference points or guide posts. In a sense, you are the CEO of your own retirement.

Second, retirement may move you to the "unknown." You've never done this before, you've had no practice, coaching, mentoring, or trial run in this area. You may not have identified what you're retiring to. You may have been too busy working to think about it.

Third, you may feel a sense of loss. You may be concerned about losing friends from work, suddenly lacking a sense of purpose, or not being part of something larger than yourself. Many retirees find the potential loss of power, influence, and prestige difficult to acknowledge and even more difficult to discuss. You may find the retirement transition particularly complex if you are unaware of the possible losses and have no plan to compensate for them.

Fourth, you may be surprised with an early retirement offer. The thought of retirement may be a shock. You may never have thought of yourself as old enough to retire. In fact, you may have envisioned yourself working for your company for another 3 to 10 years. In making the early retirement decision, the first step is to understand whether you can afford to retire. After that, consider additional questions. For example, do you *want* to retire? What will you do with this newly found time? If you really don't want to retire, what are the consequences of turning down the retirement offer? Will your department be phased out? Will your job change? Will you be demoted? Will your position be eliminated in the next round of downsizings? Will the next early retirement package offer you less? In addition to knowing whether you can afford to retire, these other questions should be asked. What is unsettling is that the answers are often based on your best guess at the moment, not on a column of figures that easily add up to the right answer.

A NEW IDENTITY IN RETIREMENT

You may have met people who've been retired for years and continue to identify exclusively with their former profession or job: "I'm a retired engineer." "I'm a retired salesperson." This response is understandable. However, the question remains, what additional roles or activities are important to these people now in retirement?

Do You Want a Second Career?

Tip

Let us tell you about an interesting study by Caroline Bird. She placed a series of questions in *Modern Maturity* magazine (published by the American Association of Retired Persons (AARP)) which has 27 million subscribers. Expecting a response from 2,000 to 3,000 people, she asked, "What's your second career?" But a staggering 36,000 retired people answered her question.

Why did they continue working? Some of their answers may make you reconsider work:

- Work provided additional sources of income.
- It organized their daily life.
- It was good for their mental health.
- It improved their family life and relationships.
- Work gave them a feeling of being needed and a sense of satisfaction.
- The nature of the work was enjoyable.

Source: Caroline Bird, "What's Your Second Career?" 31, No. 1, *Modern Maturity*, page 30.

American society has been criticized throughout the world because we do not have clear roles for retirees. This may be a curse or, more likely, a blessing. By having loosely defined roles in retirement, you have choices. There is no typical U.S. pensioner. You truly have the opportunity to choose and even create the role you want in retirement.

Here are four roles that you might relate to. Consider some or all of them.

- **Consider work.** Why would you want to work in retirement? Isn't work what you wanted to get away from? We'll answer this question in Chapter 3, but keep in mind that part-time work in particular has become the choice of many retirees. Many employers seek part-time employees because they don't need to provide benefits and can gain a great deal from the experience and skills of seasoned workers. Working for someone else is not the only approach. Becoming a self-employed entrepreneur is gaining popularity. You might turn a hobby into a money-making venture, do consulting, or venture into something completely new.

- **Become a student.** It's never too late to learn. In fact, retirees are moving into classrooms in large numbers, pursuing degrees or just taking courses out of personal interest. Elderhostel, a successful Boston-based organization has signed up close to 250,000 students age 60 and up in classes ranging from "Japanese Brush Painting" to "Prehistoric Art of Southwest New Mexico." Colleges and cultural institutions in 52 countries host these week-long classes, even while regular classes are still in session. The average cost comes to a modest $350, including tuition, room, and board. To register, call (617) 426-8056 or write to Elderhostel, 75 Federal Street, Boston, Massachusetts 02110 for more information.

- **Become a volunteer.** There are ways to apply what you love to do as a volunteer. Approximately 25 percent of men and women 55 years and older volunteer. Their combined efforts are equivalent to 500,000 full-time workers. To be part of this growing, vibrant segment of our society, you will have to reach out to create that volunteer opportunity. The need for effective volunteers is greater than ever. Contact your local Volunteer Action Center for a list of positions available in your community. Remember, volunteering can be part-time, be on your own terms, and give additional meaning to your retirement years.

- **Don't forget leisure.** Leisure may have the strongest appeal for you. There are hundreds of ways to spend leisure time: travel, crafts, carpentry, fishing, golf, movies, reading. The list is endless. What do you enjoy? What new leisure activities do you want to try? White-water rafting? Going on an archaeological dig? Gardening? This is your opportunity for fun and enjoyment. As the Nike commercial boldly proclaims: "Just do it!"

But do it with a bit of thought. Do you want to spend 100 percent of your time in one or two leisure activities? If you think of retirement as a week full of Saturdays, your retirement experience may turn shallow or boring. So think about how much time you'll be allocating to leisure and the type of activities that bring meaning and pleasure to your life.

Also, think about whether you want to spend your leisure time alone or with your spouse, family, or friends? There's no right answer. It's important to decide how much of your leisure time you want to spend in solo activities and how much time with someone else. You might want to define who that someone is.

RELATIONSHIPS IN RETIREMENT

Although most people retire as one-half of a couple, a large segment of retirees are single, divorced, or widowed. Members of the latter group in particular should examine their current relationships, plan how to create new ones, keep up with old ones, and stay connected. Specialized retirement programs have been developed for single people, specifically women. For information on *Retirement Planning for Women*, write to PREP, Long Island University, Southhampton, New York 11968.

And Then There's My Spouse

Oddly enough, marital relationships are not usually addressed in many corporate sponsored retirement planning programs—for lots of reasons. First, there never seems to be enough time to discuss this issue. Second, marriage is a personal subject, and having an outsider discussing your relationship appears intrusive. Third, couples who have been doing fine for the past 30 to 40 years may see no reason to discuss their relationships. Well, these are weak excuses. Remember, retirement is a time of change, and that includes changes in your marital relationship.

Where do you begin in this reexamination? Look at your need for privacy and your current work environment. Most likely, you leave your home daily to go to work. You go to a cubicle, office, suite, or desk—a space that's yours. When you retire, you give up that space. In moving home, many retirees take over their house as though it belonged to them, exclusively, just like the office.

You most likely have heard stand-up comedians talk about the typical husband who retires and takes over his wife's kitchen. He reorganizes all the shelves, cuts coupons, writes a daily grocery list (whether it's needed or not), buys in large quantities to save money, and even alphabetizes the items in the refrigerator! He cannot believe that his wife has managed all these years without him. What he may not realize is that he and his wife have a need for some private physical space.

Ask yourself, do I need some area that is just for me? Look at your home and determine what space can be allocated as yours. Perhaps an area can be converted into a den, computer room, wood shop, library, or art studio.

Men, let's not forget about your wife. She has privacy needs too. So wives, assess the space you need and speak up. Now comes the most important part. TALK! Yes, you need to discuss this with one another.

Aside from physical space, ask yourself if you need some private "mental space." Do you need to do some things alone without accounting for every minute of your time? Comedians have gotten many miles from monologues where the husband asks the wife, "Where are you going, when are you coming back, who are you going to see, and call me as soon as you get there."

Casey Stengel summed it up well when he said to his wife, "I married you for better or worse, but not for lunch." The point is, examine your own needs for private time, independence, and time away from the home. This applies to both husbands and wives.

Also try to remember why you married each other. In the first few years of marriage, you never had enough time to be together. Well, here's your chance. Rediscover your spouse. But having a splendid marital relationship in retirement doesn't require spending 100 percent of your time together. Each of you is an individual. In retirement, think of this relationship as a wonderful new merger, not a takeover!

Also consider helping each other with household tasks, giving mutual support, and sharing exciting activities. At the same time, give each other the "space" that is needed to be a whole person. The more complete you are as an individual, the more there is to share with one another.

With some thinking and planning about your move from work to retirement, your new roles, and your redefined relationships, you're ready to move to the path of financial planning.

A final point: To maximize your long-term retirement experience, a healthy lifestyle becomes increasingly important. Be an informed consumer of health and lifestyle information. Write a list of health behaviors you would like to achieve. Then apply what you know about nutrition, exercise, smoking, and the importance of both physical and mental activity to your own life. The journey and ultimate destination will be even better! You can learn more about healthy behaviors by reading Chapter 2, "Healthy Behaviors and Aging."

HEALTHY BEHAVIORS AND AGING

In this chapter, we discuss the effects of aging and your overall health and wellness during retirement. Read it to understand:

- Effects of aging.
- Actions to slow the aging process.
- Benefits of exercise and sound nutrition.
- Obstacles to health behaviors.

A chapter on health and wellness may seem unimportant in a financial planning book. But remember, to know if your retirement assets will be sufficient to reach your goals, you must know how long retirement will last! Is it five years? Ten years? Twenty years? Of course, no one can answer this with any certainty. But a fundamental understanding of what influences longevity and fitness is critical to making knowledgeable decisions on the adequacy of retirement resources. No matter how good your financial plan, you need a healthy, physically fit body and mentally active mind to enjoy your retirement!

THE AGING PROCESS

Your overall health and wellness is a combination of many factors, both physical and mental. For purposes of our discussion, health will be defined as being the best you can be or performing at your highest level during your retirement years. We will focus on two recurring themes:

- What can you expect to happen to your body as you age?
- How can you slow the normal aging process? How can you bring about a more active, vital life?

Of course, aging is an inevitable process for all of us, but it's one of those "bad news–good news" stories. The good news is that there is much we can do to slow it down. Researchers in the field of aging have found that:

- We are living longer and healthier lives than ever before.
- Healthy behaviors have been proven to slow down the normal aging process.
- The potential for fitness and vigor throughout one's lifetime is great.
- Intellectual growth and mental sharpness are evident in one's 70s and 80s.

Genetics and Lifestyle

Although aging is inevitable and universal, it is important to recognize that we all age differently—at different rates—because of our unique genetic makeup and lifestyles. Some people argue that up to 60 percent of how we age is genetic and 40 percent is due to lifestyle. Well, we cannot do much about our genes, but we do have some influence over our lifestyles.

Aging versus Disease

Note

Before going farther, it's important to make the distinction between normal aging and disease. Normal aging is universal. Aristotle (384–322 BC) said it well: "Aging is not disease because it is not contrary to nature."

Aging is a gradual process since we age one cell at a time. Disease is quite different. It is not universal and it is not as gradual. Here's an example how aging and disease can be confused.

You wake up one morning and try to get out of bed. Suddenly you get severe pain in your knee and can't move it. (Yesterday your knee was perfectly fine.) You say to your spouse, "Honey, I must be getting old." You may be getting older, but the pain in your leg isn't necessarily related to your age. The acute pain in your leg would suggest a more focused physical condition (a strain perhaps) rather than aging. Remember, aging is a gradual and universal process.

What Can You Expect from the Normal Aging Process?

As we age, many of the following changes occur in our bodies, but with the proper actions, we can significantly slow the process.

Change in the ratio of lean (muscle) tissue and fat tissue. As you age, your fat tissue increases, while your muscle tissue decreases. One reason for this is that your metabolism slows down with age.

Here's the bad news. If you don't change your caloric intake or activity level, on the average, you'll gain about one pound a year between ages 35 and 65. Yes, that is a possible 30-pound weight gain, depending on your height, frame, and so on.

More bad news. Fat tissue redistributes with age. For example, it often seems to disappear from just under the skin in your face and "mysteriously" appears in other areas such as your hips and waist. Yes, this is part of normal aging. **THE GOOD NEWS IS THAT YOU CAN SLOW DOWN THIS PROCESS!**

Action—To decrease your fat tissue and increase your lean muscle tissue, as well as maintain your body weight, eat fewer calories and increase your level of activity through exercise. (Of course, before adopting any exercise program, you should consult your physician.)

Why Do We Age?

Note

There are more than 100 theories of aging. Here are brief descriptions of just a few of them.

- **Hayflick genetic theory.** This theory states that a genetic "clock" is programmed in our cells. This clock controls how we age and how long we will live. It assumes that our life span is predetermined on a cellular level through heredity.

- **Wear-and-tear theory.** This theory states that as we use our bodies over time, the various systems wear out—somewhat like the tires of a car. It also suggests that our bodies are unable to repair themselves. The wear-and-tear theory has been less accepted recently because it is now known that our bodies can repair and heal at almost any age. And we can improve our physical condition through activities such as exercise.

- **Free radical theory.** This is one of the more widely accepted theories of aging. It states that cell membranes (remember, aging occurs on the cellular level) are damaged by something called free radicals, which are oxidized chemical components.

These free radicals latch on to a normal cell and cause irreversible damage. An example of a free radical is ozone. The body has its own natural defenses against actions of these free radicals. Additionally, antioxidants such as vitamins C and E seem to interfere with their damaging effects. According to researchers, there appears to be sufficient evidence that free radical damage does accumulate with aging. Whether it's the single cause of aging needs to be proven.

- **Immunological theory.** This theory deals with the immune system. When working properly, our immune system protects us from viruses, bacteria, and other foreign substances. The thymus gland, located at the base of the neck, regulates this important system. It is largest during the teenage years, then begins to shrink, and is barely detectable after age 50. As we age and the thymus gland shrinks, the immune system becomes less efficient. This decline in function may be responsible for older adults' susceptibility to infections and diseases.

Skin changes. We also know that skin becomes less elastic with age. You may recall your first recognition of aging when you looked in the mirror and saw a little wrinkle. The wrinkle was caused by two factors: the protective lining of fat under the skin decreased and your skin was less elastic. Since the skin does not shrink, a wrinkle formed. Too much sunlight over a period of years causes the skin to become even less elastic.

Action—To maintain skin elasticity, stay out of the sun and/or use sunscreen. Some people also choose cosmetic surgery, which of course isn't for everyone.

Changes in bone or musculoskeletal system. Bones tend to lose calcium with age. The common result is loss of bone mass and height. An abnormally large loss of calcium can indicate osteoporosis, a bone disease characterized by an increased risk of fractures. This is a particular problem for women.

Action—To retain bone mass, eat foods that are rich in calcium, take a calcium supplement (after consulting with your physician), and adopt an exercise program that creates impact, such as walking or jogging. The recommended daily calcium supplement is 1,000 mg for premenopausal women and 1,000 to 1,500 mg for postmenopausal women. Estrogen supplementation has also been effective in maintaining bone mass in women although some believe it may also increase cancer risk. Consult your physician.

Changes in vision. Changes in vision typically begin during our 40s. The pupil decreases in size, allowing less light to reach the retina. Also, the lens of the eye becomes less elastic, causing farsightedness, meaning it's hard to focus on things that are close. You may already be reading the newspaper with an outstretched arm!

Action—You guessed it! Glasses.

Changes in hearing. It is normal for hearing to begin changing in our 50s. The loss is so gradual that many people don't notice it. High-pitched sounds and consonant sounds of *z*, *s*, *g*, *f*, and *t* often become hard to hear. Also, with age, background noise seems to interfere with hearing.

Action—You guessed it again. A hearing aid and selecting a more quiet restaurant. But after getting a hearing aid, you may not want to sit next to the band at the next wedding reception you attend.

Changes in reaction time. Reaction time slows down with age. This begins in the 20s at a very slow rate. Reaction time is related to many of our daily activities such as driving, playing tennis, typing, and even dodging a car or falling object.

Action—To improve your reaction time, practice reacting quickly. Reaction time can be improved at almost any age. That's very good news.

Changes in the digestive system. With age, there are lower secretions of acid in the small intestines. This means that nutrients are not absorbed as well as when we were younger.

Action—Eat well! Have a nutritious diet that is low in fat and high in complex carbohydrates. The latter refers to anything that grows in the ground such as fruits, vegetables, and whole grains. At 21, you could get by with Twinkies, a soda, and chips—at least for a while. This diet does not work as well in your 50s.

Changes in the connective tissues. With age, cells in the connective tissue tend to lose water. The problem is dehydration. Connective tissue is located in every joint in our body, and is vital for flexibility and mobility.

Action—If the problem is dehydration, what do you think is the action? Most people say drink more water. Good answer, but not the right one. Exercise, particularly exercises that increase flexibility and range of motion, help the cells retain water. And yes, with exercise we'll still be able to play the piano, enter data in our computers, pick up a screw from under our RV, and cross the street with some agility before the light turns red!

Changes in bone growth. With age, bones tend to calcify. For example, hips tend to "grow" a bit, the bone at the top of the spine gets larger, and earlobes (which aren't exactly bones) tend to get longer. And here's the best—the nose tends to grow a bit.

Action—None known.

Here's a familiar picture of aging: someone with wrinkles, a long nose, long earlobes, large hips, short neck, and possibly a hearing device and glasses! But even if you experience these changes, must they affect your productivity, creativity, or what you want to do with your life? The answer is, *only if you let them!* These changes have no impact on intellectual capacity, performance, or abilities.

THE VALUE OF EXERCISE

Twenty-five years ago, experts believed that physical conditioning after age 40 had little effect. And after age 60, experts assumed that exercise produced no observable improvement in functioning. In fact, people in these age categories were considered "untrainable." In 1967, Dr. Herbert A. deVries, professor emeritus of exercise sciences at the University of Southern California, challenged this notion.

Studying men and women in the Leisure World community in Laguna Hills, California, deVries found that healthy older people who engaged in appropriate physical exercise benefited as much as younger people. His results have been corroborated by investigators all over the world.

More recent studies show that men in their 80s can still build muscle mass, which means they can get stronger. Frail older people have been found to benefit from training designed to increase their strength. With strength training programs, nursing home residents averaging age 87 increased their walking speed and ability to climb stairs. Some no longer needed walkers and used canes instead.

Master senior athletes continue to perform well between ages 40 and 65. And athletes who continue to train are competitive in their 70s, 80s, and even 90s.

Exercise is valuable at any age, but it's probably more important the older people get. Different kinds of exercises have different purposes. Here are three examples:

- Range of motion exercises help to maintain a joint's complete movement.
- Strengthening exercises help a muscle contract and do work.
- Endurance or aerobic exercises improve the body's capacity to use oxygen.

Exercise Is Effective in Slowing Down the Aging Process!

Exercise decreases body fat as well as heart rate and blood pressure. It improves endurance with increased circulation. It increases strength, building up muscle. And it increases flexibility. Some studies show that exercise can even decrease certain kinds of depression, particularly if the individual exercises with someone.

But not everyone likes to exercise. You may be one of them. The following quote attributed to James Thurber may apply to you. "Oh exercise! When I feel like exercising, I lie down until the feeling goes away."

In general, people do not continue a particular physical activity that they don't like. The key is finding an exercise that's enjoyable and fun. Then go do it!

NUTRITION

Research has long confirmed the link between nutrition and health. The following are Dietary Guidelines for Americans published by the U.S. Department of Agriculture and the U.S. Department of Health and Human Services:

- Eat a well balanced diet.
- Maintain healthy weight.
- Choose a diet that's low in fat, saturated fat, and cholesterol. It's recommended that 30 percent or less of your calories per day come from fat.
- Choose a diet with plenty of vegetables, fruits, and grain products.
- Use sugars in moderation.
- Use salt and sodium in moderation.
- If you drink alcoholic beverages, do it in moderation.

Nutrition

Note According to nutritionists' guidelines, older adults need the following:

- Breads, cereals, rice, and pasta: 6 to 11 servings a day.
- Vegetables: 3 to 4 servings a day.
- Fruits and fruit juices: 2 to 3 servings a day.
- Dairy products: 2 to 3 servings a day.
- Meat, poultry, fish, and alternatives (such as dry beans): 2 to 3 servings a day.

OBSTACLES TO GOOD HEALTH BEHAVIORS

The information in this chapter probably isn't new to you. Most of us have been bombarded with health data in newspapers, magazines, and TV. Perhaps the real issue is not a lack of information, but rather the obstacles preventing each of us from adopting a healthy lifestyle.

Over 3,000 preretirees we have worked with have reported the following obstacles that prevent them from incorporating exercise and a nutritious diet into their lifestyle:

- There is no time to exercise.
- I feel fine and look good. Why change?
- This information is not relevant to my life.
- Rich food tastes great.
- I'm exhausted after work. The last thing I want to do is exercise.
- It's hard to break a habit and change.
- My husband (or wife) isn't very supportive of a change.
- I'll have more time in retirement for this healthy behavior business.

THE MESSAGE

There are actually two messages: you are in charge and it's never too late to change. George Burns said, "If I had known I was going to live this long, I would have taken better care of myself."

Elevate your health plan to an equal level of importance as your financial plan. You need both for a happy, healthy retirement!

CHAPTER 3

CHOOSING TO WORK IN RETIREMENT

In this chapter, we explore concepts related to working during retirement, such as:

- Whether retirement as we know it will become obsolete.
- Reasons to work during retirement.
- Assessing your skills.
- Finding or creating a job.

Why would you want to work during retirement? For many retirees, work represents not only a means of supplementing retirement income but also a continuation of personal productivity and growth well into their retirement years. In this chapter, we explore some reasons, both financial and nonfinancial, why you may want to continue working in some capacity during your golden years.

THE CHANGING FACE OF RETIREMENT

Many people facing retirement do not consider work as an option. They
look forward to a period of time without a fixed schedule, pressure, or
a long commute. They want to live life on their own terms, feeling free
to do what is truly important to them. A worry-free retirement with a
healthy pension and Social Security payments is in effect a reward for
long, faithful service to an employer. This image of retirement has been
reinforced by employers (via lifetime security with good company benefits), the federal government (via special tax breaks for retirees), and
particularly by the financial service industry, which plays on the fear of
a "lesser" retirement to market a vast array of products.

But this thinking probably won't last much longer. Due to increased
longevity, life may not be as easily separated into "working years" and
"retired years." As we explored in the Introduction and Chapter 1, the
workforce is changing—second (and even third and fourth) careers are
becoming much more common. With increasing life expectancies and
changing job descriptions, the retiree of the future may manage a business from her home using today's fax machines and tomorrow's computer technology, while still having enough free time to truly enjoy her
retired years. According to a recent study at the University of Michigan, 75 percent of people between ages 51 and 61 would prefer a gradual phaseout of work to full retirement.

Furthermore, the workforce may adjust to support these workers.
Management consultant Peter Drucker cites Japan as an example.
There, the "official" retirement age is 55, yet many workers are
encouraged to remain in the workforce as temporary workers long after
age 55, perhaps with reduced benefits and seniority. Employers often
look favorably upon part-time and temporary employment for at least
two reasons. First, in most cases, they do not pay benefits to these
workers. Second, they are not locked into an employment agreement.

In the 1990s, part-time work has become a growing trend creating
something called a *contingent work force*. Contingent workers usually
are employed part-time and/or on a temporary basis. They receive
no benefits and frequently piece together multiple jobs to equal one
full-time position. This particular trend may work well for retirees,
who want part-time flexible work opportunities.

Assuming continued good health, many of today's retirees want
to work, primarily to supplement their income—and many are still

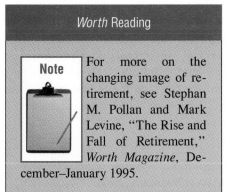

Worth Reading

Note For more on the changing image of retirement, see Stephan M. Pollan and Mark Levine, "The Rise and Fall of Retirement," *Worth Magazine*, December–January 1995.

working. As stated in the *Columbia Retirement Handbook* (New York: Columbia University Press, 1994) in 1990, half of the people between 55 and 61 years and 25 percent of those between 62 and 64 years were both collecting pensions and in the labor force.

With all these potential changes, the best advice is to keep an open mind. Focus on your skills, not your job. Whether you're 45 or 65, consider what working after "retirement" can bring in both income and psychological benefits.

REASONS TO WORK IN RETIREMENT

From a psychological viewpoint, work has many benefits:

- *A sense of purpose.* For many people, work may be the reason for getting up in the morning. It offers a place to go, a place where you have a role and where people depend upon you. In fact, leaving the workplace often constitutes a major loss for those who count on a job to give them a sense of accomplishment and the rewards of working closely with others. Many retirees report missing the challenge of work and the high level of activity. They miss the feeling of being needed, of someone counting on them, of contributing to something larger than themselves and of being part of a highly respected organization. Work also can provide the rewards of power, influence and status. If you believe that these aspects of work will be important to you after you leave the workplace, then your challenge is to find these rewards in retirement—perhaps through new work opportunities or volunteer pursuits.

- *Structure.* Work helps organize daily life. It can help you plan your activities so you won't have to determine how to spend all of your time. Work can protect against boredom. It can break up the week and provide something to look forward to. In fact, work may even make leisure hours more important, fun, and exciting.

- *Social contacts.* Over the years, you may have spent more time with your coworkers than with your family. The workplace often provides a built-in opportunity for social relationships and friend-ships. Just wanting to be with people is a significant motivation to place you back in the job market. If you're retiring alone, the social aspects of work may be even more important. Think about your relationship to the people you work with and your own social needs. Building new social contacts when work no longer exists can often be overwhelming.

- *Learning opportunities.* If you're a curious person who thrives on learning—whether it is a new computer system, management techniques, or the technological or financial market—work may provide that learning environment. Formal training programs or access to libraries, databases and the knowledge and experience of others often results in exciting learning opportunities in the work arena.

- *The work itself.* You may be one of those who loves the very nature of your work. For example, people working for railroad companies love trains, railroading, travel and all that goes with it. Scientists rarely stop becoming scientists. Bookkeepers, astrono-mers, professors, attorneys, writers, strategic planners, and sales-people often love their work. Does this describe you?

- *Keeping the marriage fresh.* Togetherness can be wonderful, but for some, too much togetherness may have diminishing returns. One way to avoid this is to work outside the home. Even though you love your husband or wife, you both may need some relief time from each other's company. Besides providing both spouses a feeling of separateness and privacy, relief time offers the oppor-tunity to be your own person. Each mate can bring something new into the relationship and enjoy one another even more.

- *The chance to be together more.* Your reason to work may be the opposite. Some retirees choose work that brings them closer to their mates. For example, a retired architect wrote a book because it involved travel and the opportunity to co-author the book with his wife. Bed-and-breakfast businesses have been started by many couples who want to work together in their later years.

- *Income.* In spite of your best-laid financial plans, you may want to work to help maintain your accustomed standard of living in

Note

Ability and Age—Don't Be Led Astray

Studies have shown that intelligence, memory, and learning capacity remain constant for most persons until age 70 and—for many people, even longer. So don't let myths about age and ability influence your pursuits.

Remember, Winston Churchill won a Nobel Prize for literature at age 79. Goethe wrote *Faust* at 82. Michaelangelo began work on St. Peter's Basilica at 70. And Casey Stengel managed the New York Yankees to an American League pennant at age 76!

retirement. Even if your income and expenses are in line, you may just want a few extra dollars to spend on luxuries or just for fun. Or you might just want some of those extra dollars as security for unplanned expenses such as caring for aging parents, adult children, young children, or even former spouses.

FINDING OR CREATING A JOB

Once you've decided work is for you, whether full- or part-time, here are some pointers to get you thinking about the process of discovering what you want to do.

Step 1. Assess Your Skills

Self-assessment requires you to examine your skills, capabilities, and experiences. To get a better sense of your qualifications, write your skills, capabilities, and experiences on a piece of paper and review them.

Step 2. Set Employment Goals

A goal is a target. Given your skills, capabilities, and experiences, what kind of work appeals to you? To answer this, think about what you want from the job. Consider the amount of income you want, whether you want part-time or full-time employment, work that is similar or different from your previous job, work that is close by or far away, and work that provides you with a sense of challenge and accomplishment or work that is not mentally or physically stressful.

Step 3. Assess the Marketplace

Explore both traditional and "hidden" job markets. The traditional job market includes newspapers, personnel departments and employment agencies. The "hidden" job market requires a little more creative thinking. A classic work on this subject, *What Color is Your Parachute*, by Richard Bolles, is now in its 23rd printing.

Step 4. Find the Best Job Opportunities

Midlife adults are advised to look for jobs with employers that are small or new; ones that specifically recruit mature workers; employers who sell to or serve mature adults; or ones who hire temporary or part-time employees.

Are there industries with a good track record in hiring competent, mature adults? Fortunately, yes. Leading the field in employment opportunities are technology, science, and health care. And the need for financial services, marketing, and sales help on all levels is increasing.

Hospital and restaurant industries are looking for qualified older employees. Service and manufacturing industries are seeking professional, technical, and administrative help as well as clerical workers.

CREATING YOUR OWN CAREER

Why not do what you've always wanted? Starting your own business and working out of your home may be attractive to you, especially after years in the dog-eat-dog office world. According to the *New York Times*, an estimated 24 million Americans have some sort of home-based business. And with the advent of fax machines, modems, and sophisticated home computers, managing that business is easier than ever.

> ### Over 50 and Job Searching?
>
> **Note**
>
>
>
> A study conducted by J. Robert Connor, author of *Cracking the Over 50 Job Market*, found that companies that hired employees over 50 years old were looking for the following skills and experience:
>
> Communication skills.
> Problem-solving skills.
> Sales and customer service.
> Banking experience.
> Technical skills.
> Scientific knowledge.
> Accuracy and accounting experience.
> Sales experience.
> Industry experience.
> Computer-related (e.g., engineering, design, manufacturing, and peripherals) skills.
> Finance experience and math skills.
> Hospitality experience.
> Marketing background.
>
> Connor found that personal qualities also were important. Industries (particularly science, technology, banking, and manufacturing) were looking for the following personal qualities:
>
> Positive attitude.
> Steady personality.
> Ability to learn.
> High energy.
> Intelligence.
> Good work ethic.
> Commitment.
>
> Source: Excerpt from CRACKING THE OVER 50 JOB MARKET, by J. Robert Connor, © 1992 by J. Robert Connor, p. 196. Used by permission of Dutton Signet, a division of Penguin Books USA, Inc.

I'M AGE 40, SO WHY SHOULD I CARE ABOUT THIS CHAPTER?

If you quickly scanned this chapter, thinking that it was for people at or nearing retirement, you might want to take a closer look! The difficulty with many older adults who are struggling with thoughts of working or not working in retirement is that they've mentally conditioned themselves long beforehand that they wouldn't work. Throughout your youth and adult life, how many times have you heard, "Be flexible!" and "Never say never!" Let your mind be flexible to the possibility of something new and different. After all, 25 to 30 years in retirement is a long time! And as a productive member of society, you have much to give!

As you complete the retirement sufficiency analysis beginning with Chapter 4, experiment with the effect of part-time work on retirement

Table 3–1	Effect of Working Part-Time on Annual Retirement Savings	
Period	**Rate of Return on Savings**	**Reduction in Annual Savings Required until Retirement (in Today's Dollars)**
5 years	7%	$3,732
10 years	7	6,940
15 years	7	9,246

(Table assumes the employee is currently age 50, will retire at age 62, 90-year life expectancy, and will work part-time for $15,000 per year. A 4 percent inflation rate is also assumed.

Note: Includes reduction in Social Security benefits due to earnings limitations. See Chapter 7.

income. As you can see in Table 3–1, working for five years part-time in retirement provides the equivalent of saving an additional $3,732 annually for retirement.

If you find yourself short on ideas, there are many books and magazines on this subject. Check out the listing at the end of Chapter 1. Remember Apple Computer was started in a garage, and Colonel Sanders founded his chicken empire at age 66!

BOOKS AND PUBLICATIONS

Careers: New Ways to Work After 50. By Caroline Bird. 1992. Boston: Little Brown and Company.

Cracking the Over-50 Market. By J. Robert Connor. 1992. New York: Penguin Books.

50 and Starting Over: Career Strategies for Success. By Karen Kerstra Harty. 1991. North Hollywood, CA: Newcastle Publishing Co., Inc.

Working Options: How to Plan Your Job Search; Your Work Life. AARP. Washington, D.C.

Comfort Zones, third edition. By Elwood Chapman. 1993. Menlo Park, CA: Crisp Publications, Inc.

How to Stay Employable: A Guide for the Midlife and Older Worker. By AARP. 1992. Washington, D.C.

Career Encores (Job Search Manual for Mature Workers.) By Fred Merrill. 1987. Los Angeles: Los Angeles Council on Careers for Older

Americans. 5225 Wilshire Boulevard, Suite 204, Los Angeles, CA 90036; (213) 939-0391.

Occupational Outlook Handbook. 1988. Washington, D.C., United States Government Printing Office.

What Color Is Your Parachute? A Practical Manual for Job-Hunters and Career-Changers. By Richard Nelson Bolles. 1992. Berkeley, CA: Ten Speed Press.

New York Opportunities for Older Americans. By Robert S. Menchin. 1993. Englewood Cliffs, NJ: Prentice Hall.

Retired? Get Back in the Game! By Jack Wyman. 1994. Scottsdale, AZ: Doer Publications.

Think of Your Work Future. AARP. 1991. Washington, D.C.: AARP.

ORGANIZATIONS

American Association of Retired Persons, a membership organization that consists of 34 million people 50 years and older. Approximately one third of their members are working; the remaining two thirds are retired. For information on employment (or retirement), write to Work Force Programs, AARP, 601 E Street, N.W., Washington, D.C. 20049. (202) 434-2277.

Forty Plus, a nonprofit, member-managed organization offering peer support, job search strategy, member networking, career guidance, PC training, interviewing techniques, and how to reenter the job market. A one-time membership fee is required. There are 16 Forty Plus organizations in the U.S. Write to Forty-Plus, 1718 P Street, N.W., Suite T-4, Washington, D.C. 20036. (202) 387-1582.

National Council on the Aging, a nonprofit membership organization that serves as a national resource for consultation, publications, special programs and training to meet older persons' needs. Write to the National Council on the Aging, 600 Maryland Avenue, S.W., West Wing 100, Washington, D.C. 20024. (202) 479-1200.

Operation ABLE, a Chicago-based, nonprofit organization that places mature job seekers with employers and provides computer training programs. ABLE also works with employers to encourage them to hire competent mature applicants. It is located at 180 North Wabash Avenue, Suite 802, Chicago, IL 60601. (312) 782-3335.

RETIREMENT FINANCIAL PLANNING

CHAPTER 4   Retirement Financial Planning—An Overview   43

CHAPTER 5   Setting Retirement Goals   57

CHAPTER 6   Understanding Your Retirement Income Sources   65

RETIREMENT FINANCIAL PLANNING—AN OVERVIEW

This chapter introduces our approach to retirement financial planning. Read on to understand the basics of:

- Analyzing, refining, implementing, and monitoring your retirement financial plan.
- Understanding your retirement income goals and resources.
- Developing a retirement sufficiency analysis to show if you will have enough to reach your retirement income goal.
- Understanding the key economic "levers" that drive your retirement plan: inflation, time horizon, and investment rates of return.

The next three chapters expand on each aspect of the retirement planning process.

To paraphrase the English philosopher Bertrand Russell, what most of us want in retirement is enough money to meet our wants and needs, and enough time to enjoy it. For people who start reasonably early and commit to a plan, this is not an unreasonable goal. As we saw in the Introduction, planning for retirement is less a one-time financial event than a process with four simple steps:

Analyze your goals, resources and time frame.

Refine your analysis based on potential changes, different options, or personal circumstances.

Implement your plan to achieve your objectives.

Monitor how your retirement plan is progressing over time.

We will carry this theme throughout the next several chapters.

Analyze means to take a "first cut" at a retirement sufficiency calculation. Our basic goal is to take some raw, unrefined data, do some calculations, and get an answer. (For example, is there a shortfall or a surplus?) Put another way, you look at your income goals in retirement, compare them to your current and projected resources, and determine whether you will have enough to meet your goals using reasonable assumptions about rates of return, inflation, and life expectancy.

Refine means to take what you learned in the analysis phase and challenge some of the fundamental premises that you used. For example, will the shortfall be less if you can get a better investment return? What happens if you work during retirement? If you retire earlier or later? If you save more? At the end of the refinement phase, you will have a good idea of how changing circumstances or economic variables (investment return, inflation) will affect your shortfall or surplus, and what planning strategies can be employed to ensure your meeting your retirement goal.

Implement means that once your plan is in place, you take the proper action steps, such as choosing the appropriate savings and investment options for accumulating retirement assets or using proper distribution and tax strategies once you start to withdraw those assets. In essence, implementation means "Now that you know what you need to do, go do it!" For example, change your savings plan investment options, increase your savings percentage, or roll your company retirement plan assets over to an IRA.

Finally, **monitor** means (1) understand how you are progressing toward your retirement goal and (2) make changes as needed over time. For example, if your investment return is better than expected, determine how it affects the plan you originally put in place. Or, if you receive an unexpected inheritance or have another child, decide what changes those events suggest. "Keeping in touch" with your plan and making the appropriate adjustments when needed gives you the best chance of reaching your retirement goals over the long haul.

Now this approach may seem simplistic, and it isn't rocket science to be sure. However, when the shortfalls loom large and you're tempted to throw up your hands, remember that there are hundreds of different variables that can determine whether you meet your goal or fall short. Using this step-by-step approach, planning becomes easier than you might think, doesn't require advanced education or expensive professional help, and can actually be fun. So let's come to grips with the process of planning for your retirement!

ANALYZING YOUR SITUATION

When you do any sort of financial planning, a good starting point is to answer three basic questions:

- What do you want?
- What do you have?
- How do you get what you want?

Now you might look at these questions and think the most important is the last, How do you get what you want? Put another way, how do you get from where you are today financially to where you want to be? Unfortunately, too many people at this point jump ahead of themselves and think that the most important task facing them is to identify and then implement specific savings and investment plans.

For most people, it's far more important to understand a plan's specific goals and objectives. That's because once you put a strategy into action, you'll need to understand the goals to see if the plan is working and whether it still meets your needs.

You should go through this exercise periodically (say, every year or so) to make sure you are still on track in meeting your goals and that your assumptions still hold true. And it is especially important if something in your retirement plan changes (for instance, if you change your job or your marital status).

Important Considerations

Caution

Some of the retirement plans we have seen don't consider several important factors, such as:

- They only look at first year of retirement, which doesn't consider changing income streams and long-time horizon.

- They focus only on the level of achievable retirement income, not on the income goal needed to maintain a current lifestyle.

- They look at future dollars and minimize the effect of inflation.

- Investment plans are oriented to income but ignore the need for growth to preserve purchasing power.

- They ignore the use of principal during retirement.

WHAT WILL RETIREMENT COST ME?

To come to grips with the cost of retirement, think about our first broad question, **What do you want?** This really means, **What is your income goal?** (How much will you need to spend to support yourself during retirement?) Now you might say, who knows?, especially if you have many years to go before your retirement lifestyle is even a thought. Yet the cost of retirement is fundamentally based on three questions:

Figure 4–1

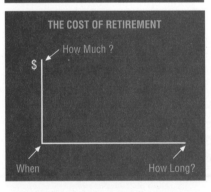

- When will I retire?
- How much will I need?
- How long will I need it?

As Figure 4–1 shows, to determine the total cost, we need to define our first three major assumptions: when we plan to retire, our income goal and our planning horizon, and the number of years between our retirement age and life expectancy.

Figure 4–2

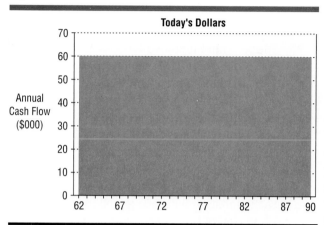

Let's take a hypothetical couple: John and Sharon, both age 50. John, a product manager at RAO, Inc. (a major software company), earns $55,000 per year. Sharon is a freelance writer earning $20,000. They have about $5,000 of annual investment income.

John and Sharon haven't given retirement much thought, but they agree that they will probably retire at age 62, and would like to stay fairly close to their accustomed lifestyle today throughout their golden years. They know that some of their expenses will change. For example, they won't have Social Security taxes anymore and hope to have lower income taxes. They look at 80 percent of their earnings ($60,000) as a reasonable goal throughout retirement. (For more on setting a retirement income goal, see Chapter 5.) Finally, John's and

Figure 4–3

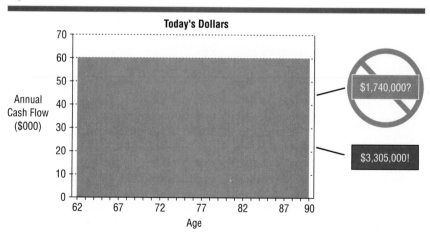

Table 4–1	Retirement Income Sources
Social Security	44%
Pensions and investments	43
Employment	10
Other	3

Source: Reprinted with permission of Employee Benefits Research Institute from *Pension Funding and Taxation, Implications for Tomorrow*, 1994, page 11.

Sharon's parents lived well into their 90s so they figure a life expectancy of age 90 is reasonable.

And there we have our three variables: a $60,000 goal, retirement at age 62, and a life expectancy of age 90. (See Figure 4–2.) Simple math says that the cost of John and Sharon's retirement is $60,000 times 29 years (the difference between age 62 and age 90) or $1,740,000. Except . . .

John and Sharon also know that inflation will take its toll, and that $60,000 income goal means what $60,000 can buy today. A $60,000 lifestyle will cost quite a bit more in 20 years. They know that they need to factor inflation into their

Today's Dollars versus Future Dollars

Note

We are showing all amounts in today's dollars (today's purchasing power) instead of future dollars (what things will actually cost tomorrow). By a "today's dollar" analysis, we mean that John and Sharon want to maintain $60,000 in purchasing power through retirement because that is roughly what it takes for them to maintain their current lifestyle, with adjustments for expenses they know are likely to decrease.

We use today's dollars in our analysis because understanding your goals in terms of today's purchasing is easier and far less intimidating than thinking in terms of future dollars. For example, if inflation averages only 4 percent, by the time they're age 90, John and Sharon will need almost $300,000 per year in future dollars to maintain that same $60,000 lifestyle. That's right, four times what they earn today! The bigger the spending goal, the more inflation—the more years to retirement, then the worse it gets!

For this reason, we recommend that you think of retirement financial planning in terms of today's dollars rather than in inflated (future) dollars. This way, the prospect of needing a six-figure income to reach your long-term retirement goal won't cause you to throw up your hands in despair!

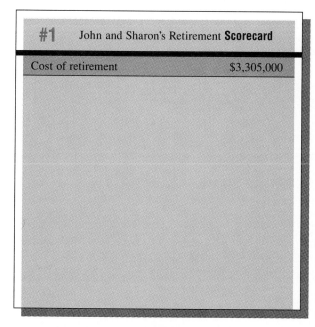

analysis; so they use 4 percent as a preliminary guess.

See all of that red on the graph? Red represents a shortfall from John and Sharon's goal. We haven't used any of their income streams yet. That's our second question, What do I have? But a retirement spending goal of $60,000 per year for 29 years (from age 62 through age 90) at 4 percent inflation means John and Sharon will need $3,305,000 at retirement to reach their goal.

Figure 4–4

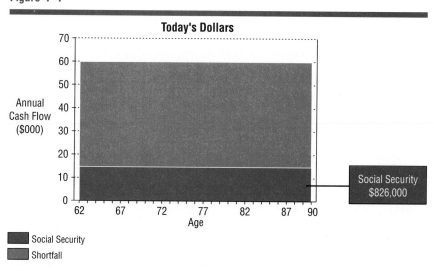

#2 John and Sharon's Retirement **Scorecard**	
Cost of retirement	$3,305,000
Social Security	(826,000)
Shortfall	**$2,479,000**

If we break that amount down into its components, $1,740,000 is the amount they would need if inflation were not a factor— 29 years times $60,000. The remaining $1,565,000 represents the additional capital John and Sharon will need to counter the effects of inflation at even a modest 4 percent rate.

WHAT ARE MY RESOURCES?

The total cost of John and Sharon's retirement seems staggering, but remember, they have just begun the analysis phase of the planning process. The next step is to identify what resources they have available.

Now of course, the likelihood is that you will have many different

Social Security Cost of Living Increases

Tip

Social Security is a flat line on the today's dollar graph since it maintains its purchasing power against inflation. This is because Social Security benefits increase every year for changes in the cost of living, as explained in Chapter 8. These cost-of-living increases keep the purchasing power of the benefit constant. John and Sharon's Social Security benefits without cost-of-living increases would total $435,000 (or $15,000 times 29 years). The remaining $391,000 (or $826,000 less $435,000) represents the value in today's dollars of the cost-of-living adjustments.

Figure 4–5

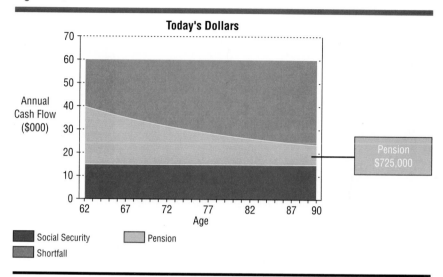

sources of retirement income. Table 4–1 on page 48 shows the sources of retirement income for many retirees:

In calculating retirement sufficiency, the challenge is to understand how each income source contributes to our ability to meet our retirement income goal over a long time. You need to ask three basic questions about each income source:

#3	John and Sharon's Retirement **Scorecard**
Cost of retirement	$3,305,000
Social Security	(826,000)
Pension	(725,000)
Shortfall	**$1,754,000**
Achievable retirement income	$28,000

- How much income can I expect?
- When will the income streams start?
- How long will the income stream last?

Figure 4–6

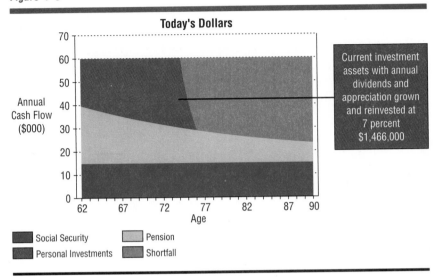

Today's Dollars

Annual Cash Flow ($000)

Current investment assets with annual dividends and appreciation grown and reinvested at 7 percent $1,466,000

Age

■ Social Security   ■ Pension
■ Personal Investments   ■ Shortfall

Having picked themselves up off the floor, John and Sharon now start to think about their resources to fund their retirement goal. They know that they have two basic types of retirement income sources. The first is **annuity plans** (retirement plans that will pay them a monthly benefit). Examples are Social Security and company-sponsored pension plans. The second type of resource is **capital balances** (lump sums of money available to them at retirement). Examples would be their company

#4 John and Sharon's Retirement **Scorecard**	
Cost of retirement	$3,305,000
Social Security	(826,000)
Pension	(725,000)
Investment assets	(1,466,000)
Shortfall	**$ 288,000**
Achievable retirement income	$45,000

Achievable Retirement Income

Note Achievable retirement spending is calculated assuming that income streams (except for Social Security) lose purchasing power each year based on a 4 percent inflation rate. We also assume that current income and principal are used as needed to reach the retirement income goal, and any excess is reinvested at a 7 percent rate of return.

401(k) savings plan, IRA, or (for the self-employed) Keogh plan.

The first resource John and Sharon think of is an annuity plan, Social Security. They know that they'll both receive a monthly benefit starting when they turn age 62, but have no idea what the amount will be. However, they've heard that Social Security would replace about 20 percent of their income, so they use 20 percent of $75,000, or $15,000 as an estimate. Figure 4–4 on page 49 shows the result.

Impressive! That Social Security benefit over 29 years is worth $826,000, and reduces the amount needed at retirement from $3,305,000 to "only" $2,479,000. John and Sharon's achievable retirement income is now $15,000, as compared to their goal of $60,000.

Encouraged, John and Sharon next look at another source of monthly income, John's pension benefits. John knows he will get a pension benefit from RAO so he calls up the RAO benefits office and gets

Figure 4–7

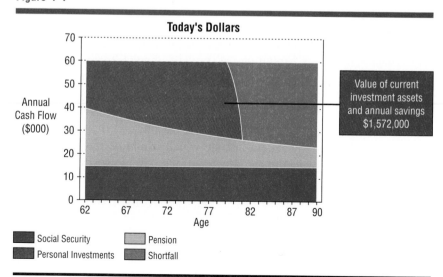

#5 John and Sharon's Retirement **Scorecard**	
Cost of retirement	$3,305,000
Social Security	(826,000)
Pension	(725,000)
Current investment assets and earnings	(1,466,000)
Savings and future earnings	(106,000)
Shortfall	**$ 182,000**
Achievable retirement income	$50,650

an estimate of $25,000 in today's dollars for his pension beginning at age 62. (Chapters 5 and 9 explain how to use a pension estimate.)

Not bad. John's pension is worth about $725,000 over the course of his retirement. These pension payments reduce the retirement shortfall from $2,479,000 to $1,754,000 and increase achievable retirement spending to around $28,000.

But notice that unlike Social Security payments, John's pension is not increased for changes in the cost of living. Thus, the total value of his pension in today's dollars is exactly $25,000 times 29 years, or $725,000. You'll find more on the need to obtain pension benefit estimates in today's dollars in Chapter 8.

Next, John and Sharon add up the amount they've saved for retirement so far in John's company savings plan, Sharon's Keogh plan, and other investments (their capital plans). It totals about $200,000. They also know they're earning about a 7 percent investment return on their money now. They use those numbers to see if the picture gets any brighter.

Quite an improvement. The principal and earnings on their current retirement assets plus any excess income which would be reinvested during the retirement years at the 7 percent rate will be worth $1,466,000 from now through age 90, reducing the shortfall from $1,754,000 to $288,000. (See Figure 4–6 and Scorecard #4 on page 52.) John and Sharon's achievable retirement spending is now around $45,000, compared to their goal of $60,000.

John and Sharon have one more resource, their annual savings. They are currently saving about 10 percent of their salary—$7,500. If they continue to save at the same rate for the next 13 years (from age 50 to 62) and those savings also earn 7 percent, their retirement shortfall drops again, as shown in Figure 4–7 on page 53.

John and Sharon think they have accounted for all of their income sources, but they still come up about $182,000 short of their goal (see Scorecard #5) and need about $9,350 in additional retirement income per year. How can they solve the shortfall or, as the Visine eye-drops commercial goes, get the red out? We cover that in the next three chapters! In the Appendix are worksheets that allow you to do the same analysis by hand.

A PLANNING PHILOSOPHY

See how the process works? Not until you've gone through this process of figuring out what your specific goals are (or of checking on them from time to time) are you ready to start planning and implementing a savings and investment strategy. Knowing you can achieve your retirement goals with, say, a $10,000 savings strategy and 7 percent annual compound investment return provides great direction as to the type of investment strategy you should design and the accompanying investment risk you need to take.

The key is to ask the broad questions first and then keep narrowing down and fine-tuning the analysis. The advantage to this approach is that you end up with manageable problems to solve instead of an overwhelming feeling that leads to a "whatever happens, happens" approach and philosophy.

In the preceding example, we went from asking how we were ever going to generate enough income to retire, to address the specific need of accumulating enough to produce just $9,350 in additional retirement income. If you don't break the task down, it may seem too discouraging even to contemplate. Breaking the retirement planning task down into small, specific elements makes the plan easier to reevaluate from time to time. You only need to check on the continuing validity of each simple element. If they're all working, then your whole plan remains valid. If one element has changed, you know by what amount you need to alter your plan.

In summary, key elements in reaching your retirement income goals include:

- When do you plan to retire?
- How much income do you want?
- How long do you think your retirement will last?
- How much will pensions and Social Security provide?
- How much do you currently have set aside?
- What investment rate do you want to use?
- How do you withdraw your funds during retirement?
- What will the long-term inflation rate be?

EVERYTHING WORKS TOGETHER

The analysis phase requires us to understand what we want and what we have, and how some basic economic and investment assumptions can work for (or against) us in the long run. It's important to understand that all of these factors work together, yet many people believe their ability to meet their goals is based on one critical factor. How many of the following sound familiar?

- I can make it if I only save more.
- All I need to do is increase my rate of return (but that means take more risk)!
- I'll be OK if I just retire as late as possible.
- I'll only live until my mid-80s.
- I'm fine as long as inflation doesn't skyrocket.

Yet, any sufficiency analysis depends on many related factors all working together, and any shortfalls or surpluses from your goal can be affected dramatically by a small change in any one factor. Remember, the most important thing to understand is that you can't afford to leave the answers to these questions to someone else. You can leave the calculations to someone else, but understand your retirement goals, your financial resources, and the levers that drive your ability to reach your retirement goals. Next we consider how to think about those factors that drive the sufficiency calculation.

CHAPTER 5

SETTING RETIREMENT GOALS

As we have seen, you should look at your retirement goals as much more than just financial. However, every retirement goal has a financial implication. In this chapter, we focus on the financial side by looking at our lifestyle today and determining how much of that lifestyle we want to maintain during retirement. Questions we answer include:

- How should you develop a spending goal?
- When should you plan to retire?
- For how long a retirement should you plan?
- How will inflation affect your retirement goal?

As we saw in Chapter 4, to answer the question **"What do I want?"** you need to decide when you want to retire, how long you anticipate retirement will be, and how much you want to spend each year. In this chapter we begin to refine that analysis by looking more closely at the third item, our retirement spending goal.

Figure 5–1   U.S. Inflation, 1926–93

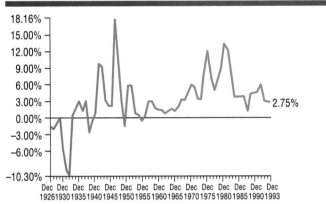

THE BURDEN OF INFLATION

A word about inflation is necessary in any discussion of retirement planning. Even though most economists feel that inflation will remain relatively low over the next 20 years (averaging 4 to 6 percent annually), don't think that a low rate won't affect you. Rising prices (and rising incomes) will affect both your future spending needs and future resources so failure to take inflation into account can leave you behind in reaching your financial goals. For example, assuming inflation averages 4 percent a year, John and Sharon would need almost $100,000 in their first year of retirement (12 years from now) to buy what $60,000 does today. And by

Figure 5–2

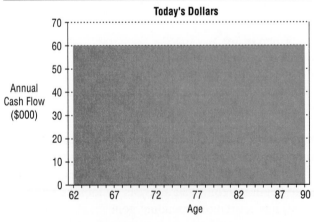

Figure 5–3

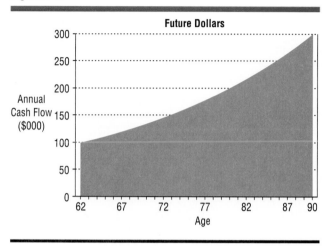

Future Dollars

Annual Cash Flow ($000)

Age

age 90, they would need almost $300,000 to buy what $60,000 buys today! Or let's say that you expect to draw a $30,000 pension over a 20-year retirement period, and inflation averages just 4 percent. In 20 years, the buying power of your pension will be reduced to $13,700! If your pension is not indexed for inflation (and most aren't), you'll need to put away an additional $111,000 and invest it at 7 percent just to maintain the $30,000 buying power you started with. Thinking in terms of inflated dollars can certainly lead to a form of "sticker shock"!

Figure 5–2 in today's dollars and Figure 5–3 in future dollars display John and Sharon's spending goal for each year of their retirement. Figure 5–2 shows their $60,000 spending goal as a flat line, which means that they will need the same amount of purchasing power throughout their retirement years. But in Figure 5–3's future-dollars graph, their spending goal increases each year because of inflation.

Let's see how we account for inflation's dramatic effects on retirement planning.

HOW MUCH WILL YOU SPEND DURING RETIREMENT?

In Chapter 4, we took a first look at our goal by estimating it

---

Less Means More

Tip

Keep in mind that the lower your current income, the more likely you are to need a greater percentage of it during retirement. For people who currently have household income under $50,000, many financial planners assume a retirement goal as high as 90 percent of current income.

Table 5–1 Retirement Spending Plan		
Expense Category	**Currently**	**Retirement**
Home mortgage	$_____	$_____
Other housing expenses	_____	_____
Utilities	_____	_____
Automobile	_____	_____
Life and health insurance	_____	_____
Long-term care	_____	_____
Food	_____	_____
Clothing and grooming	_____	_____
Travel and entertainment	_____	_____
Family gifts	_____	_____
Charitable gifts	_____	_____
Loan repayments	_____	_____
Income taxes	_____	_____
Social Security deductions	_____	_____
Savings	_____	_____
Other	_____	_____
Total	$_____	$_____

as a percentage of our current income. We can now refine that estimate further. If you're close to retirement age, determining the goal is fairly easy, since you pretty well know what you are spending your money on today. But what if you're 30 years from retirement? Who knows what your lifestyle will be like then? For all you know, inflation will make that $1.50 loaf of bread cost $10.00!

The answer is to use today's lifestyle as a guideline. If you eat bread today, it's likely you will eat it longer-term. While we can't predict what inflation will do, we know *how* we live today and *what* things cost today. If you have a long way to go before retirement, simply plan for a long-range goal that approximates today's lifestyle. It gives you something to shoot for in the long run and, given that long time frame, precise estimates aren't that critical. As we saw, an easy rule of thumb is to plan for an average spending goal of 60 to 80 percent of your current pretax income during retirement and then refine it as you go along.

As you get closer to retirement, you can use Table 5–1's worksheet to answer this question for yourself. For each expense item on the worksheet, make the best estimate you can about how it will change

Figure 5–4	Variable Retirement Goal			
	Working	**Active Years**	**Less Active**	**Passive Years**
Starting at Age	Current	62	75	85
Annual spending goal	$80,000	$60,000	$50,000	$70,000
Annual Expenses				
Home mortgage	15,000	15,000	0	0
Other housing expenses	4,000	4,000	4,000	2,000
Utilities	2,000	2,500	2,500	1,500
Automobile	3,000	1,000	1,000	1,000
Life and health insurance	1,500	3,000	4,000	4,000
Long-term care	0	0	0	40,000
Food	6,000	4,000	4,000	2,000
Clothing and grooming	3,000	2,000	2,000	2,000
Travel and entertainment	2,000	6,000	3,500	1,000
Family gifts	2,000	2,000	10,000	6,000
Charitable gifts	2,000	2,500	4,000	1,000
Loan repayments	5,000	1,000	0	—
Income taxes	15,000	12,000	12,000	8,500
Soc. Sec. deductions	6,000	0	0	—
Savings	7,500	2,000	0	—
Other	6,000	3,000	3,000	1,000
Savings/(Shortfall)	**0**	**0**	**0**	**0**

Note: All dollar amounts in today's dollars

after you've quit working. After you're done you'll have a good feel for what you're likely to spend annually during retirement. The goal is make sure you account for all of your current spending—that is, all of your desired lifestyle.

How much should you adjust your current spending figures to reflect your postretirement needs? It varies with the item. For example, you probably won't be commuting, so auto expenses will decrease. You probably will spend less on clothing. Personal loans or a home mortgage may be paid off by that time, and you may not plan to save during retirement. If you don't work during retirement, you won't pay any Social Security taxes. Because of their lower income, their income taxes should decrease. Many retirees plan on an increase in travel and entertainment expenses. Until you push the pencil and come to grips with your current spending, and related lifestyle, you cannot reasonably understand what level of retirement income you may want or need.

Figure 5–5

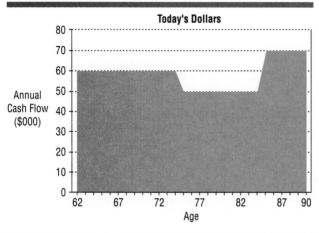

Today's Dollars

Annual Cash Flow ($000) — Age

While this may seem to be a time-consuming task and one you would rather not do, this basic activity becomes the ultimate reality check on beginning the planning process properly.

How Will Your Spending Change During Retirement?

Just as your spending pattern has changed over the years, it will likely change during your retirement as well. Experts explain retirement as having three broad phases: active, less active, and passive. In the early years of retirement, you are apt to be very active, spending a great deal on travel and entertainment. But as years go by, you are likely to become less active and you will see your activities and lifestyle change. Then in your passive years, depending on your broad family plans and whether you have long-term care insurance, you will probably see your

Caution

Don't Fail to Plan

Over and over again you have surely heard the phrase "People don't plan to fail, they fail to plan." When looking at long-term spending needs, we see an inordinate amount of conscious and subconscious hedging on life expectancy and long-term planning. It often seems that people overtly feel that if they live beyond age 85, then someone else's money can take care of them. Effective planning of retirement goals helps minimize the "overconfidence" that can occur when you expect "someone else," whether the government, family members, or your company, to come up with the funds!

#6 John and Sharon's Retirement **Scorecard**	
Cost of retirement	$3,305,000
Social Security	(826,000)
Pension	(725,000)
Investment assets	(1,466,000)
Savings	(106,000)
Variable goal	(31,000)
Shortfall	**$ 151,000**
Achievable retirement income	$50,650

spending increase again as medical and long-term care expenses grow.

John and Sharon anticipate a dramatic change in their spending plan in their "less active" years because their home mortgage should be finally paid off. They also anticipate a reduction in their travel and entertainment expenses. And finally in their passive years, they see the cost of long-term care becoming part of their spending outlays while their travel and entertainment costs continue to decrease.

In planning their retirement, one of the ways that John and Sharon could refine their plan is by using the concept of variable goal. In their case a variable goal reduced their retirement income goal to about $58,500 and reduced the amount they needed to accumulate by almost $31,000, to about $151,000, as Scorecard #6 shows.

WHEN SHOULD YOU RETIRE?

The easy answer is easy: when you want to. But in today's business and economic climate we know it's not that simple. In recent years we have watched the term *job security* be replaced with other terms such as *downsizing, restructuring,* and *rightsizing.* The notion of working for the same company for 30 or 40 years is something to which only our parents, or maybe only our grandparents, can relate. So by planning for an earlier retirement, you are in a sense ensuring that you can meet your retirement goals even if your job is eliminated.

In setting up your retirement plan, we suggest looking at a "normal" retirement, say between ages 58 and 62, and also looking at how your plan would change if early retirement, say at age 55, became an option.

FOR HOW LONG SHOULD YOU PLAN?

In essence, this means how long are you going to live—always a difficult issue. Insurance companies, pension administrators and even the IRS use very sophisticated means of estimating life expectancy. You can find the results in actuarial life expectancy tables. But the problem with these tables is that they are based on historical data and do not readily consider current advances in medical technology. To be safe— that is, to be sure that you don't outlive your savings—we suggest you plan for a retirement through age 90. If you have family members living well into their 90s, you should plan for an even longer retirement life.

Now the question becomes, What do you need to do to ensure that you can cover those expenses? That's the subject of the next two chapters.

CHAPTER 6

UNDERSTANDING YOUR RETIREMENT INCOME SOURCES

Now that we have our income goal established, we can continue to refine our analysis by evaluating retirement resources and how to use them to fund our retirement goal. Questions we answer in this chapter include:

- What are your Social Security benefits?
- How do various pension options affect the sufficiency analysis?
- What if you work during retirement?
- How do you develop a retirement savings strategy?
- What about inheritances, selling your home and extraordinary expenses?
- How should you think about spending your retirement resources?

So far we have talked about a few sources for retirement income: company retirement plans, Social Security, and company-sponsored savings plans. There are of course many others: IRAs, annuities, investments outside of company plans, part-time work during retirement, and proceeds from the sale of your home. Part of the refinement phase of planning is to understand how we can utilize these resources best to reach our retirement goal.

THE SOURCES OF RETIREMENT INCOME

Your retirement income will come in many forms. The next several chapters explain these sources in greater detail. You will have some income that will be paid monthly, such as Social Security and perhaps a pension. The rest of your retirement nest egg will probably be lump-sum amounts: your company benefit plans [401(k), profit sharing, stock bonus, etc.] and your personal investments such as IRAs, mutual funds, stocks and bonds, that are earmarked for retirement.

What exactly do we mean by *earmarked for retirement?* When you estimate your retirement resources, we want you to only include those assets that you intend to use to fund your retirement. For instance, you would not include the portion of your stock portfolio that you intend to use to pay for your children's college educations, or the mutual funds you plan to use to buy your vacation home.

When we last left John and Sharon, they were about $151,000 short of the amount needed at age 62 to fund their retirement goal. Now we begin the second phase of the planning process; refining those calculations and assumptions to see what steps they can take to solve their shortfall. So let's take a detailed look at their sources of retirement income, beginning with Social Security.

SOCIAL SECURITY BENEFITS

As you recall from Chapter 4, John and Sharon used $15,000 as their estimate of Social Security benefits, assuming that it would replace about 20 percent of their salaries. To refine that estimate, they called Social Security to get a more precise figure. You and your spouse can obtain a benefit estimate quite easily by calling Social Security at 1-800-772-1213 and requesting Form SSA 7004-SM. A copy is also available in the Appendix.

Remember that each spouse should request a benefit estimate from Social Security. The reason is that a spouse receives the higher of the benefit he or she earned based on the person's own work history, or a "spousal" benefit based on the primary wage earner's work history. In addition, to even qualify for a benefit, a spouse must be fully insured, that is, have at least 40 quarters (or 10 years) of work. (Workers born before 1929 need fewer quarters.)

Currently, you can retire and begin receiving full Social Security benefits at age 65 if you were born in 1937 or earlier. For those born after that date, the normal retirement age for receiving full benefits increases gradually starting in the year 2003 until it becomes 67 for everyone born after 1959. Because John and Sharon were born in 1944, their normal retirement age under Social Security will be age 66.

As we saw, they could draw benefits as early as age 62, but their benefit amounts would be reduced. Under current law, a spouse's benefit is generally equal to 50 percent of the worker's benefit at age 65, but because of the change in the normal retirement age, this factor will gradually decrease too. With a normal retirement age of 65, a retiree who starts collecting Social Security benefits at age 62 would receive about 80 percent of her age-65 benefit. The 20 percent reduction reflects the fact that the worker is able to collect a benefit for three additional years.

John and Sharon could further refine their analysis by thinking about when they might begin to draw their benefits. If they decide to collect their benefits at age 62, they would in fact receive a lower benefit due to the early retirement reduction. For example, John and Sharon's benefits at age 62 would be roughly 73 percent of the amount they could receive at age 66.

John and Sharon discovered from their benefit statements that their projected benefit was higher than the $15,000 they had estimated. Sharon has enough quarters of coverage to qualify, but her benefit under her own work history was less than the spousal benefit available based on John's earnings. Thus, Sharon's benefit came out to be higher with the spousal benefit of about 50 percent of John's. They used their annual benefit of $16,173 and obtained the result as shown in Figure 6–1. Refining their Social Security benefit estimate reduced their shortfall by $23,000 to about $128,000, and increased their achievable retirement spending to $51,800, as Scorecard #7 shows.

But note that if John and Sharon began drawing benefits at age 66 (their normal retirement age under Social Security) instead of age 62, it could reduce their shortfall even further, as shown in Scorecard #8.

Figure 6–1

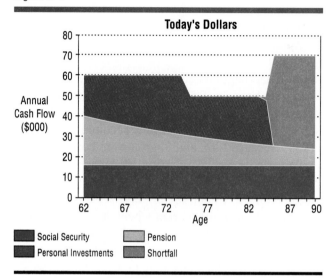

Today's Dollars

Annual Cash Flow ($000)

Social Security
Personal Investments
Pension
Shortfall

Under this scenario, their annual Social Security benefits increase to $22,054 and their overall shortfall drops to about $96,000. Waiting to draw benefits until normal retirement age can be advantageous. However, the value of this strategy depends on your actual life expectancy. The pros and cons of taking Social Security benefits at age 62 or later are discussed more fully in Chapter 7.

#7 John and Sharon's Retirement **Scorecard**	
Cost of retirement	$3,305,000
Social Security	(826,000)
Pension	(725,000)
Investment assets	(1,466,000)
Savings	(106,000)
Variable goal	(31,000)
Revised Social Security estimate—age 62	(23,000)
Shortfall	**$ 128,000**
Achievable retirement income	$51,800

PENSIONS

Of all of the retirement resources you are likely to have, you face the most choices with your pension income. As we will explain further in Chapter 8, you could take an annuity for your life, for the combined lives of you and your spouse, or for your life plus a guaranteed period.

#8 John and Sharon's Retirement **Scorecard**	
Cost of retirement	$3,305,000
Social Security	(826,000)
Pension	(725,000)
Investment assets	(1,466,000)
Savings	(106,000)
Variable goal	(31,000)
Revised Social Security estimate—age 66	(55,000)
Shortfall	**$ 96,000**
Achievable retirement income	$53,500

Your pension plan might also provide a lump sum option. And, you may be fortunate enough to have an employer that increases your pension to offset inflation.

The option you ultimately choose could have a significant effect on your overall retirement sufficiency analysis. For most people, the two most important factors to consider are (1) whether to take a lump sum distribution or an annuity if that option is offered, and (2) the potential effect of any cost-of-living adjustments on the value of their pension.

John and Sharon have been assuming that John would take an annuity from his pension. But let's say that John's pension plan allowed for a lump sum option calculated at the assumed life expectancy and interest rate specified in the plan documents. (These life expectancy and interest rate assumptions vary from plan to plan, so let's assume a 7 percent rate of return and age 90 life expectancy for purposes of illustration.) Using these assumptions, John's lump sum amount would be exactly equal to the present value of his $25,000 pension at 7 percent assuming he lived until age 90. As Table 6–1 shows, the estimated lump sum value of John's $25,000 annual pension is about $307,000.

Table 6–1 Estimated Pension Values	
Annuity value	$25,000 annually
Equals	
Lump sum value	$307,000 single payment

The many factors involved in deciding between taking a lump sum or an annuity are discussed in more detail in later chapters. However, one advantage of taking the lump sum

#9 John and Sharon's Retirement **Scorecard**	
Cost of retirement	$3,305,000
Social Security	(826,000)
Pension	(725,000)
Investment assets	(1,466,000)
Savings	(106,000)
Variable goal	(31,000)
Revised Social Security estimate—age 62	(23,000)
Additional resources from pension lump sum and other assets invested at 8%	(92,000)
Shortfall	**$ 36,000**
Achievable retirement income	$56,300

is that you may be able invest it at a rate of return higher than that used by the plan when it is calculated. For example, if John and Sharon took the lump sum, invested it along with their other assets and obtained a post retirement investment return of 8 percent, the result would look something like Scordcard #9. The 1 percent additional investment return they were able to generate reduces their shortfall to only $36,000. Since the value of the lump sum distribution was calculated using 7 percent, John and Sharon could improve their retirement situation by taking the lump sum and investing it at better than the assumed (7 percent) rate used in the calculation of the lump sum. (See Chapter 8 for a detailed discussion of lump sum distributions.)

Another factor that could affect John and Sharon's

Figure 6–2

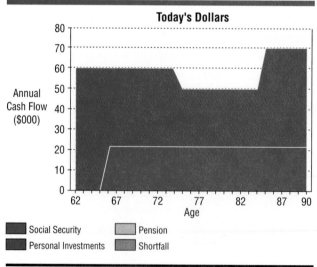

Today's Dollars

Annual Cash Flow ($000)

- Social Security
- Pension
- Personal Investments
- Shortfall

retirement sufficiency calculation is pension indexing. Pension indexing means your pension is adjusted for inflation. As explained in Chapter 8, it is common with government pensions. However, most corporate plans do not index the pension each year by an annual inflation factor, but some companies do look at overall inflation rates and adjust pensions every so often to give some protection against inflation. A typical adjustment might give a 3 percent increase once every three years. Remember two things about cost-of-living adjustments (COLAs). First, they are generally not guaranteed unless you are a government employee, and second, if you take a lump sum, you usually give up any future COLAs because the plan has "cashed you out" and has no further obligation to you.

In spite of the potential benefits of taking the lump sum, let's assume that John and Sharon decided to stick with the $25,000 annuity and assumed the 7 percent rate of return on their assets, but John's employer provided discretionary cost-of-living adjustments to his pension. If we assume John's pension is adjusted for inflation by 3 percent every three years, the result looks like Figures 6–3 and Scorecard #10. The value of periodic pension inflation adjustments drops John and Sharon's shortfall to about $100,000 and increases their achievable retirement income to $53,200.

The bottom line? Inflation adjustments to your pension can provide a meaningful benefit, but since they usually aren't guaranteed, you probably shouldn't count on them in doing your basic retirement sufficiency analysis.

Figure 6–3

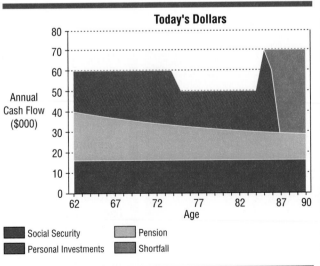

WORKING DURING RETIREMENT

As we discussed in Chapter 3, many people

#10 John and Sharon's Retirement **Scorecard**	
Cost of retirement	$3,305,000
Social Security	(826,000)
Pension	(725,000)
Investment assets	(1,466,000)
Savings	(106,000)
Variable goal	(31,000)
Revised Social Security estimate—age 62	(23,000)
Pension indexing	(28,000)
Shortfall	**$ 100,000**
Achievable retirement income	$53,200

#11 John and Sharon's Retirement **Scorecard**	
Cost of retirement	$3,305,000
Social Security	(826,000)
Pension	(725,000)
Investment assets	(1,466,000)
Savings	(106,000)
Variable goal	(31,000)
Revised Social Security estimate, age 62	(23,000)
Pension indexing	(28,000)
Consulting income	(25,000)
Shortfall	**$ 75,000**
Achievable retirement income	$54,600

who retire opt at some point to work part-time or full-time during retirement. Sometimes this is financially motivated, sometimes it's psychological, sometimes both. With respect to your retirement sufficiency calculation, working during retirement will delay the time in which you need to start drawing resources. As a rule, the longer you can defer drawing your retirement assets, the better off you will be. This is particularly true with your tax-deferred resources like 401(k)s and IRAs.

Let's assume John wanted to work on a part-time basis as a computer consultant until he reached age 65, and earned $10,000 each year.

The effect of John's consulting income would be

Figure 6–4

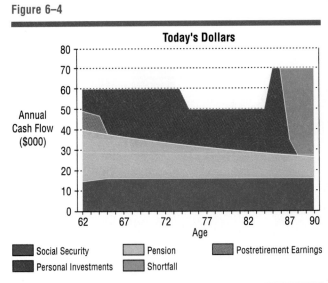

Today's Dollars

Annual Cash Flow ($000)

- Social Security
- Personal Investments
- Pension
- Shortfall
- Postretirement Earnings

beneficial, as shown in Scorecard #11 and Figure 6–4. Earning $10,000 for those three years means that John and Sharon did not have to use some retirement assets. Even after adjusting for the reduction in Social Security benefits, working part-time increased their achievable retirement spending to about $54,600 and reduced their shortfall to about $75,000.

OTHER INCOME SOURCES

In looking at other potential retirement income sources, the two most people consider are potential inheritances and using equity from the sale of their home. We give some thoughts on both in Chapter 10, but let's make some basic assumptions now for each and see how they might affect John and Sharon's retirement sufficiency analysis.

Inheritances

Let's assume that John and Sharon will each receive inheritances from their parents. Of course, we have no way of knowing exactly when that will occur, so we'll be somewhat arbitrary and assume that John will get a $30,000 inheritance at age 70 and Sharon will receive $50,000 at age 72, both in today's dollars. Using the combined inheritances of $80,000, John and Sharon's retirement situation continues to improve, as shown in Figure 6–5 and Scorecard #12. John and Sharon are able to reduce their shortfall to about $15,000 and increase their achievable retirement spending by $3,000 per year, to $57,600.

Figure 6–5

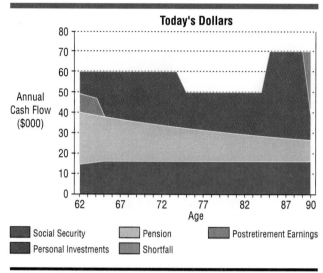

Today's Dollars

Annual Cash Flow ($000)

Age

Social Security Pension Postretirement Earnings

Personal Investments Shortfall

Selling Your Home

Well, John and and Sharon are fairly close to reducing their shortfall to zero. They know they have significant equity in their home. Of course, if they sell it, they'll have to purchase a new home, but they've always wanted to retire to a life of leisure in the Southwest. After looking at the money they could receive from selling their current home at age 75 and subtracting the cost of a retirement home, they figure they could net about $100,000 to use in funding their retirement. As Figure 6–6 and Scorecard #13 shows, John and Sharon would now have a surplus of about $120,000 and can achieve retirement income of $61,000.

#12 John and Sharon's Retirement **Scorecard**	
Cost of retirement	$3,305,000
Social Security	(826,000)
Pension	(725,000)
Investment assets	(1,466,000)
Savings	(106,000)
Variable goal	(31,000)
Revised Social Security estimate, age 62	(23,000)
Pension indexing	(28,000)
Consulting income, age 62–65	(25,000)
Inheritance, age 72	(60,000)
Shortfall	**$ 15,000**
Achievable retirement income	$57,600

THE BOTTOM LINE

It's been a long road to solving that shortfall, but remember back to when it seemed insurmountable— $3,305,000 needed for retirement when

Figure 6–6

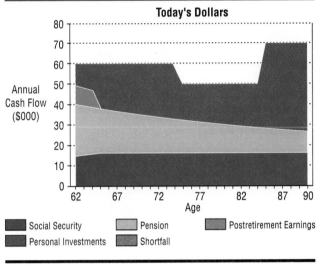

Today's Dollars

Annual Cash Flow ($000)

Age

- Social Security
- Personal Investments
- Pension
- Shortfall
- Postretirement Earnings

taking inflation into account! As we said earlier, the key is to ask the broad questions first, and then keep narrowing down and fine-tuning the analysis. If you don't narrow the task down, it may seem too discouraging even to contemplate. Breaking the retirement planning task down into small, specific elements makes the plan easier to handle. You need only to check on the continuing validity of each simple element. If they're all working together, then your whole plan remains valid. If one element has changed, you know by what amount you need to alter your plan.

The point behind this explanation is the same we made in Chapter 4: Any shortfalls or surpluses from your goal can be affected dramatically by a small change in any one factor. Remember, the most important thing to understand is that you cannot afford to leave the

#13 John and Sharon's Retirement **Scorecard**	
Cost of retirement	$3,305,000
Social Security	(826,000)
Pension	(725,000)
Investment assets	(1,466,000)
Savings	(106,000)
Variable goal	(31,000)
Revised Social Security estimate, age 62	(23,000)
Pension indexing	(28,000)
Consulting income, age 62–65	(25,000)
Inheritance, age 72	(60,000)
Sale of home at age 75	(135,000)
Surplus	**$ (120,000)**
Achievable retirement income	$61,000

answers to these questions to someone else. You can leave the calculations to someone else, but understanding your retirement goals, your financial resources, and the levers that drive your ability to reach your retirement goal is not something you should assign to someone else. No one cares about the accomplishment of your plan like you do, and no one suffers from not achieving it like you do.

DRAWING ON YOUR RESOURCES

Our discussion of John and Sharon's retirement sufficiency analysis would not be complete without introducing the concept of how they should draw on their retirement resources. Generally speaking, there are two ways to think about converting investment balances into annual income. The first way is to live off the interest and dividends the investments generate without ever spending down any principal. The second way is to consume principal as needed when cash flow is inadequate.

Of course, many retirees are reluctant to spend principal. They fear that they won't have sufficient assets available for emergencies, or are simply concerned about outliving their resources and becoming a burden to their children. These fears are understandable since most retirees don't have the option of accumulating significant assets after retirement. Yet, most planners recommend that you plan on spending at least some principal from your investments because it requires a much larger pool of assets to meet retirement living expenses if you spend income only. Table 6–2 gives some examples.

If you are planning to live off your investment earnings only, it is easy to calculate what your retirement income stream would be. Let's say your retirement nest egg amounted to $250,000, and it was generating a 10 percent return; your annual income stream would be $25,000 a year.

But don't be fooled into thinking that you would have *buying power* of $25,000 a year for each year of your retirement. Inflation will dramatically cut the purchasing power of your investment income over time. For example, if during the first 10 years of your retirement inflation averaged 4 percent a year, that $25,000 of income would buy you about $17,000 of goods in your tenth year of retirement and by your twentieth year, it would only buy $8,000 of goods!

The decision about whether to spend principal or only current income also has implications for your retirement investment strategy.

Table 6–2	Capital Needed at Retirement Assuming a 7 Percent Pretax Rate of Return, 4 Percent Inflation and 25-Year Retirement Period	
Income Goal	**Spend Principal and Income***	**Spend Income Only, Conserve Principal**
$30,000	$ 529,000	$ 803,000
40,000	706,000	1,052,000
50,000	882,000	1,315,000
60,000	1,058,000	1,578,000

*Assumes that principal is spent as needed to achieve goal, and that excess is reinvested.

Your portfolio will look vastly different if you invest only for income since you will tend toward higher-yielding assets, such as bonds, and you'll minimize assets with growth potential, such as stocks. And this type of portfolio will then offer less protection against inflation because its assets will not grow over time.

Also, it will probably offer less in the way of total return since total returns for stocks over the past 65 years have averaged about 10 percent per year, while bonds have averaged less than 6 percent per year. By the time you factor in inflation, you may actually be better off investing a portion of your portfolio in stocks and planning to spend a portion of your principal.

Here's an illustration. If John and Sharon had a retirement period of 28 years and retirement assets of $500,000 (not counting pension and Social Security), they could generate $35,000 in income per year with a bond portfolio earning 7 percent. But after taking into account inflation at 4 percent, their achievable retirement income in terms of today's purchasing power would average only $22,000. At the end of 20 years, John and Sharon would have $500,000 left for their heirs, but it would be worth only $161,000 in terms of purchasing power at a 4 percent inflation rate. (To have $500,000 in purchasing power available in 28 years, they would actually need to have about $731,000 put away at retirement.)

On the other hand, let's say they wanted to set aside $500,000 for their heirs after 20 years and were willing to invest in stocks and bonds that could earn an average 9 percent return. They could set aside a reserve of $161,000 in today's purchasing power ($500,000 in future dollars), spend down the remaining principal, and achieve retirement income of about $29,000.

This concept will be addressed more fully in Chapter 10, but for now remember that retirement will be a long period and inflation will take its toll even at the modest annual rates we have seen recently. It's likely, therefore, that you'll need to spend at least a portion of your principal during retirement. So, if you want to reserve a portion of that principal for your heirs, incorporate it in your plan today!

HOW MUCH SHOULD I BE SAVING?

That's the first question we hear from most people who are beginning to plan for retirement. The answer? It depends! Perhaps the easiest and best answer is, As much as you can! Hopefully, the retirement sufficiency analysis we just completed has shown that you can't just stop with the answer to this question. Unfortunately, though, that is precisely where many retirement plans end—with a savings goal and a time horizon. Given the many variables we have just looked at, trying to find the "right" retirement savings goal means shooting at a fast-moving target! Sound retirement planning should consider a retirement savings goal as a starting point, but also take into account the numerous other variables we have just illustrated. But to help with getting you started on a savings plan, the Appendix contains worksheets to help you set a goal, and Chapter 9 explains how to save for retirement using the tax laws to your advantage.

SO HOW DO *I* DO THIS?

Chapters 4 through 6 have illustrated a comprehensive approach to a retirement sufficiency calculation for our sample couple, John and Sharon. All of the calculations were performed using the *Price Water-house Retirement Planning System* (RPS), which is available for $45 (plus shipping, handling, and sales tax) in DOS or Windows™ versions. (Sorry, no Macintosh versions.) To perform the same calculations yourself, you may order a copy by calling us at 1-800-752-6234. Using a software application lets you look at things in many different ways using many different variables. RPS helps you to explore different life expectancies, inflation rates, investment returns, variable savings strategies, and much more.

RETIREMENT INCOME SOURCES

CHAPTER 7   Adding Up Your Social Security Benefits   81

CHAPTER 8   Maximizing Your Company Retirement Benefits   95

CHAPTER 9   The How's and Why's of Savings for Retirement   109

CHAPTER 10   Other Sources of Retirement Income   125

ADDING UP YOUR SOCIAL SECURITY BENEFITS

In this chapter, we examine Social Security income in some detail. Read on to understand:

- What benefits you are entitled to receive.
- What is the best age to begin taking your benefits.
- How Social Security indexing works.
- How to apply for benefits.
- Social Security benefits if you work while "retired."

We'll also discuss future prospects of the Social Security system and some proposals to prevent the much-discussed possibility of default.

When our lawmakers adopted the 1935 Social Security Act, they intended to provide retirement benefits for working Americans. Since

Table 7–1	Changing Ratio of Workers to Retirees	
Year	**Ratio**	
1945	42:1	
1984	3.3:1	
2020	2.4:1	

Source: Social Security Administration.

that time, a lot has changed. Today, Social Security provides retirement benefits not only for wage earners but for their spouses and dependents as well. And benefits may also be paid if you become disabled or if you die before retirement. In addition, Social Security programs such as Medicare cover many medical costs of Americans 65 years of age or older.

Probably the most-asked question these days is, "Will Social Security even be around when I retire?" Many federal budget watchers predict an end to the Social Security system in its present form by the time baby boomers reach retirement age, starting around the year 2010. Make no mistake—some reform is necessary, since Social Security deficits are projected to be staggering and can't be ignored.

Social Security's problems have several causes. First, because of the aging baby boom generation, the number of people age 65 or older in the United States is expected to double to about 65 million individuals by the year 2030. Also, demographic studies indicate that fewer and fewer workers will be available to fund the benefits payable to this growing group of retirees. (See Table 7–1.) With these constraints, Social Security is bound to exhaust its current surplus fairly soon (as early as 2036, according to some estimates).

Recent proposals for resolving the pending deficits include:

- Reducing automatic cost-of-living increases for the wealthy. This is a most difficult issue from a political standpoint. Cost-of-living increases are considered sacrosanct by most current retirees.
- Raising the normal retirement age—perhaps to age 70 or 72. Under current law, the retirement age will increase to 67 by 2027.
- Reducing benefits for the top 20 to 40 percent of wage earners. This would also meet with heavy political opposition.
- "Privatizing" the system by setting up individual pension accounts to which workers would contribute over their lifetime.

What does this mean to you? You should be saving and investing to protect yourself against future reductions in Social Security benefits! Try calculating your retirement sufficiency without some or all of your

Social Security and see what you would need to do to absorb any short-falls. Conservatively speaking, the question is not whether Social Security will be reduced, but by how much and for whom!

So what number do you use in your retirement sufficiency calculation? Use one based on the current rules. Then revise your plan to show only 75 percent of your current projected benefit. Then assume that cost-of-living adjustments won't be there. Remember, you want to understand the implications of a variety of potential future changes that may affect your current savings and investment strategies as well as future income needs.

WHAT DO YOU GET FOR WHAT YOU PUT IN?

In addition to the collapse of the system itself, many people fear that they will never get back from Social Security the amounts they paid in. This highlights part of the controversy: Is Social Security a pay-as-you-go system for current retirees or is it creating a retirement savings that a worker can draw down once retired? If you take the latter view—that is, your money is being set aside to be paid back to you once you've retired—you may be surprised. No matter what you may hear, Social Security is very much a pay-as-you-go system. Here are some numbers to illustrate the point.

Say you started working at age 25, you're married, your spouse is not employed, and you retire at age 65. Say, too, that you paid the maximum Social Security tax every year. Table 7–2 shows how benefits for you and your spouse would add up.

Now, how long will it take you to recoup the total amount of Social Security taxes you've paid over the years? The answer is not long, as

Table 7–2	Social Security Taxes Paid and Benefits				
	Current Age				
	65	62	55	45	35
Total Social Security tax paid through age 65	$58,472	$73,283	$115,197	$197,369	$310,145
Projected annual joint benefit	20,640	24,716	34,176	52,561	76,479

Table 7–3	How Long to Recoup Social Security Taxes					
		Current Age				
		65	62	55	45	35
Number of years to recoup your total Social Security taxes paid through age 65		2.83	2.97	3.37	3.76	4.06

we see in Table 7–3. Actually, the answer is a little better than the chart shows because each year the benefit is increased for a cost-of-living adjustment. So you would actually get your money back somewhat faster than the table shows.

But what if you'd invested the amount paid in Social Security taxes at, say, 8 percent instead of sending the money to Washington? If you started withdrawing your projected joint benefit at 65, how many years would your invested money last?

As Table 7–4 shows, someone who invested his contributions would probably come up short because the average life expectancy for a 65-year-old is 80.7 for men and 84.5 for women. So, for instance, a 65-year-old would run out of money in eight years—at age 73—yet she would be expected to live past 80. In that case, receiving a monthly check from Social Security would be a better deal than investing the Social Security taxes on her own.

However, Social Security is not as favorable for the 35-year-old. Paying into Social Security would only look like a better deal if he lived past 97! But, who knows, in 30 years 65-year-olds may be expected to live to 100!

Table 7–4	How Long if You Apply an Investment Return					
		Current Age				
		65	62	55	45	35
Number of years to recoup your total Social Security taxes paid through age 65 if you'd invested these dollars at a 8% rate of return		8.13	9.22	13.31	21.89	32.28

Note: Assumes benefit amount would grow each year by a 4 percent cost-of-living adjustment.

EARNINGS AND YOUR BENEFITS

Simply stated, your earnings determine the amount of Social Security benefits you ultimately receive. The more you make, the more you'll receive, although there are certain maximum contribution and benefit limits. The law bases your retirement benefits on your average earnings for a 30-to-35-year period. (The number of years used ranges from 30 years for people born in 1924 to 35 years for people born after 1928.)

You're eligible for benefits if you are—in the jargon of the Social Security Administration—"fully insured," meaning you've built up 40 "calendar quarters of coverage." In 1995, you receive a calendar quarter of coverage for every $630 per quarter you earn up to a maximum of four quarters each year.

Once you've worked the 40 quarters (the equivalent of ten years), you're fully insured for life—and entitled to benefits even if you never work again. If you were born before 1929, you need fewer than 40 quarters to qualify. Check with your local Social Security office to determine the exact number, or call Social Security at 1-800-772-1213.

The Office of Central Operations of the Social Security Administration keeps earnings records for every American who has a Social Security number. Employers—and in the case of self-employed people, the IRS—send reports of earnings to this central office.

To check your earnings, all you need to do is fill out Form SSA-7004-SM ("Request for Earnings and Benefit Estimate Statement") and mail it to the Social Security Administration. You can obtain this form from your local Social Security Administration office or U.S. post office.

It's a good idea to check your earnings record because errors, while rare, do sometimes occur.

Social Security Projections

Tip

Starting in 1995, a Social Security account statement will be sent automatically to all individuals who have reached age 60 and are not receiving Social Security benefits. This statement will show (1) the individual's earnings, (2) an estimate of the individual's contributions to the Social Security program, and (3) an estimate of the individual's future benefits at retirement. Then, starting no later than 1999, Social Security expects to send estimates annually to individuals under age 60 as well.

We recommend that you check your earnings about once every three years, especially if you've changed employers or if you work for more than one company. If you find that some of your earnings aren't on the form, contact your local Social Security office at once to get the problem corrected.

HOW MUCH WILL YOU RECEIVE?

The maximum first year benefit for someone retiring in 1995 at the normal retirement age of 65 is $14,388. If the person's spouse was also age 65 and was applying for Social Security benefits based on the retiree's earnings record, they could expect to receive an additional $7,188, for a total benefit of $21,576. Of course, if the spouse had worked for many years at a substantial salary, they might be better off collecting benefits based on the person's own individual record instead of the spouse's.

If each of you is entitled to benefits because of your own earnings, you'll receive benefits independently of one another. Your spouse may collect either a spousal benefit or his own benefit (whichever is greater) but not both.

You can draw benefits as early as age 62, but your benefit amount will be reduced. Currently, a retiree who starts collecting Social Security benefits at age 62 receives about 80 percent of her age-65 benefit. The 20 percent reduction reflects the fact that the worker is able to collect a benefit for three

Figure 7–1

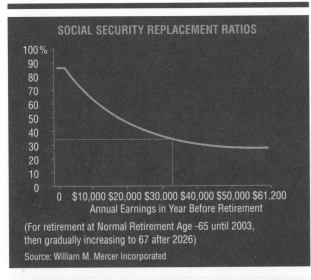

SOCIAL SECURITY REPLACEMENT RATIOS

Annual Earnings in Year Before Retirement

(For retirement at Normal Retirement Age -65 until 2003, then gradually increasing to 67 after 2026)

Source: William M. Mercer Incorporated

Age—65

additional years. As of 1995, the most that an age-62 retiree could receive is about $11,500.

Your nonemployed spouse is also eligible for a benefit. At age 65, your spouse can receive 50 percent of your benefit, whereas at age 62 the amount is 37.5 percent of your age-65 benefit. The actual benefit varies, depending on the age of each of you when you begin drawing benefits. You must begin to draw benefits before your spouse can collect based on your earnings record.

A divorced spouse can also receive benefits if he does not remarry. To collect a divorced spouse's benefit, you must have been married for at least 10 years.

Spousal benefits can be reduced if your spouse worked in a federal, state, or local government job and was not covered by Social Security when their employment ended. Under this rule, two-thirds of your spouse's pension benefits from that job will be used to reduce your spousal Social Security benefit (i.e. your spouse can receive only the Social Security benefit that exceeds two-thirds of his government pension.) There are some exceptions. Contact the Social Security Administration for more information.

Table 7–5   Normal Retirement Age—Now and in the Future

The *normal retirement* will slowly rise to age 67 for persons born after 1959. For persons born between 1938 and 1959, the normal retirement age will be somewhere between 65 and 67. Therefore, someone born in 1960 cannot receive 100 percent of her benefit, unless she begins collecting Social Security benefits at age 67. And, if she wanted to begin collecting benefits at age 62, she would only receive 70 percent of her benefit.

Year of Birth	Normal Retirement Age	Year of Birth	Normal Retirement Age
Before 1938	65	1955	66 and 2 months
1938	65 and 2 months	1956	66 and 4 months
1939	65 and 4 months	1957	66 and 6 months
1940	65 and 6 months	1958	66 and 8 months
1941	65 and 8 months	1959	66 and 10 months
1942	65 and 10 months	1960 and After	67
1943–54	66		

Source: William M. Mercer Incorporated

Table 7–6	Social Security Inflation Adjustments, 1989–94

Year	Increase
1989	4.7%
1990	5.4
1991	3.7
1992	3.0
1993	2.6
1994	2.8
1995	2.4

THE BEAUTY OF INDEXING

Unlike most corporate pension plans, Social Security benefits have an automatic annual cost-of-living adjustment (COLA). The increase becomes effective in December; therefore, your January check will be the first month to reflect the increase. Table 7–6 shows the increases from 1989 to 1994. These increases might not seem substantial, but they will ensure that your Social Security benefits do not lose purchasing power. As we saw in Chapter 6, this is a tremendous benefit: for John and Sharon, a whopping $391,000 over a 28-year period if inflation were to average 4 percent.

APPLYING FOR BENEFITS

You can apply for benefits by going to any Social Security office or by calling their toll-free number, 1-800-772-1213. The best times to call are early in the morning and early in the evening. If you can, it's best to call later in the week and later in the month. It's smart to apply for Social Security three months before you expect to begin receiving your benefits. That way, you won't have to wait for your check.

COLLECTING YOUR BENEFITS

As we saw in Chapter 6, collecting Social Security benefits before normal retirement age affects how much you'll receive. For every month before your *normal* retirement age that you begin receiving benefits, your benefits are reduced by five-ninths of 1 percent.

So if you were 62 and started collecting your benefit, your check would be 80 percent of the full benefit you would otherwise be entitled to receive (36 months early × 5/9 × 1% = 20% reduction). If you were born after 1959 and wanted to begin benefits at age 62, your check would be 70 percent of the full benefit.

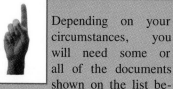

Tip

Applying for Benefits: Information You Will Need

Depending on your circumstances, you will need some or all of the documents shown on the list below. But don't delay your application because you don't have all the information. If you don't have a document you need, Social Security can usually help you get it.

- Your Social Security number.
- Your birth certificate.
- Your W-2 forms or, if you are self-employed, your last year's tax return.
- Your checking or savings account information for direct deposit.
- Your military discharge papers if you had military service.

- If your spouse is applying for benefits based on your earnings record, your spouse's birth certificate and Social Security number and a copy of your marriage certificate.
- If your children are applying for children's benefits, their birth certificates and Social Security numbers.
- If you're divorced, you may need your divorce papers.

Start obtaining these documents several months before applying for benefits. You must submit original documents or copies certified by the issuing office. You can mail or bring them to Social Security. They will make photocopies and return your documents.

Conversely, for every month after normal retirement age that you postpone collecting Social Security, the benefits go up. For those born in 1929 and 1930, future Social Security benefits increase 4½ percent a year—but only until age 70. For people born after 1930, the percent increase is even larger. It rises gradually (½ percent each two years) to 8 percent per year of delay for those born after 1942.

So if you were going to retire in the next couple of years, would you be better off collecting your benefits at age 62 or waiting until age 65? Most people are better off collecting their benefits at age 62—assuming they don't continue to work and earn more than the earnings limit (see the next section). In fact, the only people who collect more over the long haul by waiting until they're 65 to receive benefits are those who live beyond age 74, as Figure 7–2 shows.

Figure 7–2

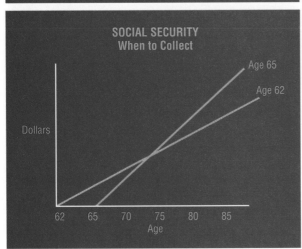

The chart looks at a worker who paid the maximum Social Security taxes until she retired this year at age 62. It assumes that her Social Security benefits will increase each year by a 4 percent cost-of-living adjustment. If she starts receiving her reduced benefit at age 62, the total of the checks she receives will be more than if she waited to receive a larger check at age 65 until she turns 74. At that point, the total of her larger age-65 checks will be over $192,000 yet the total of her smaller age-62 checks will total just over $189,000.

EARNINGS LIMITS AND WORKING DURING RETIREMENT

You can lose all or part of your monthly Social Security benefits by earning wages or self-employment income over the annual earnings limit. The amount you lose depends on your age and how much your earnings top these ceilings as shown in Table 7–7.

But in the first year you become eligible for benefits, a favorable monthly test applies that allows you to start drawing your benefits once you retire although you may already have exceeded the earnings limitation in that given year.

For example, say in 1995, you turn 65 and retire. You'd receive full benefits for any month in which your employment earnings are less than $940, even if you already earned more than $11,280 prior to receiving benefits.

If you're ages 62 to 64, you lose no benefits during your first year of retirement as long as your monthly earnings don't top $680. You should know that you can apply this monthly test only in the first year you're eligible for Social Security benefits.

Now what if in the year you retire you earn less than the earnings limitation amount. Then you should apply to have your retirement benefits begin in January even though you may not retire until later in the year.

Table 7–7	Social Security Earnings Limitations

1995 LIMITS:

Under age 65	Age 65–69
$8,160	$11,280

BENEFITS ARE REDUCED:

- Under age 65, $1 for every $2 earned over the limitation
- Age 65–69, $1 for every $3 earned over the limitation
- Earnings limitations are adjusted each year

Your Social Security benefits will not be reduced for excess earnings when you are age 70 or older.

Social Security allows you to work as much as you want once you turn 70—the earnings limitation will no longer apply so you won't sacrifice any Social Security benefits. Of course, regardless of how old you are, if you have any employment earnings, you will have to *pay* Social Security taxes on those earnings.

If you're earning more than you're allowed, call the Social Security Administration and report the information to them. You'll probably find it less painful to receive less in benefits now than face having to pay back benefits that you weren't entitled to receive.

Moreover, if you intentionally fail to report your earnings or report them incorrectly, you'll pay a penalty. The penalty equals one or more months of lost benefits. In addition to the penalty, you must repay your excess benefits.

EARLY RETIREMENT AND YOUR BENEFITS

Table 7–8	Social Security Benefits at Different Ages

Age at Which You Stop Working	Approximate Annual Benefit (Today's Dollars)
62	$11,500
60	10,800
57	10,300
55	9,900

Table assumes the individual begins to draw benefits at age 62 and had maximum taxable earnings throughout his career.

A common question from those retiring before age 62 is whether not having earnings during the few years up to retirement will materially affect the amount of benefits received. The answer: not as much as you might think. Because Social

Are Your Social Security Benefits Taxable?

Caution

Although Social Security benefits are tax-free for federal purposes for most people, up to 85 percent can be taxable for individuals with high income. So what is high income? First, let's look at the definition of *income.*

Income, for purposes of this taxability test, includes your adjusted gross income or AGI (the total of your income before you subtract your deductions and personal exemptions: it is the last line of the first page of your tax return) plus 50 percent of your Social Security benefits, plus interest on tax-free investments (municipal bonds, tax-free money market funds, but *not* interest earned in your retirement accounts such as your IRAs or 401(k) plans).

This modified adjusted gross income is then compared to two thresholds. For single taxpayers, the thresholds are $25,000 and $34,000. For married persons, the amounts are $32,000 and $44,000.

Fifty percent of any excess over the first threshold plus 35 percent of any excess over the second threshold is considered taxable

income. This amount, however, cannot exceed the smaller of (a) 85 percent of the benefits or (b) 50 percent of the benefits, plus 85 percent of any excess over the second threshold. Clear as mud? Maybe this example for a married couple will help.

Adjusted gross income	$50,000
Tax-free municipal bond interest	6,000
50% of Social Security benefits ($20,000)	10,000
Modified adjusted gross income	$66,000
Excess of income over first threshold ($32,000)	$34,000
Excess of income over second threshold ($44,000)	$22,000
1. 50% of excess over first plus 35% over second (.50 × $34,000 + .35 × $22,000)	$24,700
2. 85% of benefits (.85 × $20,000)	$17,000
3. 50% of benefits, plus 85% over 2nd (.50 × $20,000 + .85 × $22,000)	$28,700

The smallest of these three figures, $17,000, becomes the taxable portion of the Social Security benefits.

Security uses up to 35 years of earnings in its calculation, losing a few years does not have as great an effect as it might in, say, a corporate

---

Reductions in Social Security Benefits if You Work

Caution

Let's take a closer look at how working can cut into your benefits. Assume you're 63 years old and retired. You decide to work part-time to supplement your retirement income of $42,000; you earn $20,000 during the year. Before you pat yourself on the back, let's figure how much of that $20,000 you give back to Uncle Sam.

Assuming you're in the 28 percent bracket, Uncle Sam will take a hefty $5,600 (or 28 percent times $20,000) in federal taxes. Your Social Security taxes that will be withheld total another $1,530 (or 7.65 times $20,000). Let's also assume a 5 percent state tax bite of $1,000 (or 5 percent times $20,000).

Finally, you'll lose $5,920 in Social Security benefits ($1 for every $2 your $20,000 exceeds $8,160 − 50% × ($20,000 − $8,160)). In other words, because of taxes and lost Social Security benefits, you take home only $5,950—a mere 30 percent of your earnings. And we didn't even consider whether the increase in income causes more of your Social Security benefits to be taxed!

---

pension plan. Table 7–8 shows the amount of benefits you could receive if you stopped working at various ages before age 62.

WHERE TO GET ADDITIONAL INFORMATION

You can ask the Social Security Administration for free copies of "Retirement" (Publication 05-10035) and "Understanding Social Security" (Publication 05-10024). You may telephone the Social Security Administration—toll-free at 1-800-772-1213 or, if you prefer, you may write them at

Social Security Administration
Department of Health and Human Services
Baltimore, MD 21235

Social Security benefits, of course, provide only one part of your retirement income. In the next chapter, we'll look at maximizing the benefits from your company retirement plans.

CHAPTER 8

MAXIMIZING YOUR COMPANY RETIREMENT BENEFITS

This chapter covers company retirement plans by answering several basic questions:

- What are the general types of company retirement plans?
- How do pension plans work?
- Who bears the risk if plan investments don't perform?
- Who bears the life expectancy risk and why it is important?
- Why is there a rise in the number of defined contribution plans?

If you're like most people, your company retirement and savings plan will be one of the most important sources of income for you during retirement. This chapter addresses the types of retirement plans that may be available from your company and the benefits you can expect during retirement. Chapters 18 and 19 discuss how you get your money out once you're at retirement age.

To put company retirement plans in perspective, you should focus on several basic questions such as

- Who contributes to the plan?
- Who bears the risk if investments don't perform?
- How long do you get paid?
- How do you take your money out?

Answering these questions can help you understand how these plans work, their potential effects on your retirement income, and what you may need to do to maximize the income from each of them. To begin answering them, we'll describe traditional pension plans, often referred to as *defined benefit plans.*

DEFINED BENEFIT PLANS

A defined benefit plan is a retirement plan that pays a fixed monthly income at retirement, based on your salary and years of service. Over the years, companies have set up these plans, made contributions to a trust, and committed to pay employees a percentage of salary for life, regardless of how much money the company put away or how their plan investments performed in the long run. Under most traditional defined benefit plans, only the company makes contributions toward your retirement, although some so-called *contributory plans* allow you to make supplemental contributions.

With a defined benefit plan, pension actuaries calculate what future pension benefits may be payable and whether current plan assets and estimated future investment earnings will meet those obligations. If this analysis shows a shortfall (an "underfunded plan") the company must make additional current contributions. On the other hand, if the plan's assets exceed future obligations, the company may not need to make current contributions because the plan is overfunded. As Table 8–1 indicates, these calculations involve many complex variables, the use of "reasonable" assumptions, and laborious computations.

Table 8–1	Key Factors That Influence Pension Funding

Employee life expectancies
Employee retirement ages
Employee death rates before
  retirement
Vesting period for benefits
Employee turnover rates
Employee salary levels
Projected investment returns
Funding levels in previous years
Cost-of-living adjustments to benefits
  (where provided)

It's important to emphasize that your company's defined benefit plan is obligated to pay you a benefit even if plan investments perform poorly, because your payment is determined by a formula, not by the balance in "your" particular plan account. The pension plan itself bears the investment risk so the investment return assumptions used by the plan actuaries can heavily affect the plan's ability to meet its obligations. That's why some large companies (particularly in the steel, airline, and auto industries) have had to make extra pension contributions to reduce funding deficits. In some cases plans have even become insolvent. In part due to overaggressive investment assumptions, the companies put in too little over the years and came up short when plan investments did not perform as expected.

Note

What If My Company's Pension Plan Fails?

During the 1980s, the problem of pension underfunding became acute in the United States. At the end of 1992, corporate pensions were underfunded by $53 billion in the aggregate, although 75 percent of the underfunding was contained in about 50 companies. If a pension trust actually goes bankrupt, however, there is a payor of last resort, of course—the federal government.

The Pension Benefit Guaranty Corporation (PBGC) insures pensions in a way roughly similar to how the FDIC insures bank accounts. PBGC charges the plan a premium (called a *head tax*) for each participant covered by PBGC insurance.

Importantly, this insurance applies only to defined benefit plans. Other types of retirement plans are not insured. And you may not get the full value of your pension. The maximum benefit payable by the PBGC is currently around $27,000 per year.

HOW PENSION FORMULAS WORK

In a defined benefit plan, you participate in the plan but do not have an individual savings account as you would in a bank. Instead, the payment you receive each month is determined by a formula.

Figure 8–1 shows a simplified example of how a typical formula might work. Three main items determine how much you will receive from a defined benefit plan: your salary, your length of service with the company, and the "factor" or percentage that your company's plan formula specifies.

The factor is simply a percentage—here, 1.8 percent—applied to an average salary figure. Depending on the plan, the salary figure could be an average of your salary over your entire career (called a *career average plan*) or your salary over your final three to five years out of the past 10 years of employment (called a *final average plan*).

The difference between a career average plan and final average plan is significant, and can have a dramatic effect on your final pension. A career average salary can result in a smaller pension because your early salary years bring down the average over a long period of time. Final average salary only looks to your later, generally higher paid years.

Most pension formulas also reduce your pension benefit by offsetting it with a portion of your expected Social Security benefits. Your company paid for half of your benefit and the offset is a means of recovering some of that outlay.

This basic pension formula calculates a *single-life annuity,* mean-

Figure 8–1	Sample Pension Formula		
Final average salary			$60,000
Times: factor (1.8%)			1.80%
			1,080
Times: years of service with company			30
			32,400
Minus: Social Security offset			
Primary Social Security benefit		$13,000	
Times: factor (1.67%)		1.67%	
		217	
Times: years of service with company		30	
			(6,513)
Annual pension benefit payable at age 65			$25,887
Salary replacement ratio			43%

What Can You Expect?

Note

Most pension formulas are designed to provide a lifetime benefit that replaces somewhere between 40 and 60 percent of the salary figure used in the calculation. Generally, the lower your compensation, the higher the replacement ratio. For higher-paid people, certain tax rules may apply to limit the amount that can be paid through a qualified pension plan, so companies may set up excess or supplemental benefit plans to pay out the extra amounts needed to replace that higher salary. If you participate in an excess plan, some important tax rules apply. For example, you cannot roll over a lump sum distribution from an excess plan to an IRA. These are discussed in more detail in Chapters 18 and 19.

ing the amount is payable only to the employee over his lifetime. A single-life annuity is a monthly payment calculated on the basis of your projected life expectancy. A *joint-and-survivor annuity,* by contrast, is based on the life expectancies of the employee and a spouse or other beneficiary. With a joint-and-survivor annuity, the beneficiary continues to receive payments until she dies. As shown in Table 8–2, the benefit amount paid is less under the joint-and-survivor option because the company expects to pay the benefit for a longer period of time over two lives. In Chapter 17, we discuss how to choose between these and other pension options.

Table 8–2	Single-Life Versus Joint-and-Survivor Benefits
Age 65, single-life benefit	$25,887
Age 65, 50% Joint-and-survivor benefit	$23,298
Survivor's benefit after death of employee	$11,649

Note: This assumes payment of a 50 percent joint-and-survivor benefit where worker and survivor are the same age. This is a sample calculation only. Individual plan formulas will differ.

EARLY RETIREMENT REDUCTIONS

Figure 8–1 shows how the formula works for a person retiring at the normal retirement age of 65. But what would happen if he retired at age 60 instead? When you retire early, most companies "discount" your pension by a certain percentage per month. So, if in our example, the company discounts your pension by 0.25

percent per month for each month that you retire before age 65, your pension benefit would be reduced by 15 percent—that is, 12 months times 5 years times 0.25 percent per month. In the same way as we saw with Social Security, these reductions make up for the fact that if you retire early, the company expects to pay your pension over a longer period of time.

The specific terms of your pension plan formula are contained in the Summary Plan Description (SPD). This must be distributed by your company to all employees periodically, so check with your benefits office if you haven't received one.

PENSIONS AND YOUR LIFE EXPECTANCY

Remember that pension payments continue for your life (and the life of your survivors if you elect survivor benefits) regardless of the life expectancy used in calculating your benefit. Put another way, if you outlive your projected life expectancy, you come out ahead because the plan actuaries calculated the necessary plan contributions assuming that you would live to exactly your projected life expectancy. Because of this guarantee, the plan in effect takes the risk that you will outlive your life expectancy, while you take the risk that you might die shortly after beginning to draw benefits and not collect the full benefit projected under the pension formula. We'll refer to this concept as *life expectancy risk.*

Life expectancy risk has important implications to both you and the pension plan. For example, if over time the actual lifetimes of plan participants (called *mortality experience*) turn out to be longer than projected, the plan has to pay out more benefits than the actuaries might have expected. This could cause a shortfall in plan assets in the future. On the other hand, if employees die earlier than projected, the plan will have surplus assets.

Your individual life expectancy is also important in choosing how you take your benefits. For example, if your family has a history of longevity and you are in good health, you might be able to "beat the tables" and do better with a life or joint-and-survivor pension annuity. However, if your health is poor, you might elect another option, such as a term certain benefit (providing guaranteed benefits over, say, 10 or 20 years) or even a lump sum, which is calculated by the plan assuming you live exactly to your projected life expectancy. We discuss these issues further later in this chapter and in Chapters 17 and 18.

WATCH THOSE PENSION ESTIMATES!

With a defined benefit plan, your employer isn't obligated to provide you with a projection of your benefits at retirement while you are working, but many companies do. Obviously, this projection is quite valuable in understanding your expected retirement income. You need it to do an accurate retirement sufficiency calculation.

Typically, the company provides an estimate assuming you will work until age 65 and that you will have no salary increases from now until you retire. You might think that this estimate isn't accurate because you hope to have future salary increases which will increase your pension.

In reality, this is the preferred number because it is stating your pension in *today's dollars;* that is, it states the amount of purchasing power your pension check will have when you retire. The actual pension you will receive will probably be larger because of future salary increases. But, it's not the amount of your check that's important; it's how much it will buy you that's important.

Watch the factors that the company uses to prepare this estimate, however. Your employer, for example, might provide you with an estimate of your benefits for age 65. But you may plan to retire at age 62 or earlier. Or the company might give you an estimate based solely on your single-life expectancy, but you might want to elect a joint-and-survivor annuity (which, as we said before, will reduce your pension benefit amount). You can probably ask your company's benefits department for help in obtaining an estimate of your benefits tailored to your own needs.

But perhaps the biggest drawback is that the estimate is typically only applicable for your first retirement year. And the reason, as we'll explain later, is that most pension plans do not make automatic cost-of-living adjustments once you begin drawing your pension. Therefore, as we saw in Chapter 6, your pension's purchasing power shrinks with each passing year.

PENSION INDEXING—FACT OR FICTION?

An important issue surrounding corporate pension benefits in the United States is that most are not indexed for inflation. A recent Hewitt Associates LLC survey shows that between 1988 and 1992, only 33 percent of companies that have pension plans provided cost-of-living adjustments (COLAs) for retirees. And many of these companies did so

Pension Indexing for COLA

Note Pension indexing is also common in foreign countries. In the United Kingdom, for example, the majority of companies increase not only retiree benefits, but also those for employees who leave the company with a vested benefit. Many people have commented that this is a fundamental weakness of private pensions in America, but few are able to successfully argue for COLA increases in an era of corporate cost cutting.

only because the automatic increase was part of the plan design, as is common in negotiated union arrangements.

Make no mistake about it—the cost of pension indexing would be significant for most companies. In your retirement capital sufficiency analysis, unless you have a plan that mandates COLAs you should not plan on them, even on a delayed basis. If you're a federal government employee, however, pensions are regularly increased for cost-of-living adjustments by law. But, as a means of helping to achieve a federal balanced budget, this has also been thrown on the table as a bargaining chip.

Regardless of how you view the issue, you should understand its implications for your retirement. If you expect that the majority of your retirement income will come from Social Security and pensions, you must act now to supplement your retirement income through savings and prudent investing. Otherwise, as we saw earlier, inflation will have a pronounced effect on your retirement income even assuming Social Security continues to provide cost-of-living increases.

Table 8–3	Defined Benefit versus Defined Contribution Plans	
	Defined Benefit	**Defined Contribution**
Who contributes?	Usually employer only	Employer and employee
How are benefits paid?	Guaranteed monthly benefit (sometimes lump sum)	Generally lump sum
Who bears investment risk?	Employer	Employee
Is benefit insured?	Yes, within PBGC limits	No

DEFINED CONTRIBUTION PLANS

Based on what we have discussed so far, the need to supplement pensions and Social Security with other retirement resources should be apparent. As we saw earlier, when you are projecting future retirement income as part of a sufficiency analysis you need to know

- Current retirement savings.
- Future contribution levels.
- Rate of return on investments.

Most companies provide a way to accumulate those additional resources through defined contribution plans. With a defined contribution plan, you *or* your company—or you *and* your company—contribute a set amount annually (5 percent of your salary, for example). The amount you receive when you retire depends not only on the amount that was put away each year but also on how well those dollars were invested.

One advantage of defined contribution plans is that the benefits are portable. That is, if you leave your job you can usually take your benefits with you. Most pension plans, on the other hand, require you to first meet vesting requirements, and then pay you a deferred benefit when you reach your retirement age. (Some newer plans allow you to take a portable "cash balance" with you if you leave your job.) Another advantage is that it's easy to keep track of the savings balance you are accumulating. If you participate in a defined contribution plan, your company must notify you of your account balance at least once a year.

Defined contribution plans come in a number of varieties. Many companies even allow employees to participate in more than one type of plan. The most common defined contribution plans are profit-sharing plans, employee thrift plans [401(k) plans], money purchase plans, stock bonus plans, and employee stock ownership plans.

PROFIT-SHARING PLANS

A profit-sharing plan allows workers to share in company profits, usually based on a percentage of salary. It used to be that a company could make contributions to such a plan only if it posted a profit—but no more. Under current law, a company may make contributions to a profit-sharing plan even if it reports no earnings. Also, it may change

Calculating Your Company's Contribution

Tip

An employer may calculate its contributions using a formula that takes a number of factors into account, including the amount you earn each year. The rules say, however, that the employer's contribution generally may not top 15 percent of the total compensation of all workers.

Here's an example. Say your employer will contribute 10 percent of its profits to its employees' retirement accounts. The company's earnings that year equal $1 million so it plans to contribute a total of $100,000.

However, the total compensation of its work force comes to only $500,000. That means the company's total contribution for the year is limited to $75,000 (or 15 percent times $500,000), and your share is reduced proportionally. The $25,000 difference gets carried over to the following year.

the contribution from one year to the next. Normally, profit-sharing contributions are allocated to employee accounts in proportion to their current salary, and the company—not you—decides how the money in the plan is invested. (Some companies give you control, but often not until age 55 when you're getting close to retirement.)

401(k) PLANS

Employee thrift and savings plans—or 401(k)s, as they're usually known—are also defined contribution plans. In these plans, you contribute a portion of your earnings to the plan, and your employer may match all or a portion of your contributions. You decide how the contributions are invested, choosing from among the investment choices your employer makes available to you. Because 401(k) plans have become so popular, we devote much of the next chapter to them.

MONEY PURCHASE PLANS

Money purchase plans—unlike employee thrift and savings plans—are technically considered pension plans. That's because the company has a fixed obligation under the plan to make contributions whether or not it

posts a profit. The amount an employer contributes to a money purchase plan is based on a percentage of the compensation of all participants. But the most a company may contribute is 25 percent of the
earnings of employees who participate in all the employer's defined
contribution plans. Again, the company normally decides how the
money in the plan is invested.

EMPLOYEE STOCK OWNERSHIP PLANS

Employee stock ownership plans (ESOPs) invest in the stock of the
company that sponsors the plan. So your retirement benefit depends
on how well your company's stock performs. Over the past 10 years,
ESOPs have become very popular in connection with employee-led
company buyouts and as a means of encouraging employee ownership
of company stock.

ESOP rules say that when you reach age 55, you may diversify a
portion of your account into other investments. (A similar rule applies
to other retirement plans, such as profit-sharing plans, that invest primarily in company stock.)

403(b) PLANS

A 403(b), often called a *tax-sheltered annuity,* is a retirement plan for
employees of public schools, universities, and tax-exempt organizations.
Since these organizations cannot have 401(k) plans, 403(b) plans allow

---

Note

Does the IRS Cap Contributions to Defined Contribution Plans?

Yes. The ceiling is the lesser of 25 per-cent of your annual earnings or $30,000 (which is 25 percent of $120,000).

In other words, if you partici-pate in two plans—a profit-sharing plan and an employee stock own-ership plan, say—no more than a total of $30,000 or 25 percent of your annual earnings, whichever is less, could be put away in your be-half. As we will explore in the next chapter, these limits (and some oth-ers) also apply to 401(k) plans.

employees to still contribute to their retirement on a pretax basis. The current contribution limit for 403(b) plans is $9,500 per year.

WHY HAVE DEFINED CONTRIBUTION PLANS BECOME SO POPULAR?

Defined contribution plans have become more popular because they cost less than defined benefit plans, and allow employers to shift some of the investment risks to employees. As we saw earlier, some of the variables used in defined benefit plan calculations are unpredictable. Employee life expectancy, investment returns, and federal regulations all change dramatically over time, which can make defined benefit plans' long-term cost hard to predict. There's a great deal of uncertainty for the employer because the employer bears the investment and the life expectancy risk.

For example, assume that you retired from your company after working 30 years. The company has been contributing to the plan assuming you would live to age 80 (based on actuarial assumptions), but now you live until 95. Although it only planned on your living until 80, the company will have to continue providing a check until you're 95.

Also, perhaps the pension was based on an average of your final five years' salaries. What would happen if inflation was excessive in the last five years and your salary increased dramatically because of cost-of-living increases? All along the company had been making contributions based on moderate inflation, but because inflation was high in just the last five years, the company is forced to pay you a larger benefit.

And what if the stock market crashed and the value of the plan's assets decreased dramatically? Your benefits would not change, yet the funds to provide these benefits would have shrunk. The company would have to make up the difference. Defined benefit plans are also expensive to maintain and administer. Government regulations are onerous and the calculations to determine funding amounts are time-consuming and complex. Furthermore, PBGC premiums for insuring pension assets continue to soar, particularly if the plan is underfunded.

Defined *contribution* plans, on the other hand, do not have the level of uncertainty for employers that defined *benefit* plans have. Unlike a defined benefit plan, the benefit cost to the employer of a defined contribution plan is known each year and the administrative costs are far less. Take a 401(k) plan in which your employer makes matching contributions to your account. Once the employer contributes the "match" to your account, the employer's cost is known. The final amount you receive depends on how your investments perform so you're the one who bears the investment risk. And if you spend all the plan assets early on in your retirement, it's you who suffers because you also bear the life expectancy risk.

Finally, defined contribution plans also present challenges in determining a withdrawal strategy during your retirement. Years ago, your withdrawal strategy was simple—you received a monthly pension check. Now you need to calculate (1) how much you'll spend of your assets each year of retirement, (2) whether it will come from income, principal, or both, and (3) how long you can realistically expect your resources to last. We'll analyze these issues further in Chapters 17 and 18.

We've discussed a whole variety of retirement plans in this chapter. In the next chapter, we'll look further at the issue of tax-deferred savings by concentrating on 401(k) plans and IRAs.

CHAPTER 9

THE HOW'S AND WHY'S OF SAVING FOR RETIREMENT

In this chapter, we look at how to save for retirement and explore the various types of tax-deferred retirement vehicles. Read on to learn:

- The benefits of saving tax-deferred.
- Why you want to participate in a 401(k).
- The value of company matching.
- How much you can contribute.
- IRAs and annuities as alternatives.

As we saw in Chapter 6, the interplay between regular savings and a prudent investment strategy is one of the more important factors in achieving your income goals. In this chapter, we focus on saving through tax-deferred savings vehicles such as 401(k), 403(b), and 457 plans, Individual Retirement Accounts (IRAs), and the various forms of annuities. Chapter 11 will discuss how savings and investment strategies work together to help you maximize your retirement accumulations over time.

THE BENEFITS OF TAX-DEFERRED SAVINGS

As you recall from Chapter 8, retirement plans in which the employee takes the lead in contributing are becoming much more popular today. But this popularity comes at a price because of (1) early withdrawal penalties that limit access to your funds until you approach retirement age and (2) minimum distribution rules that force you to take money out before you might otherwise want to.

For most retirement savers, the benefits of tax-deferred savings far outweigh the lost flexibility and potential penalties. This is because you can build up your retirement assets in tax-deferred accounts much faster than you could with a savings account that's not tax-favored. And the best of both worlds is to save with pretax dollars (or get a current tax deduction for the money you put into the tax-deferred arrangement).

How much faster can you accumulate money? Suppose it's 1995, and you're a taxpayer in the 31 percent tax bracket. Each year for 25 years, you plan to contribute $8,000 of your earnings in a taxable investment with an average annual return of 8 percent. Actually, though, you only get to put $5,520 away because first you have to pay income taxes on your earnings, and those taxes add up to $2,480 a year—that is, 31 percent times $8,000. At the end of 25 years—after you pay your taxes each year—your investment will have grown to $269,793.

What if you set aside the same amount in your employer-sponsored 401(k)? And what if your dollars earned the same return—8 percent annually for 25 years? With your money in a 401(k), the earnings build up tax-deferred. Also, you have the *full* $8,000 to put away because you can put the money in the plan *before* taxes. In 25 years, you'd have an impressive $541,412 (or $271,619 more).

Of course, *tax-deferred* isn't the same as *tax-free*. The dollars you put away are taxable when they're withdrawn so you don't escape taxes entirely. You simply postpone them until you withdraw your money. Assuming you withdraw your money in a single sum and pay taxes at 31 percent, you'd still have $373,574, or $101,955 more than you would have had outside a tax-deferred savings plan. And you would probably put the money into a rollover IRA at retirement, take money out as you need it, and therefore pay taxes only on the money you withdraw at the time you withdraw it. In this way, the remaining balance would continue to grow tax-deferred, making the argument for the tax-deferred savings even stronger. (We talk more about IRA rollovers in Chapter 18.)

WHERE SHOULD YOU PUT YOUR SAVINGS FOR RETIREMENT?

If you can both contribute in pretax dollars and allow those dollars to grow tax-deferred, you have the best of all worlds. But even if you can only get tax deferral on the earnings, you're still likely to build your retirement assets faster. As we'll see, there is an order of investments you should consider to maximize the return on your retirement savings.

The first place to turn is to your company. You want to take full advantage of any tax-deferred plans your employer offers. For instance, if you can participate in a 401(k) plan, sign up at the first chance and put in the most you possibly can afford. Not only will you defer taxes on current income, you will defer taxes on the earnings, and hopefully you will also receive a match from your employer.

The next step is still the 401(k), but to make after-tax contributions. Not all plans allow them, but if yours does, it's similar to making a nondeductible IRA contribution without the $2,000 limitation. [Your after-tax contributions will be limited by the percent limits in your 401(k) plan, however.]

The next step is to consider an IRA. Even though you might not be able to get a tax deduction for the annual contribution, the earnings grow tax-deferred, and, as we have seen, that can be worth a lot.

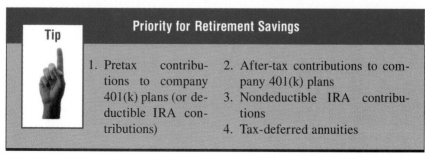

Priority for Retirement Savings

Tip

1. Pretax contributions to company 401(k) plans (or deductible IRA contributions)

2. After-tax contributions to company 401(k) plans

3. Nondeductible IRA contributions

4. Tax-deferred annuities

One other tax-deferred option is annuities. Here's another way to invest your money and let it grow for you while keeping the IRS away from the earnings for as long as possible. As we discuss later, however, annuities have their disadvantages and are generally appropriate only after you've exhausted other tax-deferred choices.

After you have exhausted these tax-deferred vehicles, what generally remains is outright ownership of stocks, bonds, real estate, and so on. Don't worry if you don't know where to begin. We devoted several chapters of this book to the different categories of investments and means to develop an investment strategy.

401(k) PLANS—WHY SHOULD YOU PARTICIPATE?

There are many reasons to participate in 401(k)s. One is to reduce your current tax bill. Another is the opportunity to accumulate retirement savings on a tax-deferred basis. Another is "forced savings"—you pay yourself first and never see the money. Depending on the type of plan, still another is to get an automatic return on your money—often as much as 50 percent—through matching contributions by your employer.

A 401(k), like an IRA and a deferred annuity, is a tax-deferred savings plan. You pay no federal and state (except Pennsylvania) income taxes on the dollars you contribute until you withdraw them, usually at retirement. And your interest, dividends, and other earnings accumulate tax-deferred until you take them out—again, usually at retirement. Many 401(k) plans allow you to borrow your funds at reasonable interest rates, although you'll have a taxable distribution if you leave the company without paying the loan back.

The term *401(k)* refers to the section of the Internal Revenue Code that created these tax-favored, company-sponsored retirement savings programs. Nearly all large employers offer them. In a little over a decade the 401(k) plan has become the largest single source of retirement assets for most Americans.

The Value of Matching Contributions

Figure 9–1 shows the value of tax-deferred compounding, but doesn't take into account any money your employer may contribute to your 401(k). A 401(k) is an even better deal if your company matches a portion of your contributions.

Tip

Does It Make Sense to Borrow from Your 401(k)?

Yes and no. Generally, 401(k) plan loans are based on current short-term market interest rates so the interest cost is less than that of, say, an unsecured bank loan. And while in most cases you can't deduct the interest on your tax return, you in effect pay it to yourself by paying it back into your account since the loan is secured by the assets in your account. So borrowing from your 401(k) may in fact be the cheapest source of funds you can find for a loan. Generally you must repay the loan in a maximum of five years (longer for loans secured by your residence), and can't borrow more than the greater of $10,000 or half your 401(k) balance, subject to a maximum overall limit of $50,000.

The problem with 401(k) loans is the yield you give up due to these relatively low interest rates. While you may pay yourself, you are only getting, say, the 4 percent interest when your account could be earning much better. For this reason, we recommend looking at your 401(k) as first and foremost retirement money, and borrowing only when absolutely necessary.

Many employers match the amount employees put away in these plans. For example, your employer may contribute 50 cents for every dollar you set aside up to limits specified in the plan. (Usually employers cap their contributions to the first 3 percent to 6 percent of your wages that you contribute.)

For most people, a key reason for participating in an employer-sponsored 401(k) savings plan is to collect the matching contributions from the company. After all, if your employer contributes 50 cents for every dollar you contribute, you're immediately getting a 50 percent return on your investment!

Now you might not *own* the company match immediately because it is subject to a *vesting schedule*. With a vesting schedule, the employee takes ownership in

Figure 9–1   Saving with Pretax Versus After-Tax Dollars

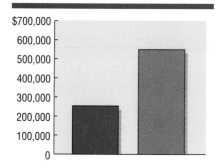

■ Taxable Account = $269,793
▨ Tax-Deferred Account = $541,412

Table 9–1	Typical Vesting Schedule
Year	**Percent Vested**
1	20%
2	40
3	60
4	80
5	100

the contributions over a period of time. The period of time is based on the employee's length of service, and it can't be longer than seven years. (Generally, five years is considered standard.) Therefore, if an employee had seven years or more of service with a company and resigned, he would be entitled to all the contributions the employer had made to his account. If the employee resigned prior to completing the full seven years, he would receive a percentage of the company contributions depending on the plan's vesting schedule.

Vesting only applies to company contributions. You are *always* 100 percent vested in your contributions.

How Do You Get In?

First, you instruct your company to subtract an agreed-upon percentage of your salary from your check every pay period and deposit that amount in a 401(k) account. The IRS doesn't tax this part of your salary—nor any interest, dividends, and capital gains that accumulate in the account—until you take your dollars out of your 401(k)—in most cases, at retirement.

Sounds similar to a deductible IRA, right. It is, except that you don't deduct your 401(k) contribution on your federal tax form. Instead, the dollars you contribute are treated as *deferred* compensation; that is, the money isn't shown as income to you on your W-2 form.

Suppose your pay adds up to $60,000 this year and you contribute 5 percent of your pay ($3,000) to your company's 401(k) plan. When you get your W-2 form, it will show taxable earnings of $57,000—your earnings of $60,000 less your $3,000 contribution to the 401(k). [You should know that the dollars you contribute to a 401(k) aren't exempt from Social Security, FICA, and Medicare payroll taxes.]

Contribution Limits

Not surprisingly, there are limits on the amount you and your employer can contribute to a 401(k) plan. IRS sets several ceilings on 401(k) contributions. Here are the most important:

- You may put aside a percentage of your wages (the percentage allowed will depend on your company plan) as a pretax contribution into a 401(k) plan, but this contribution can't be more than $9,240 in 1995. Many employers also allow 401(k) contributions to be taken out of bonuses.
- The maximum salary that can be used to figure your contribution is $150,000. This amount is adjusted annually for inflation.

Investing Your 401(k) Money

You've wisely decided to save in a 401(k). So now what? You must learn how to manage the account since all the investment decisions are yours to make. You're restricted only by the investments your company makes available to you.

As Table 9–2 illustrates, these investments include equity mutual funds, shares of stock in your company, money market accounts, guaranteed investment contracts (GICs), and government securities such as Treasury bills. Under federal law, 401(k)s must allow you to choose among at least three investment options. Furthermore, under recently issued U.S. Department of Labor rules, companies will be able to minimize their exposure to investment-related claims by providing you with detailed information so that you understand the choices available to you and the risk associated with each option.

SHOULD YOU BE SAVING IN AN IRA?

Assuming you've maximized your 401(k) savings, the next best place for your money may be an IRA. Sure, Individual Retirement Accounts (IRAs) have lost some of their luster, but they can still be a stepping

Table 9–2   Sample 401(k) Investment Options

Company A	Company B	Company C
Guaranteed income contract	Company stock fund	Money market fund
Equity index fund	Savings bonds	Bond index fund
Money market fund	Balanced fund	International fund
Growth stock fund	Intermediate-term	
Equity index fund	bond fund	
International fund		

Public and Nonprofit Employers

Note

The law doesn't allow employees of colleges, universities, state and local governments, and nonprofit institutions to participate in 401(k)s. But you have sound alternatives:

- A section 403(b) plan (commonly called a tax-deferred annuity plan) for employees of colleges, universities, and nonprofit organizations.
- A Section 457 plan for employees of colleges, universities, and state and local government entities.

Under a 403(b) plan, contributions are subtracted from your check every pay period and deposited into your account. You're not currently taxed on that amount, and the dollars you set aside, plus any earnings that accumulate, build up tax-deferred until they're withdrawn, usually at retirement.

For 403(b)s, Uncle Sam caps your annual contributions at $9,500 or 20 percent of your earnings each year, whichever is less.

A Section 457 plan works the same way as a 403(b) in that your contributions, plus any earnings, build up tax-deferred until they're withdrawn. The amounts deferred under the plan cannot exceed the lesser of 33⅓ percent of compensation or $7,500. Any amounts deferred under a 403(b) plan are taken into account in determining the $7,500 limit.

stone to a comfortable retirement. As you recall, IRAs' greatest appeal used to be that as long as you were not older than 70½, the contributions you made were fully tax-deductible. Today that's true only for people whose incomes are below specified levels or those who aren't eligible to participate in an employer-sponsored retirement plan. As we saw with 401(k)s, the benefits of tax-deductible (or pretax) contributions are compelling, and tax-deferred earnings coupled with tax-deductible contributions will almost always be the best choice. However, there are still good reasons to save on an after-tax basis in an IRA even if you can't deduct the contributions, as we'll see in a minute.

Can You Deduct Your IRA Contribution?

Under current tax law, if neither you nor your spouse participate in an employer-maintained retirement plan [including a 401(k) plan], you may contribute *and* deduct on your tax return up to $2,000 for yourself and

Table 9-3	Available IRA Deductions		
AGI	**Single/Head of Household**	**Married, Filing Jointly**	**Married, Filing Separately**
$0–10,000	Full	Full	Partial
$10,000–25,000	Full	Full	None
$25,000–35,000	Partial	Full	None
$35,000–40,000	None	Full	None
$40,000–50,000	None	Partial	None
$50,000+	None	None	None

$2,000 for your spouse. If your spouse is not employed, then his or her contribution is reduced to $250.

Now, what if you *or* your spouse actively participates in an employer-maintained retirement plan? Then another set of rules applies.

The IRS says that if you're single and an active participant, you may deduct your full contribution only if your adjusted gross income (AGI) is $25,000 or less. Your deduction drops $10 for each $50 you earn above $25,000 until you hit $35,000, when the deduction phases out entirely.

If you're married and file jointly and *either one of you* is an active participant, you get a full deduction only if your AGI is $40,000 or less. Your deduction drops by $10 for each additional $50 in income up to $50,000, when the deduction vanishes. Filing separately won't help. If married couples file separately, no deduction is allowable to either person. Table 9–3 summarizes how these rules work.

When it comes to the active participation rules, several types of plans fall into the category of qualified or tax-favored plans. Any

---

Caution

You May Not Qualify!

Remember, in the eyes of the IRS, you're an active participant if you take part in a retirement plan for just part of the year. Let's say you change jobs in November 1994 and move from Old Company Inc. to New Corp. You are not eligible for the New Corp pension plan in 1995 so you make what you think is a deductible IRA contribution for 1995. However, Old Company's pension plan does not end its tax year until January 31, 1995. Therefore, you are eligible and active in that plan for the first month of the 1995 year. You are considered to be an active participant for 1995.

Table 9–4   Retirement Plans in Which You Can Actively Participate

- Qualified pension, profit-sharing, or stock bonus plans, including Keogh plans.
- 401(k) plans.
- Simplified employee pension plans (SEPs).
- Retirement plans for federal, state, or local government employees.
- Tax-sheltered annuities for public school teachers and employees of charitable organizations.
- Deferred compensation plans for state employees.
- Certain union plans.

---

of the plans in Table 9–4 are counted. If you participate in any one of them, the law considers you an active participant, and that means you can't deduct your IRA contribution—unless your AGI falls below certain levels.

So most people with incomes above $50,000 cannot deduct the contribution. Yet, as shown in Table 9–5, saving in an IRA can still make a lot of sense. The table shows the amounts you could accumulate after paying taxes if you invested $2,000 per year in an IRA, a taxable CD, and a municipal bond. The table assumes a 31 percent tax rate. For many, saving in an IRA is a good idea since earnings—interest, dividends, and capital gains—on the dollars you set aside in an IRA still build up tax-deferred. Should you need your money before you reach

---

How Do You Know if You're an Active Participant?

Tip

Look at your W-2 form. It includes a box entitled "Pension plan" for your employer to check. If the box is checked, you know you're an active participant. If this box is blank, you'll need to understand the "active participation" rules.

The IRS says it makes no difference whether you actually participate in a defined benefit retirement plan. It matters only that you're *eligible* to participate. However, the rules are different for a defined contribution plan. Here you're considered an active participant if—during the year—you or your company contribute money to the plan on your behalf. But the law does carve out one important exception to this rule. You're not an active participant if the only money that is added on your behalf during the year is earnings from the investments already in the plan.

Table 9–5	Comparison of Savings in Three Investment Vehicles		
Years to Retirement	**Nondeductible IRA at 8%**	**CD at 8%**	**Municipal Bond at 6%**
10	$ 26,190	$ 25,775	$ 26,360
15	$ 46,770	$ 44,885	$ 46,550
20	$ 75,550	$ 69,885	$ 73,570
25	$116,385	$102,590	$109,730
30	$174,930	$145,375	$158,115

age 59½, you'll pay taxes and a 10 percent penalty on the deductible portion of your IRA contributions and on any earnings that have accumulated tax-deferred in your account. But you pay no penalty when you withdraw your nondeductible contributions.

What's the bottom line? When it comes to making nondeductible IRA contributions, there are some benefits, but make sure you have maximized your company savings plan alternatives first. You must analyze your personal situation carefully and look at these key factors: your age and liquidity concerns, the length of time you have until retirement, the rates of return you can get on competing investments, and your federal and state tax rates.

How Many IRAs Can You Have?

The IRS doesn't care if you set up one IRA or a dozen. You may set them up at as many different financial institutions as you want. However, be careful when you open multiple accounts. Most institutions charge you annual fees—up to $50 or more—to maintain your IRA. So if you maintain many small accounts—and they all charge fees—your investment return effectively drops.

You are allowed to deduct the annual maintenance fee as a miscellaneous itemized deduction. But you may write it off only if (1) you pay it out of separate funds, not the IRA funds, and (2) it and all other miscellaneous itemized deductions top 2 percent of your adjusted gross income.

And don't forget the record keeping side. If you have many different IRAs, then it's likely your mailbox is going to be filled with statements every month. By consolidating your IRAs, you will not only cut down on the paper volume but also avoid paying higher fees. Some institutions even waive annual fees if your IRA balance is large enough (usually $10,000).

Be conscious of the maximum Federal Deposit Insurance Corporation (FDIC) insurance limits if your IRA is invested with a bank.
For instance, banks will typically insure a single account for up to
$100,000. But, under a 1993 rules change, people with more than one
retirement account at the bank (for example, an IRA and a Keogh plan)
are limited to the $100,000 amount. If you have multiple retirement
accounts at one bank that exceed the $100,000 limit, we recommend
that you invest the excess—the amount over $100,000—at a different
institution.

Investing Your IRA Dollars

The trustee of your IRA may be the institution or institutions where
you maintain your IRAs: a bank, savings and loan, mutual fund
company, and so forth. You may also manage your account yourself,
investing as you see fit. If that's your preference, you'd use a bank or
brokerage house, say, as custodian of your IRA. You can invest your
IRA in most regular investment vehicles—certificates of deposit,
mutual funds, stocks, or bonds, for example.

However, you don't have total freedom when it comes to investing
your IRA dollars. Buying a life insurance contract is out, although
annuities are OK. Art objects, antiques, gold or silver coins (except
gold and silver coins minted by the United States), stamps, and other
collectibles are also forbidden when it comes to IRAs. Also, you may
not use IRA funds for "self-dealing" (buying assets from yourself or
from a company you own). For example, you couldn't use IRA dollars
to purchase stock in a company you own.

If you use IRA dollars for prohibited investments, Uncle Sam treats
the amount you invested as a withdrawal from your account. That
means you must pay tax on that amount at ordinary rates and, if you
invested in the item before age 59½, pay an additional 10 percent
penalty.

There's one more invest-
ment you should avoid when it
comes to your IRA dollars:
municipal bonds or any other
tax-free investment. As you
know, the money in your IRA
account is taxed when you
withdraw it. Municipal bonds
are tax-free. So by putting

Table 9-6	Prohibited IRA Investments
Art objects	
Antiques	
Stamps	
Other collectibles	
Gold and silver coins except gold and silver eagle coins minted by the U.S. Treasury	

these bonds in your IRA, you're converting tax-free income into taxable income.

Switching from One Investment to Another

You say you want to switch your IRA from one investment vehicle (bonds, say) to another (stocks, for example)? Or you want to shift your IRA from one institution to another. Go right ahead, but make sure you know the rules first.

The law allows for two types of IRA transfers. The first is known as a *direct trustee-to-trustee transfer;* the second is known as a *rollover.* In a trustee-to-trustee transfer, you never get your hands on your IRA funds. Instead, you tell the institution that maintains your IRA to send the funds in your account to an IRA at a second institution. Or it sends you a check made out to the institution. Either way, you don't get your hands on the money because there is no check made out to you.

You can transfer your IRA in this way as many times as you like during the year. Likewise, you won't be hit with a penalty if you shift funds from one investment vehicle to another within the same institution—again, as long as you never withdraw the money. In other words, if you maintain an IRA at a financial institution that offers a number of investment vehicles, you may shift funds from one vehicle to another—within that institution—as many times as you choose. You'll pay no tax penalty.

You should know, though, that shifting investment vehicles does present one potential problem. You might get slapped with a penalty that your financial institution imposes—the loss of two month's interest, for example, for withdrawing funds from a CD before its due date.

The rules are different for a rollover IRA. In this case, you actually withdraw your money from your IRA and deposit it in another IRA account. Here's the key distinction: The money is, at least temporarily, in your possession.

Be careful. You have only 60 days to roll your money over into another IRA. If you miss the 60-day deadline, Uncle Sam will assume you've made a withdrawal and tax you currently on the amount, and you won't be able to put the money back into the IRA. You may also pay a 10 percent early withdrawal penalty on the amount you've withdrawn if you are not yet 59½.

Here's another important rule: You may withdraw your money and roll it over into another IRA only once in a 365-day period. If you do

Can You Borrow from Your IRA?

Tip

Sort of! While the law states that you can't borrow from or pledge your IRA as collateral, you can withdraw your money, use it for up to 60 days, and then roll it into the same or a different IRA without penalty. The IRS recently ruled that you can take out IRA funds for personal use without penalty as long as you redeposit them in the same or a different IRA within 60 days. This ruling only applies to the taxpayers involved, although it gives a hint as to what the IRS position is on the subject.

it more often, you'll pay ordinary income taxes on the amount you take out and maybe even a 10 percent early withdrawal penalty if you're not yet 59½. The 365-day rule applies separately to each IRA.

You can avoid this whole problem by using a trustee-to-trustee transfer, in which you instruct your IRA trustee to forward your funds to another IRA trustee. In this way, you've never "touched" the money so the 365-day rule doesn't apply.

IRAs in Perspective

In spite of the limits on deducting your contributions, IRAs are still a valuable way to supplement your retirement savings. And they may become even more valuable with recent proposals to add a new type of IRA, the "American Dream" savings account. This new IRA would allow each spouse to contribute (but not deduct) $2,000 each year, and would allow tax-free withdrawals after age 59½ and for certain purposes if you leave your money in for five years. If passed, this legislation would certainly provide more incentives to utilize IRAs for retirement savings.

ANNUITIES: ANOTHER TAX-DEFERRED OPTION

An annuity is a tax-deferred investment contract that is underwritten by an insurance company. Although annuities come in a variety of types, the two primary types are immediate annuities and deferred annuities. With an immediate annuity, you usually purchase the contract with a lump sum and begin receiving benefits 30 to 90 days later. A deferred

Tip

Hints for Managing Your IRAs

When managing your IRAs, keep these key thoughts in mind:

- Make nondeductible contributions only after you have maximized your savings in 401(k) plans (both pretax and after-tax).

- Pay IRA fees with a check (i.e., outside of your IRA).
- Consolidate your IRAs to reduce overall fees.
- Integrate your IRA strategy with your total retirement investment strategy.

---

annuity, on the other hand, pays you benefits starting at some future date, usually at retirement.

You buy your annuity contract by paying a lump sum, by making installment payments, or by some combination of the two. With a fixed annuity, the amount you receive is paid out in regular equal installments. You decide how frequently you want to receive payments (for example, monthly, quarterly, or annually). Furthermore, the payout can be over a fixed period, such as 20 years, or for the rest of your life.

The most popular annuity for retirement investors is a variable deferred annuity. Variable annuities allow you to invest in a portfolio of investment options (such as guaranteed interest contracts or bond and stock mutual funds) that you select. With a variable annuity, the interest, dividends, and capital gains you earn accumulate tax-deferred until they're paid to you under the terms of your annuity. The price for tax deferral is the same 10 percent penalty that we saw before. You will pay ordinary income taxes plus a 10 percent penalty if you take the money out before age 59½.

Annuities certainly have their advantages if you want tax-deferred growth, but can sometimes be a very expensive way to buy your investments. Over and above any sales commissions you pay to get in, these contracts (like mutual funds) charge investment management fees and have administrative costs. And because they also offer a death benefit, these contracts charge for the life insurance protection! There may also be surrender charges imposed if you take funds out of the contract too soon. All of these fees are in addition to those charged by the funds themselves so you need to stay in the annuity for a long time before the benefits of tax deferral outweigh the commissions and additional costs. While your actual break-even period depends on the investment return

| Table 9–7 | Calculation of Break-even Period for Variable Annuity |

	Investment Return			
Tax Rate	**7%**	**8%**	**9%**	**10%**
28%	29 yrs.	20 yrs.	15 yrs.	12 yrs.
31	31	23	18	14
36	36	28	23	18
39.6	39	31	26	20

Table assumes annuity expense of 1 percent.

and your tax bracket, 20 years is a good rule of thumb.

At times we are asked to compare differences in saving pretax in a 401(k) plan to saving in an after-tax manner through a tax-defered annuity. Table 9–8 shows one such analysis.

Before we move on to investments, are there any other sources of retirement income? Indeed there are. In the next chapter, we look at some other options.

| Table 9–8 | Equivalent rate of return required if purchasing a tax-deferred annuity |

If This Is Your 401(k) Investment Return	10 Years to Retirement Combined Federal and State Tax Rate		25 Years to Retirement Combined Federal and State Tax Rate	
	35%	**45%**	**35%**	**45%**
4%	6.6%	7.3%	6.4%	7.0%
6	9.0	6.9	8.6	9.3
8	11.2	12.3	10.8	11.4
10	13.4	14.6	12.8	13.5

ASSUMPTIONS:
(1) This analysis assumes a 1.3% average annual expense for the insurance charge of the annuity.
(2) Annual contributions are not eligible for any company match within the 401(k). Any company matching contributions would create a greater required rate of return within the annuity than those specified above.
(3) Annual contribution to 401(k) is $5,000 on a pre-tax basis.
(4) Annual contribution to tax-deferred annuity is $3,250 on an after-tax basis assuming a 35% combined federal and state tax rate.
(5) Annual contribution to tax-deferred annuity is $2,750 on an after-tax basis assuming a 45% combined federal and state tax rate.
(6) Balance in the 401(k) is distributed in equal installments over 15 years and is taxed at the same combined federal and state tax rate as the annuity in each respective scenario.
(7) Balance in the tax-deferred annuity is taxed at retirement assuming payout over 15 years utilizing the specified combined federal and state tax rate.

CHAPTER 10

OTHER SOURCES OF RETIREMENT INCOME

In this chapter, we review how you might supplement your retirement income through some other sources, such as:

- Working after retirement.
- Using your home equity as a retirement resource.
- Selling your home.
- Reverse mortgages.
- Canceling or borrowing against life insurance.
- Inheritances.

As we saw in doing our retirement sufficiency analysis, you can sometimes tap into other sources of retirement income besides the obvious ones (company-sponsored retirement plans, personal savings, and Social Security). We look at some other potential sources in this chapter.

HOW ABOUT WORKING AFTER "RETIREMENT"?

Pensions and other retirement plans aren't the only way to get what you need for retirement. Another option is to work part-time after you retire. You might even take on a second career.

One businessperson we know lectures on entrepreneurship at a local university. Another writes a column about real estate for a local newspaper. A longtime collector of Civil War memorabilia, for instance, set up shop as an antiques dealer after he took early retirement. Still another fulfilled her dream to run her own restaurant.

Working after retirement may not provide you with a lot of extra cash. For one thing, you must consider how your earnings will reduce your Social Security benefits. (Chapter 7 gives the rules.) But working does give most people a purposeful activity and a sense of self-worth— two benefits that can sometimes be more valuable than money. Chapter 3 gives you more information on working after retirement.

USING THE EQUITY IN YOUR HOME

People of all ages are planning to use the equity in their home to fund at least a part of their retirement income, and why not! For most of us it represents our single largest asset. A recent study by The Oppenheimer Funds found that 70 percent of preretirees and 85 percent of retirees believe buying a house is one of the best ways to save for retirement. This is probably because this generation has just been through the largest period of residential housing appreciation in history. During the past 50 years, housing provided an average annual return of 7.2 percent.

If you're close to retirement, you may want to capture some of the value from your home for retirement by selling it and moving to a less costly residence. "Trading down"—the choice for many retirees—can be especially attractive if you're age 55 or older because of the one-time $125,000 tax exclusion of gain on the sale of your home. As explained later, reverse mortgages can also help you get at some of the equity to provide cash during retirement.

However, if you're farther away from retirement, you might not want to rely as much on your home to provide as significant a retirement nest egg. Much of the increase in real estate prices over the past 50 years was due to huge demand for housing from the baby boom generation. When that generation retires, the market for potential buyers will be far smaller and price appreciation less likely. For example, since the mid-1980s real estate has yielded just a 4.4 percent return, which is barely over the average inflation rate for the period. If future housing prices just keep pace with inflation, the value of your home equity isn't likely to provide significant income in real dollars. For this reason, many financial planners don't include home equity as an available resource when planning younger families' retirement.

The message: Your home may be another source of retirement security years from now, but don't count too much on it. It probably won't provide the nest egg that it might have for your parents. Continue to save in the types of plan we've described and treat your home as only a potential supplement to your long-term retirement income.

Relocation Issues

For people close to retirement, trading down and possibly relocating are likely options in retirement. But remember, selling a house and moving to smaller quarters is a big step—one you need to consider carefully and discuss with your family. Before making the move, consider four issues: taxes, housing costs, lifestyle, and quality of life.

- *Taxes.* Many people move to states with low income taxes (or states that don't tax pension income) at retirement. But consider the whole picture. Many low–income-tax states have high sales and personal property taxes which can make your overall tax savings much smaller than it appears. Also, some popular retirement states have high gift and inheritance taxes.

- *Housing costs.* If you decide to move to reduce your cost of living, make sure that in fact the new location gives you a saving. Real estate agents can help you assess the purchase costs and living expenses for a particular community or region.

- *Lifestyle.* When you move, you might miss friends and relatives more than you think, or the lifestyle may not be what you expected. Compare the social and religious activities and entertainment options in your current community and the new community. You might also consider renting for a year or so before you make a final decision to buy.

- *Quality of life.* Look at the climate, lifestyle, transportation, and safety of the new location.

Table 10–1   Taxes on Pensions and Personal Income

	Maximum Personal Income Tax Rate	Pension Amount Exempt From State Income Tax			Maximum State/Local Sales Tax
		Private	State	Federal	
Alabama	5.0%	100%	100%	100%	12.0%
Alaska	—	—	—	—	7.0
Arizona	6.9	0	$ 2,500	$ 2,500	8.5
Arkansas	7.0	$ 6,000	$ 6,000	$ 6,000	7.5
California	11.0	0	0	$ 40	8.25
Colorado	5.0% of federal income tax	$20,000	$20,000	$20,000	8.5
Connecticut	4.5	0	0	0	6.0
Delaware	7.7	$ 3,000	$ 3,000	$ 3,000	—
Florida	—	—	—	—	7.0
Georgia	6.0	$11,000	$11,000	$11,000	6.0
Hawaii	10.0	Partial	Partial	Partial	4.0
Idaho	8.2	Partial	Partial	Partial	7.0
Illinois	3.0	100%	100%	100%	8.75
Indiana	3.4	0	0	Partial	5.0
Iowa	9.98	0	0	0	6.0
Kansas	7.75	0	100%	100%	7.4
Kentucky	6.0	0	100%	100%	6.0
Louisiana	6.0	$ 6,000	100%	100%	10.75
Maine	8.5	0	0	0	6.0
Maryland	6.0	Partial	Partial	Partial	5.0
Massachusetts	5.95	0	0	0	5.0
Michigan	4.4	Partial	Partial	Partial	6.0
Minnesota	8.5	Partial	Partial	Partial	7.5
Mississippi	5.0	100%	100%	100%	7.25
Missouri	6.0	0	Partial	Partial	7.725
Montana	11.0	Partial	Partial	Partial	—
Nebraska	6.99	0	0	0	6.5
Nevada	—	—	—	—	7.0
New Hampshire	5.0	—	—	—	—
New Jersey	6.65	Partial	Partial	Partial	6.0
New Mexico	8.5	0	0	0	6.5
New York	7.875	Partial	100%	100%	8.5
North Carolina	7.75	$ 2,000	$ 4,000	$ 4,000	6.0
North Dakota	12.0	0	Partial	Partial	6.0
Ohio	7.5	Partial	Partial	Partial	7.0
Oklahoma	10.0	0	$ 5,500	$ 5,500	10.5
Oregon	9.0	Partial	Partial	Partial	—
Pennsylvania	2.8	100%	100%	100%	7.0
Rhode Island	2.75% of federal income tax	Partial	Partial	Partial	7.0

Table 10–1	Continued				
	Maximum Personal Income Tax Rate	**Pension Amount Exempt From State Income Tax**			**Maximum State/Local Sales Tax**
		Private	**State**	**Federal**	
South Carolina	7.0	$10,000	$10,000	$10,000	6.0
South Dakota	—	—	—	—	6.0
Tennessee	6.0	—	—	—	8.75
Texas	—	—	—	—	8.25
Utah	7.2	Partial	Partial	Partial	7.125
Vermont	9.0	0	0	0	5.0
Virginia	5.75	Partial	Partial	Partial	4.5
Washington	—	—	—	—	8.2
Washington, D.C.	9.5	0	$ 3,000	$ 3,000	5.75
West Virginia	6.5	0	Partial	Partial	6.0
Wisconsin	6.93	0	Partial	Partial	5.5
Wyoming	—	—	—	—	6.0

Finally, if you do plan to move or maintain residences in two states, remember to follow the rules regarding establishment of a new domicile for tax purposes. Otherwise, you risk being taxed as a resident of both states. The ways you establish your new domicile in a new state include:

- Registering cars and changing your driver's license.
- Registering to vote.
- Changing banks and brokerage accounts.
- Executing a will in the new state.
- Resigning from business and social organizations in the old state.

Some states, such as Florida, have official declarations of domicile that evidence your intent to be a resident of a particular state. For the particulars, check with your tax advisor.

Tax Breaks for Selling Your Residence

When it comes to selling a principal residence, the tax law offers two significant tax breaks to homeowners. The first is a one-time exclusion of up to $125,000 in capital gain on the sale of a primary residence. The second is more familiar—you can defer the taxes on your home-related capital gains by purchasing a more expensive residence. Used

What Is a Principal Residence?

Note

An obvious question, perhaps, but not to the authors of the Internal Revenue Code. A residence—in the eyes of the tax law—is a place that includes basic living accommodations. So houses, apartments, condominiums, and mobile homes qualify as residences. So do houseboats. A principal residence is the home where you spend most of your time. In other words, it's your primary residence. Just owning a house doesn't make it your principal residence. The rules say you must actually live in that house for it to qualify as your primary residence.

The IRS sets no limits on the amount of time you must spend in your home before you consider it your principal residence, but we suggest you use common sense. You should look to the address you use for voting, registering your car, having your checking account, or getting a driver's license. If your home doesn't qualify as your primary residence, you're not entitled to the tax breaks provided to homeowners.

together, these tax breaks can allow you to trade down (buy a less expensive home), pay less tax on the gain, and free up some cash for your retirement.

How Do You Calculate Your Gain?

All you need to do is subtract your basis from your selling price. Then subtract your fixing-up expenses to determine your gain.

Your basis is the cost of your home plus the cost of any improvements you've made (but not fixing-up expenses). Your basis also includes some of the costs you incurred when you purchased your house and while you owned it, such as attorneys' fees, appraisal fees, costs of defending title to the property, costs of title search and insurance, recording fees, closing charges, and survey expenses.

Here's an example. Assume the original cost of your home was $50,000. Your appraisal fees, attorney's fees, and other purchase expenses added up to $2,000. Over the years, you've added a new bathroom for $8,000 and installed central air conditioning and heating for

Don't Forget about Home Improvements

Tip

Fixing-up expenses are the costs you incur in getting your home ready to sell. Ordinarily, you don't profit—taxwise, at least—when you fix up your house. For example, you can't write off the cost of, say, painting or wallpapering on your Form 1040. However, you can subtract them from your selling price to get your *adjusted selling price*. Also, you must incur the expenses during the 90 days before you sign the papers to sell your house, and you must pay for the repairs within 30 days after the sale. Otherwise, you may not subtract them.

Improvements, on the other hand, are anything that adds to your home's value or appreciably prolongs its life. Adding a room, installing central air conditioning, and putting up new gutters count as improvements. So do less obvious costs such as installing venetian blinds, provided you leave them to the new owners. Improvements are added to your basis in calculating your capital gain.

$3,000. Fixing-up expenses (painting and cleaning) added up to $1,000.

Now, say you sell your old home for $90,000 and your broker's commission and other selling expenses come to $5,000. Is your gain $40,000—that is, your $90,000 sale price less your $50,000 cost? Definitely not. You calculate your gain by adding your purchase expenses and the cost of improvements to your basis, and then subtracting your selling expenses from the sales proceeds. So in our example, your cost basis comes to $63,000—your $50,000 original cost plus $13,000 in improvements and purchase expenses. The amount you receive after you subtract your selling and fixing-up expenses is $84,000. So your gain is

Table 10–2	Calculating Gain on Sale of Your Personal Residence	
Selling price, old home		$90,000
Less: Selling expenses		(5,000)
Fixing-up expenses		(1,000)
Adjusted selling price		$84,000
Original cost, old home	$50,000	
Closing fees, original purchase	2,000	
Improvements	11,000	
Cost basis		(63,000)
Gain on sale		$21,000

Table 10–3	Cost Basis of New Home	
Purchase price		$86,000
Purchase costs		4,000
Less: Deferred gain		(21,000)
Cost basis of new home		$69,000

$21,000—that is, $84,000 minus $63,000.

Deferring Your Gain. Once you've calculated the gain, you can defer paying income taxes if you meet two conditions:

- You must buy or build *and occupy* a new principal residence within 24 months before or after the date you sell your old home.
- You must buy or build your new principal residence for an amount that equals at least the adjusted selling price of your old home.

Let's return to our previous example. You pay no tax on your $21,000 profit as long as you purchase or build a new home that costs $84,000 or more—or at least you don't pay any tax now.

Say you buy a new house for $86,000, and your purchase costs add up to $4,000. Under the rules, you must reduce your basis in your new home by the amount of gain from your old house that you rolled over or deferred. That means your basis in your new home adds up to only $69,000—that is, $86,000 plus $4,000 minus the $21,000 gain you deferred.

Now, suppose it's a year later, and you decide to tour the world for two years. You sell your home for $90,000, but decide not to buy a new one. The IRS requires you to report on your Form 1040 the difference between your selling price—$90,000—and your basis, $69,000. And your gain of $21,000 is now taxable, since you didn't buy or build a new principal residence within the two-year time period. The only good news is that the gain is long-term capital gain if you held the property for more than one year.

Buying Down after Age 55

Using the once-in-a-lifetime exclusion is the key question for retirees wanting to fund a portion of their retirement income needs with their home equity. If you're age 55 or older on the date of sale, you can use

Age 55 Means 55

Caution

The rules state that you're eligible to exclude your gain only if you're 55 years of age or older *before* the day you sell your home. The IRS interprets the sale date as the date title passes the closing date under most states' laws.

The rules treat a married couple filing jointly as one person. So you qualify for the tax break if either you or your spouse is age 55 before the sale, and you own the home jointly.

the once-in-a-lifetime $125,000 exclusion rule to sell your primary residence and exclude up to $125,000 of profits from taxation. Any amount in excess of $125,000 is taxed as a capital gain. The $125,000 limit applies to a single person or a married couple filing jointly. If you're married and file separately, the ceiling comes to $62,500 per spouse. Furthermore, if either you or your spouse were previously married and used the exclusion, neither one of you may claim it again.

You qualify for the exclusion only if your home was your principal residence for at least three of the five years immediately prior to the sale. However, the house doesn't have to be your principal residence at the time it's sold. The IRS says that up to two years may pass between the time you vacate the house and the actual sale, as long as you lived in your home for three years before you vacated it.

Combining the Tax Breaks

You can make a really impressive tax-free maneuver by using both the $125,000 exclusion and the rollover-of-gain break. By combining these two provisions in the tax code, you may collect more than $125,000 in profit and buy a home that costs as much as $125,000 less without paying a single penny in taxes.

Here's an example of how this strategy can work. Let's say you paid $145,000 for your house in 1974. Then 20 years later you pay off the mortgage and sell it for $380,000 plus $20,000 in selling costs. You collect $215,000 profit. Since you're 56 years old, you sensibly opt to

Table 10–4 Capital Gains

Selling price	$380,000
Less: Cost basis	(145,000)
Less: Selling costs	(20,000)
Capital gain	$215,000

Table 10–5 Taxes Payable

Capital gain	$215,000
Less: Exclusion	(125,000)
Potential gain on sale	$ 90,000
Cost of new home	260,000
Taxes payable	$0

Table 10–6 Funds Available

Selling price	$380,000
Less: Cost of new home	(260,000)
Less: Selling costs	(20,000)
Funds available	$100,000

take the one-time exclusion so $125,000 of your $215,000 gain is tax-free to you—forever.

Now you want to purchase a new home. You may think you have to find one of equal value to your old one so you'll qualify for the rollover-of-gain break. But in figuring how much you must spend on a new home, the rules allow you to subtract the amount of your exclusion ($125,000) from the selling price of your old home ($380,000). So you must spend only $255,000 for a new house—not $380,000.

As long as your new principal residence costs $255,000 or more, you defer paying taxes on your remaining gain of $90,000. And you reduce the basis of your new home by only the $90,000 gain that you don't pay taxes on now. Remember, the $125,000 is excluded from taxes forever.

Let's run through how you'd project income from selling your house. When we factor in the age-55 exclusion, the sale of your home looks like Table 10–4.

Now, we figure in the age-55 exclusion. (See Table 10–5.)

So, after giving Uncle Sam his due, you have funds left to invest as shown in Table 10–6.

If you invest the $100,000 and receive a return of 6 percent after-tax, you would add about $6,000 a year to your income without touching the principal.

So, as you near retirement age—and if you're not wedded to your house—you may want to evaluate the costs of other housing options, plus use some of the equity in your home to support your postretirement lifestyle.

REVERSE MORTGAGES

In the midst of their retirement years, some retirees find that their fixed income that once seemed plentiful just isn't enough anymore. They look around for additional sources of income. The big resource surrounding them is their home that they own free and clear. In walks the reverse mortgage idea.

A reverse mortgage may rescue older homeowners who are "house rich and cash poor." They essentially "borrow" against the home from a lender. And the homeowners can have the loan paid to them under several pay-out options: (1) a lump sum, (2) a monthly check based on a mortgage for the rest of their lives or as long as they live in the home, (3) a monthly check based on a mortgage for a specific length of time, (4) line-of-credit advances when needed, or (5) some combination of options 2 through 4. To be eligible for a reverse mortgage, the homeowner and any other coborrower or person named on the title of the house must be at least age 62 and have little or no mortgage debt on the home.

The reverse mortgage becomes payable in full, *up to the current market value of the home,* upon the earliest of the sale of the home, the homeowner's permanent move out of the home, or at death. The amount owed would never exceed the lesser of the loan balance or the value of the home so no other assets except the home are needed to pay back the loan.

You might wonder how someone financially strapped would be able to even qualify for this type of loan. Because there is no repayment requirement and since the home is the only security for the loan, the homeowner's ability to repay is not considered in the determination of whether to make the loan. However, many planners view this as a last resort for most older people. Why? First of all, there are transaction costs involved and they can be considerable. Second, the amount borrowed will leave the borrower or his heirs with reduced equity in the home.

LIFE INSURANCE AS A RETIREMENT INCOME SOURCE

Many people think of life insurance as something they'll never be around to enjoy. That's true of term life insurance, which provides only a death benefit. But for other life insurance policies with investment components (whole life, universal life, and variable life), the accumulated cash values may provide a source of retirement income.

If you no longer need the death benefits, you can simply cancel your life insurance policy and get back its cash value, a useful option for people who want to supplement their retirement income and no longer need the coverage. You'll pay ordinary income tax, however, on any accumulated cash value that exceeds your policy basis (i.e., the amount of premiums you paid in).

You could also borrow against the cash value of your life insurance policy. Most companies will loan up to 95 percent of the accumulated cash value at reasonable interest rates. The loan is generally not taxable to you, and if you die before it is paid back, the unpaid portion is simply deducted from the death benefit.

If you purchased your policy before June 21, 1988, you can borrow on your life insurance tax-free. However, if you bought it after that date, be aware of limits that can affect the tax-free nature of the loan. If your life insurance premium payments top certain limits outlined, your policy will fall into the category of a modified endowment contract (MEC).

The MEC rules are intended to prevent you from using a life insurance policy as a tax shelter. Remember, the growth of cash value is not subject to current income taxes. Prior to these new rules, many people would invest large sums in universal or variable policies, which allow for flexible premium payments. They would then let the cash value grow handsomely, and borrow out the cash (never intending to pay it back), all without paying taxes.

The MEC rules closed this loophole by limiting the amount of premiums you can pay in and still have tax-free loans or withdrawals. If your policy qualifies as an MEC, the IRS assumes that the first dollars you borrow or withdraw are your accumulated earnings. And these dollars are subject to federal income taxes. Also, if you're under age 59½, the IRS hits you with a 10 percent penalty on the amount of earnings you borrow from such a plan. The amounts you contribute to your policy continue to accumulate tax-deferred until you borrow or withdraw them, or assign or pledge the policy as collateral for a loan. When you assign or pledge a policy, the amount is treated as a distribution to you for tax purposes.

Check with your insurance agent if you want to contribute more than the normal premiums to your life insurance policy. They should be able to tell you if your proposed contribution would cause the policy to become an MEC.

THERE'S NO GUARANTEE WHEN IT COMES TO INHERITANCES

Some people make the big mistake of doing little retirement planning because they *know* they will inherit enough to take care of their retirement needs. But inheritances are by no means a sure bet. First of all, there's no telling when the bequest will occur. You surely can't plan that in 13 years and 7 months you'll inherit your parents' estate, or whomever else's you have been designated as beneficiary.

Furthermore, even if your parents are elderly and not in good health, there's no telling what the wonders of medicine have in store. And what if there is no medical answer to their ills, but they still continue to live for a very long time. A long-term illness or a lengthy stay in a nursing home can dry up a big savings in no time at all. So if you're planning for retirement, treat an inheritance the same as you might treat your home equity. If it's there when you retire, that's great, but don't base your whole retirement plan on it.

Now you know about the sources available to you for retirement income. In the following chapters, we show you how you can make your investments pay off for your retirement years.

INVESTING FOR RETIREMENT

CHAPTER 11   Sound Investing for Retirement   141

CHAPTER 12   Investing by Lending—Cash and Fixed Income
Investments   155

CHAPTER 13   Investing through Ownership—Equities and
Hard Assets   173

CHAPTER 14   The Importance of Asset Allocation   187

CHAPTER 15   Implementing Your Investment Strategy   197

SOUND INVESTING FOR RETIREMENT

A sound investment strategy is one of the most important factors in your ability to achieve your retirement goals. This chapter discusses the overall concepts behind retirement investing, including:

- The investment life cycle.
- The four different investment categories.
- How these categories perform in different economic climates.
- Investment risks and how to manage them.
- The effect of your investment time horizon on risk.
- The importance of diversification.

Consistent investment returns over your retirement time horizon are one of the most important aspects of a long-term retirement plan. Once you understand your goals and the resources you have available for retirement, you're ready to develop investment strategies for every aspect of your retirement plan. This chapter discusses fundamental strategies that will help you invest successfully for retirement.

KEYS TO SUCCESSFUL RETIREMENT INVESTING

In general, successful retirement investing involves five key factors:

- Understanding your retirement goals and objectives.
- Understanding your investment time horizon.
- Focusing on the investment return you will need to achieve your goals.
- Developing an investment mix that maximizes investment return while minimizing risk.
- Monitoring and rebalancing your investment mix as circumstances change.

As an individual investor, you need to look at investments in relation to your personal circumstances and retirement goals over the long term. Yet, many investors ignore these factors, instead paying too much attention to current market or economic conditions and making short-term decisions. Remember, as an individual investor, you're quite different from an institutional investor (such as mutual funds, pension funds, etc.), whose actions can influence that market. Institutional investors are under short-term pressure to perform so they try to outguess other institutional investors and the market. And they do it on a full-time basis. Most individuals don't have that kind of time to spend focusing on their investments—nor do they want to.

GET RICH, OR GET WHAT YOU NEED?

Investments are volatile, and if you invest solely by trying to predict changing market conditions, you'll probably make serious mistakes. But if you invest with your long-term retirement goals and objectives in mind, you can usually ignore short-term market fluctuations. Unfortunately, many times people invest for retirement either by taking too little risk and sacrificing the potential for long-term growth, or by trying to "get rich" and taking more risk than they need to. Neither of these strategies makes a lot of sense for the retirement investor—the former because an overly conservative portfolio won't keep pace with inflation and the latter because the "home runs" tend to be few and far between!

We believe that your fundamental investment strategy needs to be tied to your retirement sufficiency analysis. Thus, you can't really develop an effective strategy until you understand your personal circumstances and all of the factors discussed in Chapters 4 through 6: your retirement goals, resources, savings, life expectancy, and time horizon. Once you understand your goals, resources, and projected time horizon, then your ability to achieve your retirement goal is tied to your retirement savings and investment return so, all things being equal, if you have shortfalls, you can either can save more or invest for higher returns. Thus, once your sufficiency analysis is in place, you can answer a very critical question: **What investment return do you**

The Investment Life Cycle

Tip

One convenient way to understand your current situation is to place yourself within what is known as the investment life cycle. For example, if you're young and just starting out, you have little need for current investment income and can have a more growth-oriented retirement portfolio. Your longer time horizon allows you to accept short-term market fluctuations in exchange for long-term growth. By contrast, most retirees are more concerned with capital preservation and inflation protection than investment growth so their portfolios tend to the low-risk, income-oriented investments.

Figure 11–1 The Investment Life Cycle

	Years to Retirement			Early Retirement	Later Retirement
	10–30+	**5–10**	**1–5**		
Risk tolerance	High	High	Moderate	Low	Low
Current income need	Low	Low	Low	Moderate	High
Holding period	Long	Long	Intermediate	Intermediate	Short
Liquidity need	Low	Low	Moderate	Moderate	High

Source: 1995 Mutual Funds Coursebook, Investment Education Seminars, page 63, published by the American Association of Individual Investors, 625 N. Michigan Ave., Chicago, Ill. 60611; 312/280-0170.

need to achieve your retirement goal? This is much different than the investment return we **want** to have. Everyone wants great investment performance, but financial markets are volatile and involve many different types of risk.

Furthermore, you don't want to take completely unnecessary risks when a lower-risk investment might get you where you need to go. If, for instance, you can reach your retirement income goal with a 7 percent annual return, then why would you choose an investment strategy that could potentially produce a 15 percent return, but had a chance of producing a 20 percent loss? You would be taking on more risk than you need to achieve your goal. If you *like* to try for home runs occasionally, then set aside a small portion of your funds for those kinds of long-shot investments.

Likewise, you don't want to lock in an investment strategy forever. In retirement, your goals are constantly changing so the same strategy isn't going to work for the next 20 or 30 years. You may want to travel for five years, for example, and then provide for your grandchildren's college education. As your goals change, your investment strategies should change with them!

We believe your goal should be to find the middle ground—the optimum level of return for a given level of risk. By completing your retirement sufficiency analysis before investing your money, you will understand that level of investment return you need to reach your goal. Then you can develop a sound savings and investment strategy that focuses on the return you need and takes the minimum amount of risk necessary to provide that return over the long haul.

MAJOR INVESTMENT CATEGORIES

No matter how cluttered the investment marketplace seems to be with fancy new products, there are really only four broad investment categories:

- **Cash and cash equivalents** such as money market funds, checking accounts, and short-term certificates of deposit.
- **Fixed-income investments,** a group that includes tax-exempt bonds, corporate bonds, mortgages, and long-term certificates of deposit.

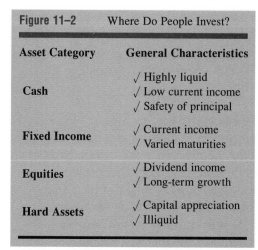

Figure 11–2   Where Do People Invest?

Asset Category	General Characteristics
Cash	√ Highly liquid √ Low current income √ Safety of principal
Fixed Income	√ Current income √ Varied maturities
Equities	√ Dividend income √ Long-term growth
Hard Assets	√ Capital appreciation √ Illiquid

- **Equities,** including both domestic and international stocks.
- **Hard assets,** such as real estate, gold, silver, oil, and natural gas.

Within these categories there are, of course, wide variations. Utility stocks, for instance, don't behave much like the stocks of young, high tech companies. But as we'll see, one economic fact remains clear: Each investment category performs differently in different economic environments so diversification across investment categories is critical to investment success when the economic climate changes. As we'll explain, studies have shown that how you divide your assets among these categories is the single most important factor in determining long-term investment results.

With this broad background in mind, let's look at the relationship between risk and return in each of these different investment categories.

UNDERSTANDING INVESTMENT REALITIES

Figure 11–3

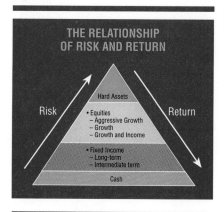

THE RELATIONSHIP OF RISK AND RETURN

Risk

Return

Hard Assets

• Equities
 – Aggressive Growth
 – Growth
 – Growth and Income

• Fixed Income
 – Long-term
 – Intermediate term

Cash

To properly develop an investment strategy, you must understand the following investment realities:

- Investment categories and subcategories have different ranges of investment return and volatility.
- Your holding period (the amount of time you actually own the investment) affects both investment return and volatility.
- As you progress through the

investment life cycle, your investment mix should change in both the accumulation and withdrawal phases.

- Your retirement sufficiency analysis should reflect these changes in investment mix during preretirement and postretirement periods.

Make no mistake about it, investment markets are volatile! Look what happened in 1994. Due to increases in interest rates many bond portfolios lost value, and stocks for the most part broke even. Now look at the first six months of 1995. Both long-term bonds and blue chip stocks rose almost 20 percent. For an individual investor, these short-term peaks and valleys certainly take their toll on the nerves!

Unfortunately, investment risk is often misunderstood because it's hard to measure. Some people would just say that risk means the likelihood that you will lose the entire value of your investment. Others look at the probability that the actual return will turn out to be different than what was expected. A more accepted definition equates risk with volatility (fluctuations in investment returns over a given time period).

In assessing volatility of returns, one of the most common measurements used by investors is a statistical concept called the *standard deviation,* which means the degree to which annual returns varied above or below an average. Generally speaking, the more volatile the investment, the larger the standard deviation.

As Table 11–1 indicates, using historical performance as a guide, we can get a sense for how different investments perform as a class and how returns vary around the averages.

Over time, investors have been rewarded for taking on the risk posed by more volatile returns. In Table 11–1, for example,

Table 11–1	Historical Asset Class Returns and Risk, 1926–93	
Asset Class	**Compound Average Annual Return**	**Standard Deviation***
Small-company stocks	17.6%	34.6%
International stocks	15.8	23.8
Large-company stocks	12.3	19.6
Government bonds	5.4	8.6
Treasury bills	3.7	3.3
Inflation	3.2	4.6

*95 percent of the returns varied around the compound average by plus or minus the percentage shown.
Source: Ibbotson Associates.

large-company stocks posed more than twice the risk of U.S. government bonds, as measured by the standard deviations of their returns. But the returns of large-company stocks were also more than twice as large as those of government bonds. Even more volatile, but more rewarding were small-company stocks.

THE DRAMATIC EFFECT OF TIME HORIZON

Now that we have seen an example of the volatilities of different investment classes, how can we minimize volatility in our own portfolio? The answer is by designing an investment portfolio that makes sense given our investment **time horizon.**

For retirement investing, your time horizon is generally defined as your proximity to retirement age. For example, if you are one year from retirement, it wouldn't make much sense to have your entire portfolio in small-company stocks. They're simply too volatile—a short-term market downturn would have devastating effects. On the other hand, if you're 30 years from retirement, you shouldn't invest 100 percent of your money in Treasury bills that barely keep pace with inflation. Your time horizon will govern the amount of risk you can afford to take since history shows that the passage of time will always smooth out short-term market fluctuations. To emphasize this point, let's look at the historical performance of each asset class over time. We'll start with 90-day Treasury bills, which we will use to represent the asset category of cash and cash equivalents.

As you can see from Figure 11–4, average annual returns on Treasury bills are almost identical throughout 1-, 10-, and 20-year holding periods. Furthermore, the range of returns doesn't vary a great deal. The highest one-year return was 14.7 percent, and the lowest return was less than 0.5 percent. This makes sense given the nature of cash and cash equivalents as short-term, virtually risk-free investments.

Figure 11–4

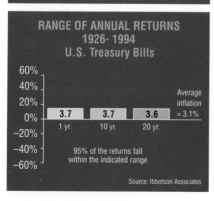

RANGE OF ANNUAL RETURNS
1926- 1994
U.S. Treasury Bills

60%
40%
20%   Average
 0%   3.7   3.7   3.6   = 3.1%   inflation
       1 yr. 10 yr. 20 yr.
-20%
-40%   95% of the returns fall
-60%   within the indicated range

Source: Ibbotson Associates

Figure 11–5

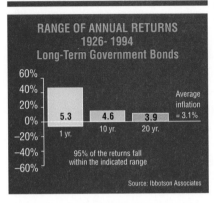

Long-term government bonds see a greater range of returns (volatility) over short time periods. For example, as shown in Figure 11–5, the average annual return for one-year holding periods was 5.3 percent. The best return for any of the one-year holding periods between 1926 and 1994 was 40.4 percent in 1981. The worst was a loss of 9.2 percent in 1967. But for 20-year holding periods, the average return was 3.9 percent with a best return of 10.1 percent from 1973 to 1993 and a worst period of less than 1 percent. Overall, long-term U.S. government bonds topped inflation by less than two percentage points a year.

The effect of a long-term time horizon is best seen with equity investments. Only stocks have returned a comfortable margin above inflation, over time, but in the short run, they can be very volatile. Stock prices fell 22 percent on a single day in 1987. They rose 54 percent in one year (1933) after dropping 43 percent two years earlier. The bear market of 1974–75 took 37 percent out of the value of stocks over a two-year period, while stocks almost doubled during the booming four years of 1988–91.

Figure 11–6

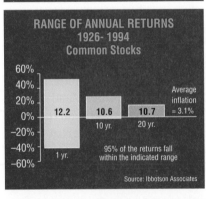

Over longer periods, however, the stock market's ups and downs have been much more moderate. Figure 11–6 shows that the best annual return for any of the one-year holding periods between 1926 and 1994 was 54 percent in 1933. The worst was a loss of 43.3 percent, the average was 12.2 percent. For the 20-year holding periods, the average return was 10.7 percent, while the range of returns fell between 16.9 and 3.1 percent. As you can see, the longer you held a stock investment, the smaller

Tip	Variable Rates of Return and Your Retirement Sufficiency Analysis

Remember that as you change your portfolio to reflect a shorter time horizon, you should reflect these variable returns in your sufficiency analysis. At a minimum, we recommend that you use different returns for the preretirement (higher-return) and postretirement (lower-return) periods to take into account the need to shift to a more conservative portfolio in retirement. Chapter 14 will consider expected returns on a number of suggested portfolios.

the range of returns—and hence the less volatility! Stocks, for example, never had a losing 20-year period. Returns were always positive.

So the investor with a long time horizon can afford to invest in more risky investments because that time horizon averages out short-term market fluctuations. As you get closer to retirement, however, your portfolio should change from higher risk to lower risk to reflect the fact that you can't afford to take as much risk. Changing your portfolio to a more conservative one (called *rebalancing*) will of course reduce your returns, but in the meantime you'll have had the benefit of portfolio growth over time. As we'll see in Chapter 14, a portfolio that is well diversified across different investment categories can achieve significant returns with moderate risk, primarily because of the time horizon.

A WORD ON PURCHASING POWER RISK

As we have noted, one of the biggest risks to your long-term retirement security is purchasing power risk (the risk that your money won't keep pace with inflation). To reduce purchasing power risk, you should invest for the long term in assets whose returns have traditionally outpaced inflation, such as common stocks. Put another way, you should invest to maintain a "real" rate of return over your investment time horizon.

How do you calculate your real return? Figure your after-tax rate of return, and then subtract the current rate of inflation. The result is your real rate of return. For example, say you invest in a bond yielding an after-tax rate of return of 5 percent. If inflation is running at 4 percent a

Figure 11-7   What Is a Real Rate of Return?

	Cash	Fixed Income	Equities
Current yield	3%	6%	4%
Appreciation	—	—	6%
Total return	3%	6%	10%
Less: Federal and state income taxes	(1%)	(2%)	(3%)
After-tax return	2%	4%	7%
Annual inflation	(3%)	(3%)	(3%)
Real return	(1%)	1%	4%

year, your real rate of return is 1 percent. What if inflation jumps to 12 percent a year? Your investment is actually declining in value by 7 percent a year.

By focusing on your *real* rate of return, you can calculate if your investments are staying ahead of inflation. Investment experts point out that a 1 percent to 4 percent real rate of return in a moderately risky portfolio mix is a significant accomplishment.

PUTTING IT TOGETHER—ASSET ALLOCATION AND DIVERSIFICATION

What's asset allocation? It is simply the process of dividing your investable assets among the four investment categories in the most appropriate manner given your investment goals, need for current income, and time horizon until you will need the money. More than any other factor, asset allocation has been shown to explain the majority of long-term investment performance in a portfolio.

The basic idea behind asset allocation is to have a mix of assets over all four categories that gives you the best chance of achieving good returns with moderate risk. We will cover asset allocation in detail in Chapter 14, but for now let's review a study of the benefits of asset allocation and diversification done by Bailard, Biehl & Kaiser (B,B&K), an investment management firm in the San Francisco area.

The study showed that even a naive approach to asset allocation— that is, investing equally in asset categories—was effective in dramatically reducing the overall portfolio risk in any single year. B,B&K used five asset categories (treating international investments as a separate category) and a 20-year time horizon. The five categories were cash and

Table 11–2   The Naive Portfolio, 1974–93

	Compound Annual Return	Standard Deviation (+ or −)*
S&P 500 index	12.8%	31.8%
Long-term bonds	9.9	15.1
Foreign securities	14.5	46.2
T-bills	7.4	5.3
Real estate	8.0	13.4
Naive portfolio	**11.1**	**15.3**
Inflation	5.9	6.8

*95% of the returns varied around the average by plus or minus the percentage shown.
Source: Bailard, Biehl & Kaiser.

cash equivalents (Treasury bills), fixed income (government and corporate bonds), equities (Standard & Poor's 500 composite index), international securities (foreign stocks and bonds), and hard assets (real estate).

The firm hypothetically invested 20 percent in each of these categories. At the end of every year, it reduced the amount in the winning asset categories and purchased more in the losing categories to keep a constant 20 percent mix in each category.

As you can see, the naive portfolio had excellent returns and only moderate risk, as measured by its standard deviation. To further emphasize this point, let's compare the returns of the S&P 500 and the naive portfolio. In the 20-year period, 95% of the S&P 500 returns were between −19% (or 12.8% minus 31.8% standard deviation) and 44.6% (or 12.8% plus 31.8%). On the other hand, 95% of the naive portfolio's returns were between −4.2% (or 11.1% minus 15.3%) and 26.4% (or 11.1% plus 15.3%). The naive portfolio was therefore half as volatile as the S&P 500 yet its compound rate of return was almost as great— 11.1% versus 12.8%. It is this ability to achieve close to market returns with less

Table 11–3   How to Reduce Investment Risk

Type of Risk	Techniques to Reduce Risk
Inflation risk	Invest in stocks or hard assets
Volatility risk	Hold investments for the long term
Business risk	Diversify within an asset category
Market risk	Diversify among asset categories
Marketability risk	Choose investment according to time horizon
Interest rate risk	"Ladder" portfolio with different maturities
Currency risk	Diversify among countries or hedge

The Parable of Diversification

Tip

In early 1975, a man we'll call Ron wins $100,000 in a lottery. He decides to invest his windfall conservatively. Because 1973 and 1974 were terrible bear markets, he opts for purchasing long-term government bonds.

In 1979, interest rates skyrocket, and the value of his bonds plunges to $72,000. Well, he decides, I'm going to get out of the bond market and cut my losses. But what to do now? He remembers that gold was selling for $35 an ounce in 1972; today it's at $800 an ounce. Moreover, he just heard someone on the radio predict that gold will soar to $2,000 an ounce. So he decides to buy 90 ounces of gold with his $72,000.

Now the year is 1982, and gold has fallen to $300 an ounce. Ron has only $27,000 left of his lottery winnings, but this time he's going to be smart. In the early 1980s, he knows, the only investments that have performed well are oil and gas and real estate. As Ron sees it, only one investment makes sense. He decides to buy a condominium in Houston. He locates a $100,000 condominium, puts $27,000 down, and takes out a mortgage of $73,000.

The years pass and it's 1987. He's paid his mortgage down to $70,000, but Houston's real estate prices have crashed, and his condo is worth only $60,000. He now has a negative net worth of $10,000!

The moral of Ron's story: Diversify.

---

overall risk that makes strategic asset allocation the strategy of choice for most individual investors.

DO INVESTMENTS INVOLVE MORE THAN ONE KIND OF RISK?

You bet they do. Investments often involve many types of risk to one degree or another. But some investments are affected more than others by certain types of risk. (Chapters 12 and 13 explain the types of risk.) For example, real estate is especially prone to illiquidity risk and bonds are prone to interest rate risk. As Table 11–3 indicates, you can minimize all of these risks by using a number of techniques, primarily a

Figure 11–8

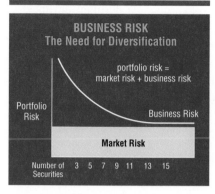

long time horizon and diversification within and across investment categories.

THE VALUE OF DIVERSIFICATION

Of course, asset allocation is first and foremost a type of diversification, in this case across asset categories. One of the most important ways to reduce risk is by having a diversified portfolio.

There are three levels of investment diversification. The first level is among asset categories (i.e., cash and cash equivalents, fixed income, equities, and hard assets). This is the basis for asset allocation, and is significant because the greatest differences in investment behavior exist between assets in different categories rather than between different investments within a class. For example, bonds and real estate generally have opposite reactions to inflation. Having investments in each category will hedge the exposure to inflation present in both categories.

The second level of diversification is among subcategories. For instance, equities have subcategories of aggressive growth, growth, growth and income, and international stocks. Diversifying among these subcategories recognizes that each subcategory behaves differently during different parts of the economic cycle. Investing in more than one subcategory will cushion the blow when a particular subcategory is adversely affected. (We discuss these subcategories further in Chapters 12 and 13.)

The third level of diversification is representation of an adequate number of individual securities within an asset subcategory so that the performance of the subcategory is reflected in your portfolio. As Figure 11–8 shows, generally, once you have about 12 to 15 individual securities in the portfolio, you should be sufficiently diversified against market risk. Good or poor performance of each stock should average out to approximate the market so long as an adequate number of securities is held.

WHAT'S NEXT?

The next three chapters will expand on the concepts outlined in this chapter. We discuss the investment performance of each broad investment category and how to best structure a portfolio for long-term investment success. Then we wrap up by discussing how best to implement your investment strategy using the principals we have outlined.

CHAPTER 12

INVESTING BY LENDING— CASH AND FIXED-INCOME INVESTMENTS

With the framework of Chapter 11 in mind, let's turn our attention to the cash and fixed-income categories. Read on to learn about:

- Cash equivalents and why they are appropriate.
- The types of fixed-income investments.
- Interest rate risk and how to protect against it.
- Managing credit risk.
- Taxable versus tax-exempt bonds.

In this chapter, we cover the special qualities of cash and fixed-income investments that have a practical impact on your investments while you're still working and after you reach retirement age.

155

Table 12–1	Cash Equivalent Investments

Money market accounts
Money market funds
Short-term CDs
Commercial paper
U.S. Treasury bills
Savings /NOW accounts

Note: Cash and fixed-income investments can be separated by their maturities. Generally speaking, anything with a maturity of two years or less is a cash equivalent investment; anything longer is a fixed-income investment.

Cash and fixed-income investments play an important role in any portfolio, whether you're 30 years from retirement or already retired. Younger investors invest in cash and bonds to provide a stable level of income and reduce overall portfolio risk. Older investors and retirees look to these investment categories to provide steady, predictable income streams while maintaining safety of principal. In this chapter, we examine the value of each of these investment types, starting with cash and cash equivalents.

CASH AND CASH EQUIVALENT INVESTMENTS

Of the four asset classes, cash equivalent investments offer investors maximum liquidity and stability of principal. Dollars invested in these vehicles don't typically fluctuate in value. Cash investments are issued by borrowers such as government agencies, large corporations, and banks with strong financial positions. There is little, if any, credit risk, and the short maturities of these investments protect against significant loss of principal due to interest rate changes. On the downside, however, when interest rates plunge, the return on your cash investments can drop to very low levels. (Recall 1993, when money market fund returns dropped to around 2.5 percent.)

As we saw in Chapter 11, however, you pay a price for safety and liquidity in the form of lower yields. Historically, cash and cash equivalent investments have provided yields that have barely exceeded the annual rate of inflation. As Figure 12–1 shows, $1 invested in U.S. Treasury bills between 1926 and 1963 would have grown to $11.73, equal to a 3.7 percent average annual return. However, after adjusting for inflation over the same time period, the real value of that $1 investment grew to only $1.44. Because of these low returns, the primary reasons to invest in cash equivalents are (1) to maintain a reserve for emergencies and (2) as a short-term, low-risk place to put funds awaiting investment in other vehicles.

Although cash investments are low-risk, they aren't entirely risk-free. Inflation risk (purchasing power risk) is the primary risk of investing in

Figure 12–1   Growth of $1 Invested in 30-Day
U.S. Treasury Bills, 1926–93

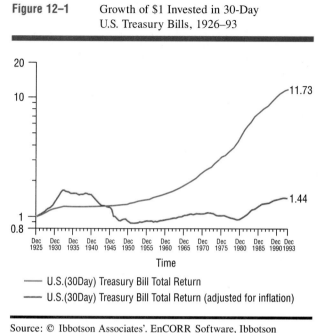

Time

—— U.S.(30Day) Treasury Bill Total Return

—— U.S.(30Day) Treasury Bill Total Return (adjusted for inflation)

Source: © Ibbotson Associates'. EnCORR Software, Ibbotson
Associates, Chicago. Used with permission. All rights reserved.

cash equivalents. Inflation risk means that the dollars you earn on your investments each year buy less and less. The greater your time horizon, the greater the purchasing power risk. This is bad news for people in retirement. Many people in retirement live on fixed incomes, and inflation can wreak havoc on their purchasing power. To maintain the purchasing power of investments, short-term cash equivalents should make up only a relatively small portion of a retirement investment portfolio.

Types of Cash Equivalent Investments

Cash investments tend to be packaged in various ways, but all exhibit essentially the same performance characteristics. Let's look at the major types of cash and cash equivalent investments.

Money Market Accounts and Funds.   Don't confuse money market accounts, offered by banks and savings and loans, with money market funds, offered by brokerage houses and mutual fund companies. Think of money market accounts as limited checking accounts (you can write only a few checks a month) that pay daily interest in relation to market rates. Because they are offered by banks and savings and loans, these accounts carry Federal Deposit Insurance Corporation (FDIC) insurance up to $100,000 and are thus generally risk-free.

Unlike money market accounts, money market funds are not insured by a government agency. But that shouldn't cause you much concern

---

 Tip

Watch Fees of Your Money Market Funds

You probably won't find that much variation in gross returns among money market funds anymore because in 1993 the SEC set rules that require funds to invest at least 95 percent of their assets in securities of the highest grade, and average maturities in the fund must be 90 days or less. These rules mean that the fund manager is constrained when it comes to investing in lower-quality (higher-yielding) investments or those with a longer maturity. However, it still pays to shop around because fees (which lower returns) can vary dramatically. Look at the expense ratio of the fund, which can vary from around .25 percent all the way up to 2 percent annually. The higher the expense ratio, the more fees will affect your investment return.

---

because these accounts invest in the highest quality U.S. government securities, commercial paper, banker's acceptances, and other securities. And the funds usually pay a higher rate of interest than bank money market accounts. We'll talk more about money market funds in Chapter 15.

Certificates of Deposit.   Banks and savings institutions may offer certificates of deposit (CDs) at whatever amount, maturity, and interest rate they choose. This means that you can shop among banks to find the CD package that's best for your current needs. Since you can buy and redeem CDs by mail, it's just as easy to do business with a bank in another state as with the one across the street. You can also purchase CDs from brokerage firms. You'll pay a brokerage fee, of course, but brokerage houses often pay a higher rate of interest because they buy in large quantities so they can frequently negotiate a higher rate.

When investing in CDs, some cautions are in order. First, if the interest rate a bank offers is substantially higher than the going rate for CDs of similar amount and maturity, be skeptical. The bank may be in a shaky financial condition and so must offer the higher rate to attract new money. Of course, if the bank is an FDIC institution, FDIC insurance would cover your loss if the bank went belly up, but not necessarily the interest that is due you. Also, your money could be tied up for weeks or even months. This possibility is particularly distressing if, as a retiree, you rely on your bank CD for income every month.

Also, when buying a CD, make sure to find out about getting your money out before the CD matures. In some cases, a bank or savings and loan can slap you with an early withdrawal penalty that totals the entire amount of interest that's due you. You may not be hit with a penalty if you withdraw your CD before its due date from a brokerage firm. That's because these firms make what's known as a secondary market in CDs so your broker can simply sell your certificate to some other investor.

U.S. Treasury Bills.   Treasury bills (T-bills) are short-term obligations of the U.S. government. Since they're backed by the full faith and credit of the U.S. government, there's no safer place for your principal, which is why they're favored by both retirees and younger folks who want at least a portion of their money in ultrasafe instruments.

With an investment in T-bills, many people, especially if they're retired, worry that they might need their cash before the year is up. But that's not much of a problem since T-bills are completely liquid. You can sell them through a broker at any time. But when you sell a bill before its maturity, you may realize a gain or loss, depending on whether current interest rates are lower or higher than the rate in effect when you bought the bill.

Where Do You Buy T-bills?

Tip

You can purchase T-bills through a broker or bank, in denominations of $10,000 and higher— and thereafter in multiples of $5,000. Brokers and banks charge small commissions—usually $25 to $50 per transaction. T-bills can be purchased in several different maturities: 90 days, 180 days, or 52 weeks.

You can eliminate commission charges by buying T-bills directly from Federal Reserve Banks or their branches. The Federal Reserve Banks and branches, acting as agents for the U.S. Department of the Treasury, sell U.S. government obligations to the public with no sales commissions.

If you telephone the Federal Reserve Bank nearest you or write the Bureau of Public Debt, Division of Customer Services, 300 13th Street SW, Washington, D.C. 20239-0001, you can receive a free brochure on how to buy Treasury securities from a Federal Reserve Bank or branch.

Table 12–2	Fixed Income Investments
Longer-term CDs	
U.S. Treasury notes and bonds	
Corporate bonds	
Federal agency bonds	
Mortgage-backed securities	
Municipal bonds	
Bond mutual funds	

Note: Most bonds mature in anywhere from 2 to 30 years. So-called notes are types of bonds that mature in 10 years or less.

In sum, deciding on the right cash equivalent investment depends on what matters most to you: safety, liquidity, convenience, or return. Investing in cash equivalents is a function of trade-offs. For example, with T-bills, you get a high degree of safety but a lower return. With money market funds, you get liquidity but less safety. Compared with both T-bills and money market funds, bank CDs give you convenience and a higher return, but less liquidity.

FIXED-INCOME INVESTMENTS

Like cash, bonds and other fixed-income securities have their special functions in a properly diversified investment portfolio. And they have always played a special role in a retirement portfolio.

Figure 12–2 Growth of $1 Invested in Long-Term Government Bonds, 1926–93

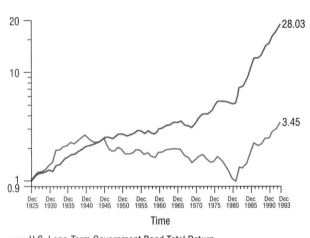

U.S. Long-Term Government Bond Total Return

U.S. Long-Term Government Bond Total Return (adjusted for inflation)

A bond is nothing more than a contract between the issuer of the bond, the borrower, and the person who holds the bond—you, the lender. The issuer agrees to pay interest at a fixed rate, or *coupon rate,* at specified times, usually twice a year. When the bond matures, the issuer must pay you the bond's face value—that is, the value that's

Figure 12-3   U.S. Corporate Bond Volatility, 1980–93

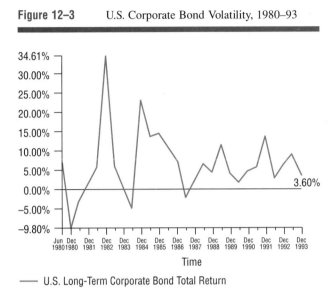

— U.S. Long-Term Corporate Bond Total Return

marked on the bond.

Historically, fixed-income investments have outperformed cash and cash equivalent investments, but generally haven't outperformed inflation to a significant degree. As Figure 12–2 indicates, $1 invested in long-term U.S. government bonds between 1926 and 1963 would have grown to $28.03, equal to a 5.02 percent average annual return. However, after adjusting for inflation over the same time period, the real value of that $1 investment grew to only $3.45.

Furthermore, while the coupon rate of a bond may be fixed, its price is not. When we measure the total return on bonds (that is, earnings plus price appreciation/depreciation), bonds are not the secure, stable investment most people think. (See Figure 12–3.) Interest rate risk can wreak havoc on the value of a bond portfolio. As we saw when interest rates rose in early 1994, bonds can be as varied and as volatile as any of your investments. In fact, most people don't know it, but from March to October 1987—before the 1987 crash in the stock market— bonds lost from 10 to 25 percent of their value, depending on their term and quality.

Nonetheless, bonds are attractive investments because (1) they provide higher yields than cash equivalents and (2) the income stream from a bond is usually fairly predictable. Also, bonds can provide additional diversification in a portfolio. While they do fluctuate in value, bonds are generally less volatile than stocks so they can moderate the effects of short-term swings in stock prices. Said another way, often when stock prices go down, bond values stay the same or increase. Thus, the overall value of a portfolio may stay the same.

The fact that fixed-income securities can be volatile doesn't mean that they aren't good investments. Most people who are either looking toward retirement or already retired should include bonds and other fixed-income investments in their portfolios because they offer a steady flow of income and often an attractive rate of return.

MORE ON INTEREST RATE RISK

As we explained earlier, most of the volatility associated with fixed income investments is due to interest rate risk, or the vulnerability of bond prices to movements in interest rates. To keep up with market rates, issuers of bonds and other fixed-income instruments have to pay higher rates on their new issues when interest rates go up. So older issues, paying lower rates of interest, are worth less if sold before maturity, as shown in Figure 12–4.

In other words, an increase in the interest rate paid on some particular debt instrument—five-year corporate bonds, for instance—has the effect of lowering the value of existing debt instruments previously issued at lower rates. The 7 percent five-year bond you bought last year would fall in value if similar bonds issued this year paid 9 percent.

While rising interest rates hurt bond prices, falling rates pose a type of risk as well. Many corporate and municipal bonds can be redeemed

---

Tip

Focus on Current Yield

You'll often hear the terms *par value* and *current yield* when dealing with bonds. Par value is the face value of a bond (what the issuer will actually pay you when the bond matures). Current yield is the annual return a bond pays and is calculated as a percentage. To figure the yield, divide the income a bond pays in a year by the bond's current price. Another yield measure, *yield to maturity*, is similar to the compound rate of return you'd have to earn on a comparable investment to equal the total return you'll get on your bond if you hold it until it matures. This yield takes into account the interest payments you receive reinvestment of that interest as well as the net rise or fall in the price of the bond as it nears its maturity value.

Figure 12–4	Interest Rate Risk . . . How Can It Affect Me?

You own a $1,000 bond at 6% maturing in five years. If interest rates rise from 6% to 7½% after 2 years, the value of your bond will fall by $45 because:

	Your Bond	New Bond
Face value	$1,000	$1,000
Rate	× 6%	× 7.5%
Annual interest	$60	$75
Years to maturity	× 3	× 3
Future earnings	$180	$225

Earnings on new bond	$225
Earnings on your bond	180
Bond discount	$ 45

(called) by their issuers. When interest rates fall, issuers take advantage of that privilege and call in their bonds. So a high-interest bond may be redeemed for cash at a time when investments available in the market yield much less.

You should know that, as a rule, a bond's value is affected by its maturity date. The price of long-term bonds— those that don't mature for many years—is influenced more by interest rate fluctuations than is the price of shorter-term bonds, as Table 12–3 shows. The table assumes that bonds of various maturities are worth $1,000 when they mature. It assumes, too, that you buy a bond when interest rates are 8 percent. The chart shows what may happen to these bonds if interest rates fell to 6 percent or rose to 10 percent. As you can see, long-term bonds can be especially volatile, and it usually makes sense to buy them only if you plan to hold them to maturity to fund a specific long-term income need or goal.

REDUCING INTEREST RATE RISK

Table 12–3	Impact of Interest Rate Changes on Bonds' Underlying Values		
Years to Maturity	**Market Rate Moves to 6%**	**Coupon Rate Is 8%**	**Market Rate Moves to 10%**
1	$1,019	$1,000	$981
5	1,085	1,000	923
10	1,149	1,000	875
20	1,231	1,000	828
30	1,277	1,000	810

You've probably heard of bonds referred to by their maturities: short-term, intermediate-term, and long-term. Usually short-term bonds mature in 1 to 2 years, intermediate-term bonds in 2 to 10 years, and long-term bonds in more than 10 years.

If you're planning to hold your bonds until they mature, consider staggering their maturities so they come due at different times. (This concept is referred to as *bond laddering*.) That way, you won't be taking as big a chance on interest rate fluctuations over a period of time.

Say you want to allocate $100,000 of a portfolio to bonds. To stagger your maturities, you might take 60 percent of your $100,000, or $60,000, and buy 12 intermediate bonds (bonds maturing in 3 to 10 years). So you would purchase 12 $7,000 bonds that are slated to mature in stages over the 7-year period. Then you'd allocate 30 percent of your $100,000 to short-term bonds (those maturing in less than three years). So you might buy three separate $10,000 bonds maturing in 1 year, 18 months, and 2 years.

As we saw, long-term bonds are riskier than short-term ones. The longer the period of time, the harder it is to predict economic conditions. To attract buyers, bonds that have longer maturities usually offer a higher current yield than medium- or short-term bonds.

However, in recent years we've seen that the extra yield on long-term bonds isn't significant enough to justify the increased risk. Figure 12–5 shows that in early 1989, yields on intermediate-term government bonds actually exceeded the yields on long-term bonds. This phenomenon, called an *inverted yield curve,* usually results from the Federal Reserve Board attempting to slow down the

Figure 12–5   Yield on Long-Term versus Intermediate-Term Government Bonds

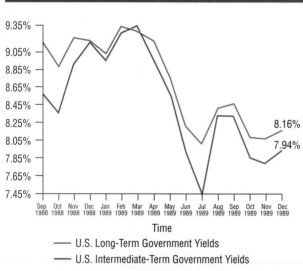

Time

—— U.S. Long-Term Government Yields

—— U.S. Intermediate-Term Government Yields

economy by keeping short-term interest rates high. An inverted yield curve sometimes can predict a fall in interest rates because sooner or later the Fed will free up the money supply.

CREDIT RISK

When you buy a bond, you are as much a lender as a bank is. The issuer owes you interest on your loan (investment) and must repay the loan (principal) at maturity. Thus, as a lender, you want to know that the issuer is creditworthy—you want to know the likelihood that you will be paid the interest and will receive your principal at maturity.

Bonds are rated by two primary agencies: Standard & Poor's, which rates bonds from AAA to D (AAA being the highest), and Moody's Investor Services, which rates them from Aaa to Ca. The higher the rating, the safer the bond, which means that the rating service believes the issuer is likely to make the required annual interest payments and repay the principal when it comes due. Safety, of course, carries a price—in this case, lower interest rates. Usually, the lower the rating, the higher the interest you'll earn since companies with low-rated bonds must pay a high return to attract investors.

Table 12–4	Standard & Poor's and Moody's Bond Ratings	
Standard & Poor's	**Moody's**	**Comment**
Investment Grade		
AAA	Aaa	Highest quality
AA	Aa	High quality
A	A	Good quality
BBB	Baa	Medium quality
Noninvestment Grade		
BB	Ba	Speculative element. Junk bonds are rated BB/Ba or lower.)
B	B	Speculative
CCC	Caa	More speculative
CC	Ca	Highly speculative
D	No rating	In default

Source: Investment Company Institute.

Sometimes you can invest in a bond with a high rating and see its rating downgraded. This drop usually won't matter as long as you hold the bond until it matures. But if you decide to sell your bond before maturity, its principal value may be less due to the change in its rating.

Here's an example. Say you buy a bond with a Moody's rating of A. Six months later,

Moody's upgrades your bond's rating to Aa. The bond is now considered a less risky investment than when you bought it so the company that issued it may offer a lower yield on new bonds it offers.

That's good news for you if you want to sell. A buyer should be glad to pay more for your bond than you did since the bond is now considered safer. But if the rating on your bond fell, the bond's value would fall as well. If you wanted to sell it before maturity, you may receive less than your purchase price. The buyer would have a bond with more risk; so, to compensate, the buyer would expect a higher current yield.

Now that we've looked at the basics of fixed-income investing, let's take a look at the types of securities available for your retirement portfolio.

TREASURY SECURITIES

Securities issued by the U.S. government are the safest investments you can buy because they are backed by the "full faith and credit" of the U.S. government. If the United States defaults on its obligations, none of our investments would be worth much at all. In other words, a government default is nearly impossible.

Where to Buy T-Notes

Note You may also purchase Treasury notes and bonds directly from the Federal Reserve. Just call the Federal Reserve in the city nearest you to get information on the government's Treasury Direct program. You can also write the Bureau of Public Debt, Division of Customer Services, 300 13th Street, SW, Washington, D.C. 20239-0001, to get a free brochure on this program.

The difference between Treasury bills, notes, and bonds is in years to maturity. Bills mature in 1 year or less; notes in 1 to 10 years; and Treasury bonds in 10 to 30 years. Also, Treasury bills have a minimum denomination of $10,000. Treasury notes that mature in fewer than four years cost a minimum of $5,000. However, if you opt for longer maturities for notes, you can buy these securities for only $1,000. And, of course, there are plenty of mutual funds that hold only U.S. obligations, and their minimum investment requirement is usually considerably less.

GOVERNMENT AGENCY SECURITIES

Certain federal government agencies or federally chartered organizations also issue securities. Some of these bonds are explicitly guaranteed by the U.S. government, but all are considered safe because even without an express guarantee, the risk of default is considered extremely low. The best known are mortgage pools—pools of home mortgages issued by the Government National Mortgage Association (GNMA or Ginnie Mae), Federal National Mortgage Association (FNMA or Fannie Mae), and Federal Home Loan Mortgage Corporation (FHLMC or Freddie Mac). These entities all buy mortgages from banks and thrifts, pool them, and then sell units of the pools to investors. Let's look at these three types of government agency securities.

GNMAs

When you buy Ginnie Maes, you're actually purchasing a portion of the 30-year mortgages issued by the U.S. Federal Housing Administration (FHA) and the Veterans Administration (VA). The GNMA collects monthly interest and principal payments that homeowners pay on their mortgages, subtracts a small administrative fee, and passes the payments on to its investors.

Since homeowners' monthly payments include both principal and interest, the check investors receive each month includes both interest income and some principal. Only the interest portion is taxable. The amount of principal and interest a Ginnie Mae pays each month fluctuates since some homeowners pay off their mortgages because they sell or refinance their houses. So if you invest in Ginnie Maes, you can't predict precisely how much you'll receive each month.

Bear in mind, though, that homeowners have the right to repay their mortgages at any time—and often do. Witness the refinancing boom in the early 1990s. When homeowners refinance their mortgages, the entire principal is repaid and passed through to investors, which reduces both the maturity and return of the mortgage pool. It's this *prepayment risk* that causes GNMAs, although they're government-backed, to pay a rate of return higher than those available on regular U.S. Treasury bonds. Before making a Ginnie Mae investment, you should decide whether this additional premium is large enough to offset the additional risk.

Other Mortgage-Backed Securities

Fannie Maes and Freddie Macs are other types of mortgaged-backed securities. Unlike Ginnie Maes, which return both interest and principal each month, these securities make regular interest payments, but you don't receive your principal back until the securities mature.

Fannie Maes and Freddie Macs carry more risk than Ginnie Maes because they invest in mortgages that aren't insured by the Federal Housing Administration or Veterans Administration. Even though the mortgage isn't guaranteed, however, the Federal National Mortgage Association and the Federal Home Loan Mortgage Corporation do guarantee that you'll receive your interest payments. Because these securities are more risky, they can pay a higher rate of interest than does a Ginnie Mae.

In sum, mortgage-backed securities pay a better yield than other government securities, and you don't give up much in safety. Not only are these securities backed by the government, they're also collateralized by the real estate they finance.

MUNICIPAL BONDS

Municipal bonds have long been a mainstay of people saving for retirement and those already in retirement. What could be better than bonds whose interest is free from federal income taxes and sometimes state and local taxes as well.

Apart from this consideration, are tax-exempt bonds a good deal for you if you're in a high marginal bracket? Usually—but compare the yields to know for sure.

To compare the yields of taxable and tax-exempt bonds, you must convert the yield on the tax-free bonds to an equivalent taxable yield. It's simple. Just divide the tax-exempt yield by 1 minus your tax bracket (expressed as a decimal).

Here's an example. Say you're in the 31 percent tax bracket, and you're considering purchasing a tax-exempt bond with a 6 percent yield. You divide 6 percent by 1 minus your tax bracket (31 percent)—or 0.69. The result—8.70 percent—is the amount you must get from a taxable bond to match the interest from a municipal bond. So if you can find a taxable bond that pays more than 8.70 percent at the same level of risk, it makes sense to buy it. If not, it probably makes more sense to buy the tax-exempt bond.

How Risky Are Municipal Bonds?

Tip

Public-purpose municipal bonds are also exempt from state and local taxes if they're issued by your home state. The only exceptions to this rule are Illinois, Iowa, Nebraska, Oklahoma, and Wisconsin.

Municipal bonds that are free from both federal and state taxes are advertised as double–tax-free. Those that are exempt from federal, state, and local taxes are, appropriately enough, known as triple–tax-free.

Most public-purpose municipal bonds are reasonably free of risk and are liquid, but you pay steep commissions when you sell. Some, however, are riskier than others, as evidenced by the recent Orange County bankruptcy. So-called *general obligation bonds* should be the least risky since they're backed by the full faith and credit of the government that issues them. *Revenue bonds,* however, are backed only by the income from the project they're set up to finance—a local hospital, for example, or a water or sewer project. If the project fails, you could lose the entire amount you invested.

What about insured municipal bonds? You don't pay directly for the insurance—the issuer does. However, for your added measure of safety, you must be prepared to accept a yield $\frac{1}{10}$ to $\frac{1}{3}$ of a percentage point less than on uninsured bonds.

Municipal bonds aren't cheap. Direct investments in municipal bonds cannot be made on a small scale since they sell in units of $5,000. But you can get around this hurdle by investing in mutual funds that invest in municipal bonds. You can find funds that allow you to invest as little as $250 to $500.

CORPORATE BONDS

Corporate bonds are riskier than bonds issued by the U.S. government. If the company issuing your bond goes belly up, your ability to get your money back depends on the provisions of the bond you buy. Bondholders do usually take priority over common stockholders when a company's assets are distributed. However, in practice, few people below the level of secured creditor receive any return of principal when a company goes bankrupt. As you might expect, to compensate for this extra risk, corporate bonds pay higher yields than government bonds.

Most corporations issue bonds in denominations of $1,000, but you must buy them in lots of five. You can, however, invest in a bond mutual fund, where the initial investment requirements can be as low as $250. By investing in a bond mutual fund, you'll have a very diversified bond portfolio because you'll own a share of probably 50 to 100 different bonds.

Unlike municipal bonds, the interest you earn on corporate bonds is subject to federal, state, and local taxes. Corporate bonds are liquid. You can usually sell them without too much trouble before they mature. Bonds that carry the highest ratings are the most liquid.

High-Yield Bonds

A high-yield bond is a special type of corporate bond known in the trade as a *junk bond*. These instruments pay very high yields, and for good reason—the risk you take on when you purchase these bonds is very high. If the company goes belly up, you'll probably lose every penny you invested. Recently, defaults on these low-grade corporate bonds occurred much more frequently than defaults on other corporate bonds. And, with the 1989 collapse of the investment banking firm Drexel Burnham Lambert (the firm that established much of the market for these bonds), the outlook for these bonds has become even more uncertain.

ZERO-COUPON BONDS

Zero-coupon bonds (nicknamed *zeros*) are simply bonds without a coupon rate, that is, no coupon payment. When you buy them, you receive no annual interest payment. Instead, the bonds are sold at a deep discount from face value. For example, you might pay $275 for a $1,000 bond that yields 9 percent and matures in 15 years. When the bond matures, you know exactly the amount you'll collect—$1,000.

That's one reason these bonds make sense in tax-deferred retirement accounts. The IRS says that you must pay taxes on the interest you would collect each year on zero-coupon bonds, even though you don't actually receive any money until the bond matures. The only exception to this rule is for zeros issued by a municipality since that interest is

U.S. Savings Bonds

Tip

Series EE U.S. savings bonds are zero-coupon bonds. But unlike other zero-coupon bonds, EE bonds give you the option of deferring tax on the interest earned each year until you cash in the bond.

Let's say you bought a $100 savings bond and elected not to report the interest each year. The bonds are sold for exactly half their face value so you would pay $50 for a $100 savings bond. When the bond matures, you could cash it in and receive $100. In that year, you would have to report $50 (the difference between the $50 you paid for the bond and the $100 you receive) as interest income.

The rules for EE savings bonds have changed recently. Here is a summary:

- Bonds issued between 3/1/93 and 5/1/95 still carry a minimum rate guarantee of 4% for five years, after which your return is 85% of the rate paid by 5-year treasury securities for the entire time you've held the bonds. Bonds issued prior to 3/1/93 had a 6% guaranteed minimum rate. All of these bonds will pay interest for up to 30 years, except those issued prior to November 1965 which will pay interest for up to 40 years.

- There is no longer a guaranteed minimum rate for bonds issued after 5/1/95.

- These new issues pay either short-term or long-term variable rates, and will pay interest for up to 17 years. These bonds still have a 30-year life, but the U.S. Treasury Department has not decided what rate to pay for years 17–30.

- Rates are set every May and November.

- The short-term rate is 85% of the average 6-month treasury security rate for the prior 3 months. For example, the May rate would be based on the average of the 3 months from Feb.–Apr. This is payable for years 1–5.

- The long-term rate is 85% of the average 5-year treasury security rate for the prior 6 months. For example, the May rate would be based on the average of the 6 months from Nov.–Apr. This is payable for years 6–17.

You purchase these bonds directly from the Federal Reserve Bank. You can obtain the form you need to send to the Federal Reserve from your local bank.

tax-exempt. However, if you buy taxable zeros for a tax-sheltered retirement account, such as an IRA or Keogh, you don't have to worry about paying annual taxes until you take money out of the account.

Zero-coupon securities come in nearly as many varieties as there are bonds. You can buy corporate zeros, municipal zeros, convertible zeros, mortgage-backed zeros, and Treasury zeros. If you're interested in buying the safest bonds possible, stick to Treasury zeros.

Like all bonds, you don't have to worry about fluctuations in interest rates if you hold your zero-coupon bonds to maturity. You'll collect the amount you're due when the bond matures. However, if you plan to sell before maturity, remember, the value of zero-coupon bonds fluctuates much more dramatically than other bonds. Because the bonds are locked in at a specific—and favorable—reinvestment rate, investors are willing to pay more for them than for other bonds in periods of falling interest rates.

CONVERTIBLE BONDS

Convertible bonds give you the best of two worlds. They're part bond and part stock, and, because of their hybrid nature, you can buy them for current income but still have the chance to profit later if the issuer's stock appreciates. Here's how these bonds work.

When you own a convertible bond, the company issuing it grants you the right to exchange your bonds for shares of the company's common stock. The trade-off for this privilege is a lower yield.

You can make the exchange when and if the stock's price rises a certain amount above the stock's price when the bond was first issued. Of course, the underlying stock may never rise in price, and in the meantime, you've accepted a lower yield. Also, convertible bonds aren't as liquid as other types of corporate bonds because the market for them is smaller.

Now that we've reviewed the characteristics of fixed-income investments, let's move on to the equity portion of your portfolio.

CHAPTER 13

INVESTING THROUGH OWNERSHIP—EQUITIES AND HARD ASSETS

Continuing our discussion of the major types of investments, this chapter discusses equities and hard assets. Read on to learn about:

- The types of equity investments.
- Managing market and business risk.
- Understanding international investing.
- Investing in real estate, oil and gas, and precious metals.

Equities (stocks) and hard assets play a critical role in any investment portfolio, whether you're 30 years from retirement or already retired. The reason is these investments are your primary means of providing growth within your portfolio, which in turn provides protection against inflation. Over time, common stocks have shown superior returns over other investment classes. And hard assets, while not as impressive, show significant returns in periods of higher inflation. In this chapter, we examine the value of each of these investment types, starting with equities.

BASIC CHARACTERISTICS OF COMMON STOCKS

Equities in general represent ownership of a business. Your investment return from stocks depends on the prospect for the company's business as a whole, and can be composed of dividends, capital gains, or both. Stocks have generally shown superior performance relating to fixed income securities because the businesses you own generally earn higher returns on invested capital than the interest rates they pay on debt (their bonds). Otherwise they wouldn't stay in business for long!

Of course, these returns aren't guaranteed, and the value of your stock investments will be affected by the same forces that move stock prices in general. If a bear market develops, your stocks are likely to drop. If a company experiences poor financial times, dividends may be cut. But one thing has held true—common stocks have far outperformed other asset classes, and have done the best job of keeping ahead of inflation over the long term. As Figure 13–1 shows, $1 invested in large-company stocks in

Figure 13–1   Growth of $1 Invested in Common Stocks, 1926–93

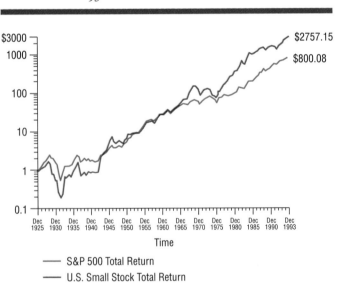

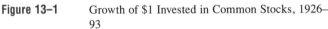

1926 would have grown to $800 by the end of 1993. Small-company stocks have performed even better; $1 invested in 1926 would have grown to $2,757 over the same period. The growth over that period, after adjustment for inflation, was $339 for large-company stocks and $987 for small-company stocks. Taking into account average inflation of 3.1 percent over the period, stocks have provided a real rate of return of over 7 percent.

As we saw in Chapter 11, while the performance of stocks has been impressive, it has also been quite volatile when measured annually. For one-year periods between 1926 and 1993, for example, returns ranged from a one-year gain of 53.9 percent in 1933 to a one-year loss of 43.3 percent in 1931. But remember, holding stocks for long periods of time greatly reduces the volatility in range of returns.

THE RISKS OF INVESTING IN STOCKS

The main risks in equity investing are market risk and business risk. Let's take market risk first.

Market Risk

Market risk is the danger that whole financial markets can rise or fall in value. As they do, these markets may affect the value of a particular investment in the market, even though the other risk factors for that investment remain unchanged. You may buy the stock of a prosperous company, but the entire market may fall as a result of uncertainties about the economy. While your company may be doing quite well, investors will become wary of stocks in general, so the price of your stock is likely to fall due to lower demand. One of the best examples of market risk is the stock market crash of 1987, when the value of stocks of rock-solid companies plunged with all other stocks in a single day.

You can protect yourself from volatility by investing for the long term. As we know, in the short run common stocks can be quite volatile—stock prices fell 22 percent on that single day in 1987. The bear market of 1974–75 ground 37 percent out of the value of stocks over a two-year period, while stocks almost doubled during the booming four years of 1988–91. Over longer periods, however, the stock market's ups and downs have been more moderate. For example, the best annualized

Figure 13–2   Market Risk of Common Stocks—
Time Horizon, 1926–94

Length	Number of Periods	Holding Period Winners	Holding Period Losers
1 Year	68	46	23
5 Years	64	51	14
10 Years	59	53	7
20 Years	49	50	0

Source: © Ibbotson Associates'. EnCORR Software, Ibbotson Associates, Chicago. Used with permission. All rights reserved.

return for any of the 10-year holding periods between 1926 and 1994 was 20.1 percent. The worst was a loss of just 0.9 percent. For the 25-year holding periods between 1926 and 1994, the best average return was 14.7 percent, while the worst was a positive 5.9 percent a year.

As we said in Chapter 11, the way to manage market risk is to invest for the long term. Figure 13–2 illustrates how your risk declines the longer you invest. When we use the term *winner* in the chart, we mean that the Standard & Poor's 500 (S&P 500) had a total return greater than inflation. The term *loser* means the S&P 500 failed to produce a total return in excess of inflation. (The S&P 500, a stock index composed of 500 of the largest companies in the U.S. equity markets, is generally accepted as a benchmark of the stock market as a whole.) The figure shows that if you held the S&P 500 during any 20-year period between 1926 and 1993, your return over the 20-year period always exceeded inflation. What if you held the equities for only one year? There's a two-out-of-three chance your return topped inflation.

The converse of investing for the long-term is to try to eliminate market risk by "timing the market" (predicting where it's going and reacting accordingly). However, people who try to determine market changes—often called *market timers*—don't consistently make the right call. Market timing is sophisticated guesswork.

Figure 13–3   Accuracy of Market Timing (1980–94)

Accuracy	Return
100%	25.2%
63	14.5
50	11

Source: Sanford C. Bernstein & Company, Inc. and Ibbotson Associates

Figure 13–3 illustrates how accurate you would have to be in timing the market in order to beat the market. It's based on the S&P 500. Assuming you could optimize your holdings every quarter, you would have to make the right call almost two-thirds of the time

Figure 13–4	Does Market Timing Work?	
		Average Annual Return
3,793 trading days		14.5%
Less: Best 10 days		11.3
Less: Best 20 days		9.1
Less: Best 30 days		7.2
Less: Best 40 days		5.4
Inflation—1980–1994		4.6

Based on S & P 500, 1980–1994
Source: Sanford C. Bernstein Company, Inc. and Ibbotson Associates.

or more for the market timing approach to work (in other words, to equal the return earned by the S&P 500). Even the experts have trouble meeting this challenging target consistently!

And what if you'd been out of the market on some of the best trading days? As Figure 13–4 shows, had you been out of the market (S&P 500) for the 40 best days between 1980 and 1993, your return would have barely outpaced inflation!

Business Risk

The second major risk with equity investing is business risk. This is the specific risk associated with the underlying business of the issuer of a particular stock, bond, or other investment. (With fixed income investments, it's called *credit risk*.) Business risk is the risk that some event, perhaps unforeseen, may reduce the return on a particular investment. If, for instance, you've invested in a company that makes a popular cold remedy, and somebody comes up with a surefire cure for the common cold, your company's product suddenly isn't worth much. The value of your investment declines.

You minimize business risk through diversification (having an adequate number of individual securities within an asset subcategory). Generally, once you have about 12 to 15 individual securities in your equity portfolio, you should be sufficiently diversified against business risk. Good or poor performance of each stock should average out to approximate the market if an adequate number of securities is held.

TYPES OF EQUITY INVESTMENTS

Equity investments can be confusing because there are many subcategories of stock within the category. The major types of equity subcategories are income stocks, growth and income stocks, growth stocks, aggressive growth stocks, and international stocks.

Income Stocks

These stocks produce steady income in the form of dividends. As a rule, these are the stocks of older, well-established companies in mature industries such as utilities and railroads. Because they don't need cash to support rapid expansion, these companies tend to return a hefty portion of their earnings to investors in the form of quarterly cash dividends. Income stocks are usually less risky—at least in the short run—than the stocks of younger, less well-established companies.

The downside? As you might expect, income stocks offer less chance for growth. In other words, don't expect the price of your stock to appreciate too much since demand for these companies' products or services is fairly stable. That's why income stocks often form the backbone of the conservative investor's portfolio.

Growth and Income Stocks

As their name suggests, these stocks combine regular dividend payments with some prospect for growth. They're slightly riskier than income stocks only in that the market value of their shares is subject to greater variation. You've no doubt heard the term *blue chip stocks,* which are also known as *widow-and-orphan stocks.* These are the equities most people think of when they refer to growth and income stocks.

Don't ask your broker for a list of blue chip stocks, though. It doesn't exist, although the S&P 500 is a good proxy for this category. Companies whose stock might qualify as growth and income stocks are American Telephone & Telegraph, Coca-Cola, Dow Chemical, Du Pont, General Electric, General Mills, ITT, Merck, and similar multinational companies. All of these companies have a proven track record of stable growth, steady profits, and regular dividend payments.

Growth Stocks

This category represents younger, but fairly well-established companies that are reinvesting their cash in the company rather than paying it out to shareholders in the form of dividends. If the company's business strategies are successful, the value of these stocks can increase substantially—and quickly. Of course, they're more volatile than established blue chip companies, and thus have a greater potential for fluctuations in returns. You'll find these companies on such lists as the annual Inc. 100 or the Forbes list of up-and-comers. Examples include many computer hardware and software companies such as Intel, Compaq, and Microsoft.

Growth stocks usually have higher price/earnings (P/E) ratios than other equities, which means that a dollar of earnings for a growth stock results in a higher stock price than for a growth and income stock. Growth stocks make few or no dividend payments to shareholders. That means you shouldn't rely on growth stocks for current income, but they can be a valuable part of a portfolio that's oriented toward long-term growth.

Aggressive Growth Stocks

Everything we just said about growth stocks applies double to aggressive growth stocks. These are issued by very young companies (often firms operating on the cutting edge of technology), where the risks of failure are as great as the potential rewards of success. Again, the companies reinvest their earnings so they pay little or no dividends.

How Are Stocks Traded?

Note

Stocks are traded on public exchanges. There are three major markets: the New York Stock Exchange (NYSE), American Stock Exchange (AMEX), and National Association of Security Dealers Automated Quotation (NASDAQ) system in the over-the-counter (OTC) market.

In addition to these markets, there are several regional stock exchanges, including the Philadelphia Exchange, Midwest Exchange, and Pacific Exchange. These regional exchanges list companies of particular interest to their geographic areas.

International Stocks

A generation ago, U.S. stocks represented two-thirds of the value of all stocks outstanding worldwide. Now it's the other way around. Two-thirds of all stock value lies in foreign markets. Currently, opportunities for investors are growing much faster overseas. Foreign stocks tend to offer higher returns—as well as greater volatility—than domestic U.S. issues. Economic growth overseas in the Pacific Rim, Latin America, and other emerging markets has recently outpaced growth rates in the United States, providing for rapid expansion of sales and profits by corporations in those countries.

Just as importantly, stock markets around the world don't move in sync with the U.S. market. Returns from Asian stock markets, for example, have tended to be down when U.S. returns are up, and vice versa. That means investing overseas could add an important measure of diversification to a portfolio of U.S.-based stocks.

Of course, there are risks to investing outside of the United States, among them political risk. The trend since World War II has been to open up national borders to flows of outside capital and investment. But at some point in the future, the world is likely once again to see trade disputes, political unrest, and wars that will disrupt international markets and imperil the value of overseas investments.

Another pitfall facing international

Table 13–1	Returns of U.S. and Foreign Stocks	
	Total Return	
	S&P 500 Index	**MSCI EAFE* Index**
1983	22.51%	24.82%
1984	6.27	8.02
1985	32.16	56.92
1986	18.47	70.21
1987	5.23	25.26
1988	16.81	28.91
1989	31.49	11.04
1990	−3.17	−22.97
1991	30.55	12.86
1992	7.67	−11.53
1993	10.06	32.56
1994	1.31	7.78
Average return	14.95	19.49
Standard deviation	12.24	26.48

*Morgan Stanley Europe, Australia, New Zealand, Far East Index

Source: © Ibbotson Associates'. EnCORR Software, Ibbotson Associates, Chicago; and Morgan Stanley International. Used with permission. All rights reserved.

Investing Internationally

Tip

Several alternatives are available for individuals who want to invest in the growth of foreign economies:

- One way to participate in the global economy is to buy stock in U.S.-based companies with extensive overseas operations. Examples include: Caterpillar, Coca-Cola, Citicorp, Exxon, and Gillette. These stocks benefit from international growth. And unlike the other alternatives listed below, they have less currency risk for U.S. investors. However, stock prices of U.S. corporations tend to move with the U.S. equity markets, even for those companies whose predominant business is outside the United States.

- Stocks listed on foreign exchanges can be purchased through major U.S. stock brokerages and international banks. Ownership of foreign stocks entails marketability risk and currency risk. Stockholders may also encounter problems with documentation and timely receipt of dividend payments.

- American depository receipts (ADRs) are listed on U.S. stock exchanges. They certify ownership of a particular number of shares of a foreign company on deposit at a foreign branch of an American bank. They avoid problems with documentation and dividend payments that can be involved with direct ownership of foreign stocks. But there are disadvantages. First, the ADR market is thin and liquidity can be an issue. Second, you're subject to currency fluctuation. The price of your ADRs will rise and fall with the exchange rate even when the underlying stock price is stable.

- International mutual funds are a final option. Some funds take a global approach, buying both foreign and U.S. stocks, while others limit themselves to non-U.S. investments. More specialized funds invest in a single region, such as Europe, the Pacific, or emerging markets. In addition, there are several dozen funds specializing in single countries (for example, Italy, Spain, India, Korea, or Mexico).

investors is currency risk. Let's say you buy a non-U.S. stock and the dollar subsequently rises 10 percent against the value of that stock's home-country currency. Even if the stock's price hasn't changed, the value of your investment in dollars has declined by 10 percent. Currency risk can result in quick and painful losses for investors who must sell after a major currency realignment. For long-term investors, however, the currency risk posed by international stocks is of less concern. The variations in return related to currency fluctuations will enhance the diversification effects provided by investing in international stocks. And if future economic growth proves to be much greater overseas, foreign currencies will tend to strengthen versus the U.S. dollar over time. Such a trend would be favorable for U.S. investors holding international stocks because the value of those stocks would rise in dollar terms.

Professional money managers sometimes take steps to hedge (limit) the effect that currency changes will have on the value of their portfolios. These steps involve such things as the use of currency options or futures contracts. As a U.S.-based investor, you can avoid currency risk only by (1) choosing investments whose underlying assets are dollar-denominated or (2) using mutual funds that hedge the currency risk posed by their foreign securities.

HARD ASSETS

The final category of investments is hard assets, so-called to distinguish them from paper assets like bonds and stocks. As the term implies, hard assets are those that you can see and touch: gold, silver, and other precious metals; natural resources such as oil and minerals; real estate; and collectibles. If you decide to allocate a portion of your assets to hard assets, you need to figure out which you want to purchase.

The common characteristic of hard assets is that they tend to hedge your portfolio against inflation because their values tend to rise along with the overall level of consumer prices. Aside from its inflation hedge, however, hard assets have generally outperformed bonds but have not provided as much return potential as common stocks. As Figure 13–5 shows, $1 invested in real estate in 1946 would have grown to $138.52 by the end of 1992. The real rate of return over that period, after adjustment for inflation, was $20.99. Taking into account average inflation of 3.1 percent over the period, real estate has provided a real rate of return of 6.9 percent.

Figure 13–5   Growth of $1 Invested in Real Estate, 1946–92

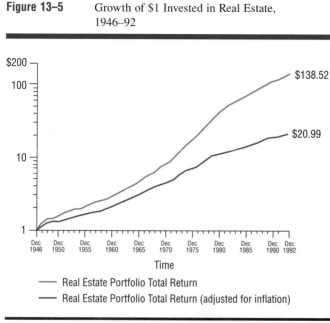

Real Estate Portfolio Total Return

Real Estate Portfolio Total Return (adjusted for inflation)

In addition, some hard assets, such as commercial real estate and oil-and-gas properties, can offer current income as well as the opportunity for price appreciation. Others, like gold bullion and raw land, provide no current income and may even carry expenses, such as real estate taxes, that give them a negative cash flow. Let's look at several principal categories of hard assets.

Real Estate

Unlike such investments as stocks and bonds, each parcel of real estate has unique characteristics, including location, type of building, improvements, amenities, and lease arrangements. For example, there is no standard price per square foot for a given type of building, even within a local geographic market. Instead, each real estate investment needs to be valued individually. Real estate may also offer limited marketability. Once acquired, a property may take months or years to sell. These factors mean that direct investments in real estate can be risky, even for professional investors with detailed information about a particular market. And let's face it, not everyone is cut out to be a landlord. Many people have neither the time nor the temperament to cope with dripping faucets and broken windows.

On the other hand, direct investments in real estate often prove to be enormously profitable. Leverage in the form of mortgage financing is available to enable an investor to acquire property with a relatively small equity investment, boosting the potential for profit. For instance, if you buy a parcel of real estate with a 10 percent down payment and then sell after just a 10 percent appreciation in price, you've doubled your money. No wonder many of the country's largest fortunes have been based on real estate investments.

Investors who want exposure to real estate without buying property directly often turn to real estate investment trusts (REITs). REITs are structured much like closed-end mutual funds and offer diversification, liquidity, and the opportunity to make a small initial investment. They pool cash from investors and issue shares, which subsequently can be bought or sold on a stock exchange or in the over-the-counter market. Like mutual funds, REITs also don't pay taxes. Instead, they pass through to shareholders the income from rents, interest, and gains from property sales. Investment strategies of REITs fall into two broad categories. Equity REITs purchase interests in real estate developments, and may specialize in a certain category of property, such as apartment buildings or shopping centers. Mortgage REITs, on the other hand, make mortgage and construction loans. As a result, their performance tends to be similar to fixed-income investments such as bonds.

The Tax Reform Act of 1986 took away many of the tax advantages of real estate ownership in general and clamped down in particular on tax-shelter–oriented real estate partnerships. The 1980s also saw a series of severe regional slumps in real estate and the collapse of the savings and loan industry. These events hurt property values in many markets and caused losses for real estate investors. However, as real estate markets have recovered recently, the investment performance of many limited partnerships and REITs has improved.

Oil and Gas

Short of drilling for oil and gas yourself, there are four ways you can invest in oil and gas: through stock in energy companies, through shares in an energy mutual fund, through a stake in limited partnerships, and through shares in master limited partnerships.

A simple way to participate in the oil and gas industry—and the least risky way—is to buy energy stocks. A major advantage of this strategy is liquidity. You can buy and sell any amount whenever you want. The downside is that energy stocks may not directly reflect changes in oil and gas prices. And they're subject to the vagaries of the stock market as a whole.

You can participate more directly in this industry through oil and gas "programs" or drilling partnerships. These programs share some characteristics with mutual funds. Both are investment pools run by professional managers. Both pass through profits and losses to investors, and both have diversified holdings. But that's where the similarities end.

The purpose of oil and gas programs is generally either to explore or drill for oil or to purchase producing oil wells. Usually these programs come in the form of joint ventures or "untraded" limited partnerships. That is, they're offered for a fixed number of months. So each program is a distinct operating business, varying in size from $1 million up to $300 million. Partnership units usually cost a minimum of $5,000 to $10,000.

You should know that investing in oil and gas programs is risky business and only for the most sophisticated investors. Also, these investments aren't traded on any public exchanges so they're highly illiquid.

Precious Metals

What are the advantages of investing in precious metals? Since metal has intrinsic value, it has traditionally been perceived as a hedge against inflation and political uncertainties.

You can invest in metals in a number of ways. You can purchase bullion (bars or ingots) or coins directly, or you can buy certificates from a dealer who holds on to the metals for you. You can also purchase futures contracts or mining stocks, or you can invest in mutual funds that invest in mining stocks.

Of course, when you buy precious metals directly, you get no current income—an important consideration for people who are already retired. Shares in mining companies can be another story. They frequently pay dividends—some of them quite generous.

As a rule, most people who invest in metals put their money in gold. But you can also invest in silver and platinum in much the same way. Again, your options are bullion, coins, certificates, metals futures, mining stocks, and mutual funds that invest in mining stocks.

So far we've discussed how to invest directly in our four investment categories. Now the question is how much should we invest in each category, or what should our asset allocation be. The next chapter deals with the process of asset allocation.

CHAPTER 14

THE IMPORTANCE OF ASSET ALLOCATION

Now that we've seen how different investment categories perform, we'll explain why asset allocation is the best strategy for a long-term investor. Read on to understand:

- The economic rationale for asset allocation.
- The benefits of asset allocation.
- Model allocations for your place in the investment life cycle.
- Rebalancing your allocation.

In previous chapters we looked at the risk and return characteristics of cash, fixed income, equities, and hard assets. If you're investing for retirement, you may believe that the particular investments that you buy—individual stocks, bonds, or commodities—determine the overall success of your investment portfolio. But in reality, of all the investment decisions you will make, your **asset allocation** decision will have

187

by far the greatest effect on your portfolio's performance. Asset allocation is simply the process of dividing your investable assets among the
four investment categories in the most appropriate manner given your
investment goals, need for current income, and time horizon until you'll
need the money.

The question you must ask, of course, is how much do you allocate
to each category? That's what this chapter is all about. Your assets
should be allocated differently depending on your age, need for current
income, and future goals. As we'll see, asset allocation will give you
the best chance of achieving the returns necessary to reach your goals
with the least possible amount of risk. As you read through this chapter, keep in mind that an allocation strategy for retirement is only the
final result of a process in which you evaluate and consider the relationship of risk and return within the context of your retirement sufficiency
analysis.

STRATEGIC ASSET ALLOCATION

The goal of strategic asset allocation is to determine the way you divide
your assets among the four major asset categories so that you can
obtain the long-term portfolio performance you need to achieve your
retirement goals with the least risk. Asset allocation is by nature a long-
term investment strategy, and has its theoretical foundation in what has
become known as modern capital market theory. This theory holds that

- Domestic and international capital markets are dominated by
  institutions with almost limitless access to information. It is
  increasingly difficult for individuals to get the information
  necessary to predict price movement given this institutional
  domination.
- Economic analysis doesn't lead to consistently profitable investment results. Trying to outguess peaks and valleys in the markets
  based on economic data has proven fruitless since markets don't
  seem to respond consistently to similar economic trends.
- Inflation is usually the best predictor of long-term investment
  behavior.
- Different classes of investments respond uniquely to the various
  kinds of risk.

- Holding periods greatly influence the suitability of particular types of investments.
- Diversification is an effective way to control risk.

Since the individual investor is constrained by a lack of timely information, and even those professionals who supposedly have it often can't outperform the market indexes, it's unlikely that any investment manager will continually obtain superior returns over the market as a whole. Given this reality and the unpredictability of markets in general, investing becomes almost a defensive strategy—achieve reasonable long-term results but protect your downside by minimizing risk as much as possible.

More than any other factor, asset allocation has been shown to explain the majority of long-term investment performance in a portfolio. Yet many investors are more concerned with the specific investments they make, like the specific bonds or mutual funds they select. "Determinants of Portfolio Performance II, an Update," a study in the May–June 1991 *Financial Analysts Journal,* showed that less than 9 percent of the total return on your investments is explained by the specific investments that you make. The authors looked at 10 years of investment performance (1982 to 1991) of 82 large corporate pension plans and considered three key decisions made by those plans: asset classes, timing, and security selection. The most important factor in the pension plan's investment performance, they concluded, is how the investment managers allocated investment dollars among categories of assets—for example, cash, fixed income, equities, and hard assets. The study showed that as much as 91.5 percent of the plan's investment return depended upon this allocation process.

Unfortunately, many people invest as if the opposite were true,

Figure 14-1

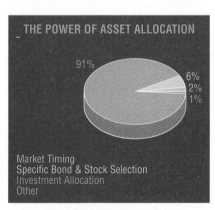

THE POWER OF ASSET ALLOCATION

91%

6%
2%
1%

Market Timing
Specific Bond & Stock Selection
Investment Allocation
Other

Source: "Determinants of Portfolio Performance II, an Update," by Brinson, Singer, and Beebower. Reprinted, with permission, from *Financial Analysis Journal*, May/June 1991. Copyright 1991, Association for Investment Management and Research, Charlottesville, VA. All rights reserved.

and focus exclusively on the characteristics of particular investments. Or, they try to "time the market" and outguess market declines or advances. With these types of strategies, investing often becomes no more than a guessing game (sometimes a very sophisticated one) with unpredictable long-term results.

ASSET ALLOCATION—WHAT'S IN A NAME?

There's often confusion as to exactly what asset allocation means. Noted investment theorist William F. Sharpe has identified four different types of asset allocation:

- *Strategic asset allocation.* The focus is on long-term asset mix with no attempt to outguess or time the market.
- *Dynamic asset allocation.* There is no market timing, but active shifting among security markets limits downside risk (creates portfolio insurance). This strategy tends to have particularly high transaction costs.
- *Tactical asset allocation.* The express intent is to beat the market using market timing or other techniques.
- *Dynamic tactical asset allocation.* Both market timing and portfolio insurance are used.

Much of what you read in the investment press focuses on tactical asset allocation. Many investment managers use asset allocation, but shift the asset allocation periodically in response to market conditions. However, since the majority of professional investment managers have been unable to consistently beat the markets, it follows that strategies that assume that you can outguess the market (tactical strategies) or have high transaction costs (dynamic strategies) should be avoided. Strategic asset allocation, on the other hand, emphasizes that investment returns (net of transaction costs) equal to overall market returns are acceptable, especially if they can be obtained with less than overall market risk.

WHAT DETERMINES THE APPROPRIATE ASSET ALLOCATION?

Individual investors should allocate their assets differently, depending upon how long they intend to invest, their tolerance for risk, and how much they have to invest. In determining your overall asset allocation, there are five basic factors to consider:

- *Your risk tolerance (the "sleep at night" factor).* Risk tolerance is often hard to measure since it involves complex psychological factors. Essentially, only you know how you feel about risk, but most of us are by nature very risk-averse—we don't want to lose money.

- *Your investable assets (how much you have to invest).* This can be explained as "the more you have, the more you can afford to lose." Although size of assets isn't as critical as some of these other factors, it can be helpful in determining the amount of risk you are comfortable taking.

- *Your age and investment time horizon.* This is probably the most critical factor since (as we saw in Chapter 11) your time horizon to a particular goal governs the amount of risk you should be taking with your investments and is a major factor in the rate of return you'll need to achieve your goals.

- *The phase of your investment cycle (accumulation or distribution).* If you're in the accumulation phase, you can have more growth-oriented investments in your portfolio and still manage market risk. On the other hand, if you need current income, you don't want to be selling your growth-oriented investments in volatile markets because of a need to generate current income.

- *Other factors, such as large concentrations in company stock.* Sometimes corporate employees have large amounts of company stock that they don't want to sell due to company culture or other factors. Asset allocation should take into account the need for additional diversification within the equity category given the large amount of business risk these individuals will be taking.

Determining the appropriate asset allocation is sometimes more of an art than a science, but investment managers will generally construct asset allocations by combining the preceding factors with an emphasis on time horizon and your phase in the investment life cycle. Many investment managers also use sophisticated mathematical calculations to determine the optimum mix of assets for a particular investment portfolio based on historical performance. In doing so, they try to achieve a portfolio that is on what in investment circles has become known as the *efficient frontier*. Simply stated, the efficient frontier is the optimum mix of assets that, based on historical performance, should generate the highest possible return for a given amount of risk you're willing to take within your particular time horizon.

MODEL ASSET ALLOCATIONS

The best asset mix is one that is consistent with your stage in the investment life cycle. As a general rule, portfolios should be sufficiently diversified so that all major asset categories are represented. Beyond that, allocation decisions depend largely on your investment time horizon. Portfolios invested for long time horizons can afford to accept the greater short-term price volatility that comes with a more significant allocation to stocks. Shorter time horizons call for less volatile mixes.

Table 14–1 provides some suggested broad model allocations based on your stage in the investment life cycle. As you can see from the table, cash and fixed-income investments should be given relatively little weight until you get close to retirement. Someone with 30 years until retirement, for example, would want 75 percent of her investment assets in stocks, 10 percent in hard assets, and 15 percent in bonds. And, even in retirement it will be important for you to allocate some of your portfolio to equity and hard-asset investments to protect the purchasing power of your funds. For retirees, playing it too safe where investment volatility is concerned can mean losing purchasing power to inflation over the long term.

SUBCATEGORY ALLOCATIONS

To further minimize risk, you should allocate among the four asset categories and then use the concept of suballocation to split up your

Table 14–1	Asset Allocations for Retirement							
	Years to Retirement					Retirement Period		
Asset Class	30	20	15	10	5	Early Years	Middle Years	Later Years
Cash	0%	0%	0%	0%	0%	10%	10%	10%
Fixed income	15	20	25	30	35	40	50	60
Equities	75	70	65	65	60	45	35	25
Hard assets	10	10	10	5	5	5	5	5

Table 14–2   Investment Subcategories

Asset Class	Classification
Fixed Income	
Short-term	Maturities of 1 to 2 years
Intermediate	Maturities of 2 to 10 years
Long-term	Maturities of over 10 years
Equities	
Growth and income	Large-company stocks (for capital growth and dividend income)
Growth	Smaller companies offering significant growth potential but little or no dividend income (for capital growth)
Aggressive growth	Emerging start-up companies with highly volatile returns
International	For global diversification

investments further within the larger investment categories. We explained the various investment subcategories in Chapters 12 and 13. We show them again in Table 14–2.

Subcategory allocation allows you to minimize risk through diversification within each asset category. For example, you could minimize market and business risk by allocating your equity category further among stocks with varying degrees of volatility—for example, 20 percent aggressive growth stocks, 35 percent growth stocks, and 45 percent growth and income stocks.

Likewise, as we saw in Chapter 13, to reduce interest rate risk, you should stagger the maturities of your fixed-income investments so they come due at different times. That way, you won't be taking as big a chance on interest rates. Finally, you can reduce liquidity risk by allocating to the cash equivalent category enough money to maintain sufficient reserves or rely on credit lines to meet your normal and unexpected needs. That way you won't be forced to sell bonds, equities, or real estate at a time when the market doesn't favor them. Table 14–3 shows our suggested subcategory allocations. Using historical returns for the period January 1977 through December 1993 as a guide for various indexes in each of the suballocation categories, the historical average returns for these allocations range from 15 percent (30 years from retirement) to 11 percent (later years in retirement) with a standard deviation of 22 percent and 9 percent respectively.

As we saw in Chapter 11, historical performance, while not necessarily predictive of future performance, gives us a good indication of the overall performance and risk characteristics of particular asset classes over time. In attempting to determine expected returns,

Table 14-3   Suballocations for Retirement Savings

| Asset Class | Years to Retirement | | | | | Retirement Period | | |
	30	20	15	10	5	Early Years	Middle Years	Later Years
Cash	—	—	—	—	0%	10%	10%	10%
Fixed Income	15%	20%	25%	30%	35	40	50	60
Short-term	—	—	—	—	5	10	10	20
Intermediate-term	15	20	25	30	30	30	40	40
Equities	75	70	65	65	60	45	35	25
Growth and income	—	—	—	5	10	10	15	15
Growth	25	20	20	20	20	15	10	5
Aggressive growth	25	25	25	20	15	10	5	—
International	25	25	20	20	15	10	5	5
Hard Assets	10	10	10	5	5	5	5	5

investment managers will measure historical performance using indexes, which tell the historical returns and risk associated with each investment category. Time horizon becomes critical in determining the expected return and standard deviation. If you were calculating the expected return of a particular mix over the next 20 years, you wouldn't want to use historical performance over the past one or three years as a guide period.

REBALANCING YOUR ALLOCATION

As Table 14-3 shows, when you get close to one of the breakpoints in the table (five years from retirement, for example), you'll want to slowly shift (rebalance) your allocation. You don't need to do this suddenly—all on your anniversary date, for example. Plan on shifting slowly—over the course of one to two years, say—to minimize market risk. A good rule of thumb is to begin rebalancing six months before your anniversary date, for example.

First, identify the amount of money you need to shift to reach your new allocation. Then move 1/12 of it each month, while adjusting for market movements during the previous month(s). At the end of the one-year period, you'll have achieved your rebalanced allocation with a minimum of risk.

A FINAL WORD

Remember too that our suggested allocations are only guidelines. Your individual circumstances may provide many reasons to modify them. For example, you may have a certain percentage of your portfolio earmarked for your heirs and have even taken steps, such as splitting your investments up into multiple IRAs and designating a grandchild as beneficiary of each, to convey that property to them. Again, you should consider weighting these investments more heavily toward stocks. Why? Because their time horizon now becomes the point at which they will be consumed by your heirs, hopefully many years in the future.

In summary, pay close attention to the allocation of your retirement investments. It will be the most important decision you make in determining your investment returns over the years. In particular, remember the risks of long-term inflation. Short-term safety of principal may mean long-term sacrifice of purchasing power.

In the next chapter, we discuss how to implement your asset allocation decisions using a variety of investments and investment managers.

CHAPTER 15

IMPLEMENTING YOUR INVESTMENT STRATEGY

In this chapter, we address how to implement your asset allocation decisions using a variety of techniques. Read on to understand:

- The types of investment advisors.
- Using mutual funds.
- Active versus passive management styles.
- Using money managers.

Once you understand the value of asset allocation and the characteristics of each investment category (and subcategory), the next step is to effectively implement your investment strategy. In a nutshell, implementation means selecting the appropriate investment vehicles consistent with your strategy, while keeping in mind the level of services you want from an investment advisor and the costs associated with investing in general.

In general, you have several different ways to implement your invest-ment strategy:

- Buying mutual funds.
- Using a professional money manager.
- Buying individual securities through a full-service or discount broker.

As shown in Table 15–1, each option has its advantages and disad-vantages, which we assess in this chapter. In general, we believe that most younger investors should use mutual funds to implement their retirement investment strategy since they offer the lowest cost and highest flexibility of all investment options. By contrast, if you're an older investor with large lump sums, you can use mutual funds or indi-vidual money management services, both of which can be obtained through investment advisors or on your own. Buying a portfolio of individual stocks or bonds can be an option if you have the time and patience to manage your own investments or want to pay the fees to have a broker or financial planner do it for you. In general, however, mutual funds or money managers provide the most cost-effective means to implement your investment strategy.

INVESTING WITH MUTUAL FUNDS

Mutual funds provide an easy means to invest in the different asset categories—cash, fixed income, equities, and hard assets—or some combination of categories. They come in all shapes and sizes, from tra-ditional stock and bond funds to international funds and sector funds, such as biotechnology or telecommunications funds. You can probably find a mutual fund that meets your needs whether you're 25 and retire-ment seems light-years away or 75 and eager to preserve your current income. In fact, you probably are already invested in mutual funds if you invest for retirement through a company-sponsored 401(k) plan.

A mutual fund is a pool of professionally managed investments that is owned by many different shareholders in proportion to the amounts they contributed to the fund. Rather than owning the specific securi-ties, the fund investor owns shares of the fund itself and sells these shares (or purchases new ones) through the fund itself. Specific fund investments are selected by the fund's managers according to the fund's

Table 15–1   A Comparison of Investment Alternatives

	Advantages	Disadvantages
Mutual funds with financial planner/advisor	Professional money management Somewhat lower fees than wrap accounts	Total costs higher due to separate fee to advisor Must depend on advisor's competence for fund selection
Mutual funds without financial planner/advisor	Professional money management	Must do your own research
Discount broker	No pressure to trade Ability to select individual securities and custom design portolio to fit personal circumstances	Must do own asset allocation and research Investment knowledge necessary
Full-service broker	Ability to select individual securities and custom design portfolio to fit personal circumstances Brokerage firm research available	Broker's income based on frequency and size of trades Higher trading costs than with discount brokers Must depend on individual broker's capabilities
Wrap accounts	Professional money management No incentive for broker to churn (excessively trade) the account	Higher total costs Manager criteria not always explicit Choice of managers limited to those offered by firm and followed by broker Must depend on individual broker's capabilities to find appropriate manager

Source: *The AAII Journal*, February 1993, p. 9. Published by The American Association of Individual Investors, 625 N. Michigan, Chicago, Ill. 60611; 312/280-0170.

investment objective—for example, long-term growth or current income.

Many investors include both *open-end* and *closed-end* mutual funds in their definition of mutual funds, although technically the two are different legal entities. Open-end mutual funds sell an unlimited number of new shares and constantly repurchase or redeem outstanding ones.

So the amount of money in the fund is always changing. The share price of an open-end mutual fund (also called the *net asset value per share*) fluctuates with changes in the value of its portfolio, except for a money market fund, which always has a value of $1 per share.

In contrast, closed-end companies have a relatively fixed amount of assets under management. Closed-end funds raise money as ordinary corporations do—with an initial offering on a recognized stock exchange. Once they're issued, the shares of closed-end companies are traded just like any other stocks—on the major stock exchanges and over the counter.

While mutual funds aren't insured or guaranteed by any government agency, their operations are regulated by the U.S. Securities and Exchange Commission and by state agencies. The Investment Company Act of 1940, the principal federal law regulating mutual funds, requires funds to operate in the interest of shareholders and to take steps to safeguard their assets. Fund sponsors must also provide extensive disclosure about their investment activities, risks, fees, and sales commissions. This information is included in the fund's prospectus, which is distributed to each prospective investor at the time he purchases shares.

Advantages of Mutual Funds

Mutual funds offer many advantages to the individual investor: professional management, lower costs, diversification, flexibility, liquidity, record keeping and performance monitoring, and administrative ease.

Professional Management.   One advantage of mutual funds is that you get expert management of your investments. The fund manager takes responsibility for following the fund's investment objectives, monitoring securities in the fund's portfolio, and keeping an eye out for new investment opportunities. In addition, your money is handled by people who devote their full time and attention to the task, whereas many individual investors don't have the time or expertise to manage investments effectively.

Lower Costs.   Mutual fund shareholders get the full-time services of these professional money managers at comparatively low cost, typically 1 to 2 percent of assets under management. Mutual funds reduce your cost of investing by spreading administration, safekeeping, and management advisory fees over a broad base of shareholders. Those costs, as a

Figure 15-1   What Do Mutual
Funds Provide?

- Diversification
- Subcategory allocation flexibility
- Low transaction costs
- Professional management

result, are less of a drag on the
investment returns of individual
shareholders. Brokerage charges and
expenses for securities bought and
sold by a mutual fund are also lower
because funds can negotiate lower
brokerage commissions based on the
volume of securities traded.

Diversification.   Except for certain types of sector funds, you also get
broad diversification with mutual funds. A typical mutual fund invests
in dozens of different securities; large funds own hundreds. Federal law
requires mutual funds to have no more than 5 percent of its assets in
any one company, so a mutual fund must own at least 20 individual
securities.

As a result, even a small investment in a mutual fund provides broad
diversification. And mutual funds enable you to take a step further by
diversifying *within* a particular asset category. To purchase stocks on
your own and achieve the same level of diversification, you would need
to invest in a substantial number of individual issues and pay significant commissions to do so.

Flexibility.   You can use a mutual fund to "buy" a particular class of
investments (such as technology stocks or utilities) or even an entire
market. For example, index funds are available that seek the same
return as the Standard & Poor's 500. Other funds aim to mirror the
returns of market indexes for global bonds, small-company stocks, or
regional groupings of foreign stock markets. As we'll see later, index
funds are attractive because of their low fees and the nature of their
performance; you'll always do at least as well as the index.

Liquidity.   Shares in a mutual fund can be sold quickly and conven-
iently. The fund is required to establish a daily price for its shares and
allow investors to redeem shares at that price. With most funds, you
can redeem shares with a phone call and have the money wired to your
bank, or transfer the sale proceeds into a money market fund in the
same fund family and write a check on it the same day.

Record Keeping and Performance Monitoring.   Mutual funds provide
detailed statements that help you to keep track of your original investment as well any reinvested dividends and capital gains. You can easily

monitor and evaluate your fund's performance through newspapers and mutual fund ratings services.

Administrative Ease.   Fund families make it easy to invest in different kinds of funds and to switch money among funds with different objectives as the need arises. Most fund families will provide you with a consolidated account statement showing the status of the fund investments you have with that family. Fund families also offer easy transferring among investments and the convenience of consolidated statements for all your funds. Also, any income and capital gain distributions can be automatically reinvested in additional shares of the fund at your option.

Understanding the Types of Mutual Funds

Because there are so many different types of funds on the market, the mutual fund industry has developed categories to help classify funds by investment objective. Most fund categories start with whether the fund is a money market fund, bond fund, or common stock fund; from there they place the fund into a subcategory, such as aggressive growth for stock funds or intermediate term for bond funds. There are also many specialty and sector funds, which tend to invest in particular types of investments (e.g., real estate or futures contracts) or sectors of the market (e.g., telecommunications or biotechnology). Common general fund categories include money market funds, bond funds, stock funds, balanced funds, asset allocation funds, and international funds.

Figure 15–2   Mutual Fund Classes

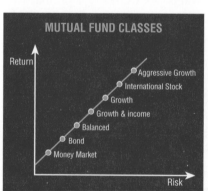

Money Market Funds.   These funds invest in short-term cash equivalent investments such as U.S. Treasury obligations and commercial paper. Money market funds offer stability of principal with interest income that fluctuates depending on current market rates. Generally, money market funds come in five varieties:

- General purpose funds investing in corporate commercial

paper, certificates of deposit, Eurodollar deposits, and U.S. government obligations.

- Federal government agency funds investing solely in obligations of the U.S. Treasury and other federal agencies.
- U.S. Treasury bill funds.
- National municipal funds investing in federally tax-exempt obligations of different states.
- Individual state municipal funds investing in tax-exempt obligations of a single state. (These are also exempt from taxation in the issuing state and are thus commonly called *double tax-exempt*.)

Money market funds have very short maturities. The average maturity of a portfolio cannot be more than 90 days under SEC rules. Most money market funds average about 45-day maturities. Also, the SEC requires that at least 95 percent of a fund's assets be invested in Treasury bills or bank CDs and commercial paper within the top two debt grades as determined by a recognized rating agency, such as Standard & Poor's or Moody's. As a result, money market funds give you the most stable principal value over time, but yields fluctuate significantly as short-term interest rates rise and fall.

Bond Funds.   These funds provide current income and can add diversification to an equity-oriented portfolio. Bond funds can be volatile (as we saw in 1994) because returns will rise and fall depending on market conditions and the maturities of the bonds in the fund. There are five major types of bond funds:

- *U.S. government.* Treasury notes (2 to 10 year maturities) and Treasury bonds (10 to 30 year maturities) as well as securities issued by federal agencies.
- *Mortgage.* Ginnie Maes, Fannie Maes, and other U.S. government agency securities.
- *Investment grade corporate.* Corporate bonds with a rating of BBB or better as rated by Standard & Poor's or Moody's.
- *High-yield corporate.* So-called *junk bond funds*, investing in bonds with below–investment-grade ratings.
- *Municipal.* Obligations of state and local governments. Fund income is tax-exempt at the federal level, although possibly

subject to the Alternative Minimum Tax. Capital gains from sale of fund securities are taxable, however.

Stock Funds.   Stock funds are classified by the types of stocks they invest in. Most common stock funds fall into one of three classes: aggressive growth funds, growth funds, and growth and income funds.

Aggressive Growth Funds.   Sometimes called *small-company funds*, these funds seek long-term growth by investing in small, emerging companies that trade over the counter. As the name implies, the objective of aggressive growth funds is to maximize capital gains. Thus, you get little if any dividends from these funds.

Growth Funds.   Growth funds invest in more established, less volatile companies with good prospects for future growth. As with aggressive growth funds, dividend income is low.

Growth and Income Funds.   These funds seek a balance between current dividend income and long-term growth. They invest in well-established companies that pay regular dividends, and attempt to avoid excessive fluctuation in returns. You can find some variation in names within this category. For example, equity income, income and total return funds all have the general characteristics of growth and income funds.

Balanced Funds.   These funds invest in a combination of stocks, bonds and cash. A typical ratio might be 50 percent stock, 40 percent bonds, and 10 percent cash. They tend to be less volatile than pure stock funds, and typically do not alter their allocation in response to market conditions.

Asset Allocation Funds.   These funds are similar to balanced funds except that they tend to alter their allocation depending on the fund manager's outlook for each investment category. Because varying an asset allocation is a form of market timing, you should carefully evaluate an asset allocation fund's investment policy to see under what conditions substantial changes in the allocation will be considered by the fund manager.

International Funds.   These funds invest primarily in overseas stocks, although some so-called global funds will also hold U.S. stocks. These funds can add diversification to your portfolio, although you do incur additional risk over and above domestic funds. The most common additional risk is currency risk, where the value of the dollar relative to foreign currencies can affect the value of your fund's investments. Political risk is also present. Your fund may be invested in third-world country stocks that could be affected by changes in governments, wars, or other unexpected political events.

Evaluating Funds

Currently more than 4,500 mutual funds are available within these categories. How do you choose which fund is best for you? Many factors enter into the decision, but the starting point for selecting a mutual fund should be its historical total return and the amount of risk associated with that return.

You can start by comparing the fund's 5- and 10-year returns. You want to see how the fund you're considering has performed in both bull and bear markets. When you evaluate the risk associated with the historical return, you're really looking at the fund's volatility.

Say you're interested in two funds of the same type (aggressive growth, for instance), with the same average annual return for the past 10 years. Which should you select? Pick the fund that's least volatile. In other words, a fund that turns in a consistent 10 percent a year is preferable to one that earns 15 percent one year and 5 percent the next.

Return and risk matter most when it comes to selecting a fund. But you may want to be aware of some other factors, such as the fund's turnover rate (the average length of time the fund holds shares before selling them). A high turnover rate sometimes indicates that the fund manager is trying to time the market—that is, judge when the market is going to go up or down—and market timing just doesn't work consistently.

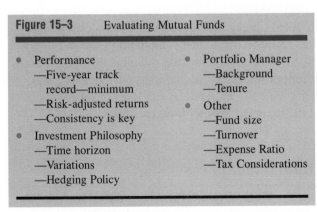

Figure 15–3   Evaluating Mutual Funds

- Performance
  —Five-year track record—minimum
  —Risk-adjusted returns
  —Consistency is key
- Investment Philosophy
  —Time horizon
  —Variations
  —Hedging Policy
- Portfolio Manager
  —Background
  —Tenure
- Other
  —Fund size
  —Turnover
  —Expense Ratio
  —Tax Considerations

Narrowing Your Choices

Once you decide on mutual funds, then it's a good idea to

Figure 15–4	Mutual Fund Selection— Sources of Information	
Barron's—Quarterly Mutual Fund Record		(800-328-6800)
CDA/Wiesenberger Mutual Fund Report/Update		(800-232-2285)
No-Load Fund Investor (Handbook)		(914-693-7420)
AAII-Individual Investor Guide to No-Load Mutual Funds		(312-280-0170)
Morningstar		(312)696-6000
No Load Fund Analyst		(510-254-9017)
Value Line Mutual Fund Survey		(800-284-7607)

use a ranking service to help you narrow your choices. Ranking services don't sell funds so they are objective. First they group the funds by the different categories. (Stock funds are classified into growth, growth and income, aggressive, etc.) They then rank each individual fund.

Be conscious of how the ranking services do their rankings. Sometimes a business magazine will do a mutual fund survey and list the hottest funds of the previous year. This isn't very valuable information. You should be interested in funds that performed well in the past 5 or 10 years, not just the past year.

You can subscribe to a number of ranking services that evaluate mutual fund performances. Among them are:

CDA/Wiesenberger's *Mutual Fund Report* (monthly), 1355 Piccard Drive, Rockville, Maryland 20850, telephone (301) 975-9600.

Morningstar (biweekly), 225 West Wacker Drive, Chicago, Illinois 60606, telephone (312) 696-6000.

Some libraries, especially good business libraries, subscribe to these services. Check your local library before you write out a check for several hundred dollars. Several magazines—including *Forbes, Money,* and *Business Week*—provide extensive annual rankings of mutual funds.

Performance is an important factor in making your decision, and performance can be dramatically affected by the level of fees you are paying. Let's look at the assorted fees with mutual funds.

Understanding Mutual Fund Fees

Obviously, mutual funds don't provide their services for free. Mutual fund costs fall into three basic categories: sales loads (front-end and

Table 15–2	Mutual Funds Fees		
	No Load	**Low Load**	**Load**
Front end (commission upon purchase)	0%	1%–3%	3%–8.5%
Back end (redemption fee upon sale)	0%	1%–2%	7%/declining
12b-1 costs (annual marketing fee)	0%–.25%	0%–.75%	0%–.75%
Annual service fee	0%–.25%	0%–.25%	0%–.25%
Annual management fee—stocks	.5%–1%	.5%–1%	.5%–1%
Annual management fee—bonds	.5%–.75%	.5%–.75%	.5%–.75%

back-end), annual fund operating expenses, and the fund's costs of buying and selling portfolio securities.

Front-End Loads. When you buy mutual fund shares from a stockbroker or other salesperson, you usually pay a front-end load (a commission on the shares you purchase). In addition, you may pay a sales charge even when you invest directly (without the help of a stockbroker or salesperson) in funds offered by some mutual fund companies.

Here's an example of how a front-end load works. Say you instruct your stockbroker to invest $3,000 in a mutual fund whose shares have a net asset value of $50 each. Your $3,000 will get you 60 shares, right? Wrong. Let's say the sales charge is the maximum allowable, 8.5 percent and adds up to $255. So only $2,745 of your money actually goes to purchase shares. The $255 went to the stockbroker who sold you the fund.

Funds sold by salespeople will typically charge a 4 to 8.5 percent front-end load or back-end load. Funds with an initial sales charge of 0.5 percent to 3.0 percent are called *low-load funds.* These are funds that can usually be purchased directly from the mutual fund company; the load will go to the mutual fund company, not to the mutual fund manager or any salesperson. Check the prospectus to see if your fund will charge you a load on any dividends or capital gains you reinvest. Most do not; shy away from funds that do.

Back-End Loads. As an alternative to front-end commissions, many load funds offer shares with back-end commissions, also known as contingent deferred sales charges or redemption fees. These charges apply

Watch Out for Front-End Loads

Note

Front-end loads are understated because they customarily are expressed as a percentage of the gross amount you pay, rather than the amount that actually gets invested. For example, a 5 percent front-end load on a $10,000 investment equals $500. But since the broker keeps the $500, your actual investment totals $9,500 and $500 is 5.3 percent of that amount. It also turns out that 5.3 percent is the return you will need on the $9,500 over the first year just to break even on your $10,000 total investment. In addition, the investment performance of front-end load funds is typically overstated because independent rating services generally ignore the effect of the load for purposes of calculating returns. Using the above example of $10,000 used to buy a fund with a 5 percent front-end load, let's assume further that the fund reported an 8 percent total return over the next year. That 8 percent applies to the $9,500 you actually invested so your return in dollar terms amounted to $760 (or $9,500 × .08). But that represents only a 7.6 percent return on your full $10,000 (or $760/$10,000).

if you sell your shares within a certain time. Funds that impose back-end loads typically charge 6 to 7 percent if you withdraw your money within one year. This percentage usually decreases 1 percentage point for each year you remain in the fund until it reaches zero after six years. Back-end loads can be costly if you withdraw your money in the early years and your investment has grown in value. In that case, you will be paying a percentage of a much larger amount than your initial investment.

Another alternative is the level load, where the front-end commission is replaced by a permanent fee. Back-end loads and level loads may sound like a better deal than front-end loads, but they often are accompanied by higher annual fees. And as we just saw, high annual fees are much more costly for long-term investors than front-end loads.

No-Load Funds.   There are also many *no-load funds*, which charge no front-end sales charge. If you invest $3,000 in a no-load fund, $3,000 will actually go to purchase shares. A few no-load funds impose a redemption fee so be conscious of any fee you might have to pay if you sell out of the fund.

Figure 15–5   Average Expense Ratios

Stock/Precious Metal Funds	Bond Funds	
Aggressive growth 1.5%	General 0.7%	
Growth 1.2%	Government 0.7%	
Growth and Income 0.9%	Mortgage-backed 0.7%	
Balanced (stocks/bonds) . .1.0%	High-yield 0.9%	
Index 0.4%	Tax-exempt 0.6%	
Small capitalization 1.3%	Corporate 0.7%	
Precious metals 1.6%		

Source: Morningstar Mutual Performance Report, May 1995, page 8.
Morningstar Mutual Funds, Inc., Chicago, Ill.

There are just as many choices in the no-loads as in the load funds. There's no evidence that load funds perform any better than low-load or no-load funds. In fact, a recent study by Morningstar, Inc., showed that no-load mutual funds actually have lower average expense ratios than load funds, which in most cases means higher returns.

Fund Operating Expenses.

Fund operating expenses are expressed as a percentage of a fund's average assets for a particular year, commonly known as the expense ratio. They fall into four general headings—management fees, 12b-1 fees, service fees, and other expenses—each listed as a separate item in mutual fund fee tables.

Management Fees.   The management fee compensates the fund's investment advisor. Management fees will vary depending on a fund's investment objective. Fees for managing specialized stock funds are relatively high, while those for bond and money market funds are lower.

Annual operating expenses also include the commissions that mutual funds pay to brokers when they buy or sell securities. These costs have the effect of reducing investment returns. The greater the rate of portfolio trading, the greater the cost of brokerage commissions and mark-ups. Mutual funds don't report these brokerage expenses as part of the management fee so they aren't listed in the fee table or included in a fund's expense ratio. But you can get a relative measure of trading activity at different funds by comparing their turnover rates. Funds with high turnover rates relative to their peers are paying higher transaction expenses.

12b–1 Fees.   Many mutual funds charge an annual 12b-1 fee. This fee takes its name from the Securities and Exchange Commission rule that allows fund sponsors to cover their marketing expenses by passing them through to investors.

The 12b-1 fee is for distribution-related expenses such as advertising and marketing costs. It can range up to 0.75 percent of assets each year.

Service Fees.   The service fee, limited to 0.25 percent of assets, is used to compensate brokers or others who service mutual fund share-holders. Many funds don't charge 12b-1 or service fees. Others collect both up to the combined 1 percent limit as a substitute for a traditional front-end load. In any case, these fees are not officially classified as sales charges.

Fees for Other Expenses.   The other-expense category covers miscellaneous costs including accounting, administration, record keeping, and legal fees.

How do you find out exactly how much each fund charges? The best source of information is the fund's prospectus and the statement of additional information. The fund is required to provide you with a copy of each either before a sale or not later than confirmation of the sale. As you can imagine, it can be quite a challenge to get through all the prospectus's legalese. Fortunately, the SEC has simplified prospectus requirements in recent years.

Mutual Fund Families

You may also want to consider investing in a fund that's part of a fund family, especially where one is a money market fund. A mutual fund family is simply a group of two or more mutual funds offered through the same sponsor organization. In most cases, the goals of the funds differ. For example, one may be a growth fund, the other an income-oriented fund.

Figure 15–6   Evaluating a Fund Family
• Variety of funds
• Minimum initial investment
• Number of free exchanges
• IRA fees/minimums
• Checkwriting
• Consolidated statements
• Basis tracking

With a fund family, you can easily move your money from

one investment vehicle to another—sometimes with no more than a telephone call. Check to see if a fund or fund family offers a toll-free 800
telephone number.

The Case for Index Funds

Instead of using a fund where a money manager researches and selects
individual stocks or bonds, you might choose index funds (which use a
passive approach) for an excellent balance of low costs and good performance. As we saw in Chapters 11 and 14, indexes are used to measure the historical performance of the various asset classes. Index funds
are mutual funds designed to track one of these market indexes, such as
the Standard & Poor's 500 Stock Index. It does so either by owning the
actual stocks (or bonds) that make up the index, or by holding a sample
of securities whose returns are expected to closely track the returns of
the index.

The notion of index investing was introduced by economists who
argued that stock and bond markets are highly efficient. Information on
each security and its prospects is widely transmitted and instantly
incorporated into market prices, the theory holds, so that stocks and
bonds at all times are accurately valued. As a result, it's hard for investors to find securities that are mispriced and consistently outperform
the market by investing in them. The economists predicted that simply
buying and holding all the securities in a broad market index would
yield better results than active management over the long run, in large
part because of the higher expenses associated with actively managed
portfolios.

Passive investing gained wide acceptance in the 1970s among institutional investors such as pension funds. Over the years, indexing has
begun to catch on with individual investors as well. Although there are
many types of index funds, by far the most popular variety tracks the
S&P 500 Composite Stock Index, a group of large-company stocks that
represent about 70 percent of the total value of all U.S. stocks. There
are other indexes used for index investing, such as the broader Wilshire
5000 Index, which tracks more than 6,000 U.S. stocks, and the Russell
2000 Index, an index of small-company stocks.

Index funds derive much of their long-term attractiveness from pre-
dictability and low costs. Index investing is predictable in the sense that

Table 15-3	Indexing Performs Well With Large-Company Stocks—Comparing Rates of Total Return	
	Index Fund*	**78 Actively Managed Funds**
3-Year	15.0%	14.0%
5-Year	12.3	9.9
10-Year	16.0	14.3

*Vanguard Index Trust 500 Portfolio tracking the S&P 500 Index.

Source: Morningstar Mutual Funds, 24, issue 3, January 10, 1992. Morningstar Mutual Funds, Inc., Chicago, Ill.

it can be relied on to deliver a market average return. By "owning the market," an index investor is buying the return of all the securities in a certain asset category, such as the S&P 500's large-company stocks. An investor in an actively managed fund, on the other hand, is buying the return of some securities chosen by the manager. Some managers will make better choices than others so their individual performance relative to the market isn't predictable.

The cost advantages of index funds are another important consideration. An index fund offers low costs because the manager's only job is to make sure that the fund's portfolio closely tracks the composition of its target index. Index funds also trade less often than actively managed funds, saving money on brokerage commissions and dealer markups. For instance, portfolio turnover for the Vanguard Index Trust 500 Portfolio, an index fund that tracks the S&P 500, was about 6 percent in 1993, compared to an average turnover of 64 percent for all funds in its category. Heavy trading and the higher advisory fees for active management can each add 1 percentage point or more in annual expenses, as compared to passive index management. That means an actively managed fund will probably have to exceed the gross return (before transaction costs and advisory fees) of an index by up to 2 percentage points to beat the net return of an index fund investing in the same asset class.

Table 15-4	Active Management Does Better with Small-Company Stock—Comparing Rates of Total Return	
	Index Fund*	**95 Actively Managed Funds**
3-Year	12.8%	15.7%
5-Year	9.6	10.3

*Vanguard Index Extended Market Portfolio tracking the Wilshire 4500 Index.

Source: Morningstar Mutual Funds, 1992. Morningstar Mutual Funds, Inc., Chicago, Ill.

Indexing can be hard to beat when investing in highly efficient markets, such as the market for large-company stocks. Table 15–3 illustrates a study conducted in 1992 by Morningstar that compared the performance of 78 actively managed growth and income mutual funds with the performance of the Vanguard Index Trust 500 Portfolio. Due to their higher fees, trading costs, portfolio holdings of some cash, and perhaps lack of stock-picking success, the actively managed funds as a group consistently lagged the index over a 10-year period.

Indexing does not always come out on top, however. In less-efficient markets, such as those for small- and medium-size company stocks, active management seems to do better. After testing large-company funds, Morningstar ran a similar study with small and medium-size company funds to see whether active management or indexing would win out. This time Morningstar's analysts looked at 95 actively managed funds owning stocks with market values of between $100 million and $2 billion. They compared the performance of the funds with that of the Vanguard Index Extended Market Portfolio, an index fund that tracks the Wilshire 4500 Index of small and medium-size company stocks. The actively managed funds in the study owned stocks with the same range of market values as the stocks represented in the index. In this instance, the actively managed funds outperformed the index fund, although with a higher level of risk.

The two Morningstar studies have implications for investments in other asset classes. Few actively managed funds may be able to add enough value to make up for their added costs when investing in large, highly effective markets. Besides large-company domestic stocks, such markets include government bonds and investment-grade corporate bonds. In these arenas, index funds merit careful consideration. On the other hand, funds in less efficient markets may thrive through astute management, offering their shareholders attractive returns and acceptable risks even if their expense levels are somewhat high. Among the categories of assets fitting in this category are stocks of small- and medium-size

Table 15–5	Typical Schedule of Management Fees— Individual Accounts	
Assets under Management		**Percentage Fee**
Wrap Accounts		3%*
$250,000–$1 million		1.5%
$1 million–$2 million		1.0
Over $2 million		.75

*Negotiable

companies, foreign-company stocks, high-yield bonds, and convertible bonds.

USING MONEY MANAGERS

We've already seen professional money managers in connection with our discussion of mutual funds, since the vast majority of mutual funds have a professional fund manager. In this section, however, we discuss managers who work with individual portfolios. A professional money manager can custom-design an individual portfolio for each client, reflecting her specific investment goals and objectives. These services were once only available to very wealthy individual investors, but today growing numbers of people can take advantage of these services.

Money management services are available from independent managers, trust or private banking departments, financial planners and stockbrokers. A professional money manager is paid an annual fee, typically as a percentage of assets under management. As Table 15–5 shows, the fee ranges from .75 to as high as 3 percent, compared with an average for stock mutual funds of 1.5 percent. For the fee, individual account managers will custom-design an investment program based on your goals and risk parameters, and provide you with professional advice on asset allocation and selection of investments. Because their fee is based on the amount of assets under management, the manager has a built-in incentive to make your portfolio grow. In addition to the management fee, you typically pay all commission expenses and possibly additional fees for consulting services or performance monitoring.

You should also know that comparative information on money managers is often much

Understanding Money Managers

Note Keep in mind that when you place assets with a money manager, you must trust the manager's judgment. Most accounts are handled on a fully discretionary basis, meaning that the manager selects what to buy, when to buy it, and how much to buy. Furthermore, you probably won't actually talk with "your" manager unless your account balance is very large. However, the manager will follow her particular style (for example, value, growth and income, or growth) in making investment selections.

harder to find than comparative data on mutual funds. Money managers run many different accounts and aren't required to make public performance data on individual portfolios. However, many of the larger money managers provide performance statistics to independent evaluation services and brokerage firms.

Wrap Accounts— Boon or Bane?

As we stated earlier, money management services were once available to only the very wealthy. But since the mid-1980s the brokerage industry has developed a service called the wrap account, which allows you to get professional money management services with as little as $100,000 in investable assets. In the past decade, wrap accounts have become one of the fastest growing types of investment accounts available.

Recent SEC Rules on Wrap Account Disclosures

Tip

In April 1994, the Securities and Exchange Commission passed new rules governing the level of disclosure required of brokerage firms selling wrap accounts. As of October 1994, each firm must give potential customers a brochure containing the following disclosures:

- Fee schedules, including what portion of the fee goes to the money manager and whether the fee is negotiable.
- How money managers are selected and reviewed, and the criteria used to judge performance.

- How performance numbers are calculated and whether the firm uses a uniform standard (such as Association of Investment Management Research) for evaluating performance.

- Under what circumstances you will be allowed to contact the manager, such as whether you need to call the broker first.

- The amount of information the broker must give to the money manager on your investment goals and objectives, risk tolerance, and so on.

A wrap account is simply a way to match you up with a professional money manager, who handles the actual investment of your money. Thus, the broker from whom you "buy" the wrap account is seldom the person who will manage your money. Wrap accounts are heavily promoted by brokerage firms, particularly for large lump sum distributions that will be rolled over into IRAs. The term *wrap account* derives from the "wrap fee," an all-inclusive fee for money management, commissions/transaction charges, ongoing account monitoring, and service charges.

For your fee, which can run to 3 percent per year (though it's often negotiable), you get access to a list of preferred money managers that have passed the brokerage firm's search process. Your money will be managed by the manager that you and your broker select, though your account will still be held at the brokerage firm. All communication regarding your account will be with your broker, who will provide confirmations of purchases and sales, quarterly performance reports, and personalized attention to your account.

Wrap accounts seem like a great idea, but are sometimes controversial because the wrap fee is significantly larger than you might pay to obtain money management services on your own or through mutual funds. For example, most wrap fees start at around 3 percent. The average fee for all wrap accounts is 2.3 percent. Often these fees are negotiable; check with your broker. By contrast, most independent managers charge around 1 to 1.5 percent (plus brokerage commissions). Mutual funds may have even lower fees. If you pay a 3 percent wrap fee, the independent manager fee is 1 percent, and trades are cleared through the brokerage firm that holds your account (they often are), clearly the wrap account can be very profitable to the brokerage firm.

However, keep in mind that wrap fees can still be lower than the commissions many people pay when managing their own stock portfolios, even using discount brokers. Also, the wrap fee is a flat, all-inclusive fee so the brokerage firm or manager can't increase commissions through heavy trading. Overall, your decision on using wrap accounts comes down to paying a higher fee for personalized attention and professional money management that might not otherwise be available based on your account balance, contrasted with putting in the time to manage your own portfolio using much–lower-cost mutual funds.

FINAL THOUGHTS

When we began the investment section of this book, we suggested that successful investment performance is much more than just selecting the right stocks or bonds, or outguessing where investment markets are headed. Rather, your asset allocation and time horizon will be the most important factors in determining your investment returns over the years. History proves that an asset allocation strategy allows you to (1) moderate investment risks over time and (2) construct a portfolio that gives you a good chance of achieving positive long-term returns in excess of inflation.

Furthermore, once your basic allocation is in place, remember that it should change over time to reflect your place in the investment life cycle. This "rebalancing" approach ensures that you aren't taking an inordinate amount of investment risk for your particular stage in life, and it responds to differing needs for stable income versus growth as you age.

Finally, keep in mind that successful investing also means you shouldn't take inordinate risk by shooting for returns in excess of what you need to achieve your goals. As we pointed out in Chapter 11, the basic goal of a retirement investment strategy should be to get the return you **need,** not necessarily the higher returns that everyone **wants.** And the return you need is directly tied to your retirement sufficiency analysis. In part by managing your expectations, you can achieve consistently good returns and meet your retirement goals over the long term.

The remainder of our book deals with the more technical side of retirement planning: i.e. distributions from retirement plans, income tax issues, risk management and estate planning. These topics, while perhaps important today for reasons other than retirement, become increasingly important as you leave the work force. We begin with a discussion of how to evaluate an early retirement offer.

WITHDRAWING YOUR RETIREMENT ASSETS

CHAPTER 16   Evaluating Early Retirement Offers   221

CHAPTER 17   How to Evaluate Your Pension Distribution
Options   229

CHAPTER 18   What You Need to Know about Lump Sum
Distributions   239

CHAPTER 19   Managing Your IRA Distributions   249

EVALUATING EARLY RETIREMENT OFFERS

In this chapter, we give some suggestions for evaluating an early retirement offer. Read on to understand:

- What pension benefits you can receive.
- What is the value of continuing to work.
- What are your options for life and health coverage.
- What about severance payments.
- How should you approach making the decision.

While the recession of the early 1990s is over, companies continue to restructure their work forces through voluntary—and sometimes involuntary—early retirement offers. Often these programs offer tempting sweeteners to encourage employees to retire early. This chapter gives you some tips to consider if you receive such an offer.

The terms of an early retirement offer vary depending on whether it is a true voluntary early retirement program or an involuntary severance

Table 16–1	A Sample Voluntary Early Retirement Offer

Enhanced pension—five years added to age and service

One week's severance pay for each year of service

Lifetime medical coverage

Life Insurance at one times salary for one year after retirement

Financial counseling

Outplacement assistance

program. As shown in Table 16–1, many voluntary early retirement offers provide employees with a host of benefits from cash severance payments and enhanced pensions to postretirement medical coverage and offers of outplacement counseling or help in finding a new job. Many companies also provide early retirees with financial planning assistance to help them evaluate the offer. Other benefits, such as educational assistance and ongoing life insurance coverage, may be available. Check the specifics of your retirement offer. Keep in mind that this list explains the most common benefits based on our experience. Your company has no legal obligation to offer these payments and its program may be very different.

If you're surprised by an early retirement offer, don't feel singled out or feel that it reflects on your job performance. Particularly over the past 10 years, companies have increasingly used early retirement programs to reduce work force levels across the board. The truth is that for many companies, offering enhanced early retirement programs is more cost-effective than continuing the work force at present levels. Harsh as it may seem, early retirement has become an economic fact of life in corporate America.

Keep in mind that you do have a choice. Under federal law, you can't be forced to take the package that is offered. However, nothing prevents your company from later eliminating your job, demoting you, or otherwise making you wish you had taken the offer. We've seen many companies follow up a voluntary program with a less generous involuntary severance program within a year or so. One company we know of offered a generous voluntary early retirement program to 6,000 workers, and followed it within two years with involuntary layoffs of up to 10,000 workers.

Also, some people have to—or want to—work after they leave their current employer. If you're one of them and you receive an early retirement offer, think about your odds of finding another job. That's where a professional outplacement counselor comes in handy. If your employer doesn't provide this service, you may want to foot the bill yourself. If you have good prospects for finding another job or starting your own business, the decision may become easier. But for many of us, the real question comes down to whether you can afford to retire now. So do a retirement sufficiency analysis along the lines of that presented in Chapters 4 through 6.

If you receive an early retirement offer, look at the pension benefits you'll receive. Will you get lower benefits because you're retiring early, or do enhanced age and years of service make up the difference? Will you receive enough to fund your retirement adequately until you qualify for Social Security benefits? How do your early retirement benefits compare with those you'd collect if you continued to work for your company? Are they more generous or less generous?

Say you hadn't planned to retire until 5 or even 10 years from now. Your early retirement benefits might be considerably less than those you'd anticipated receiving. If they are, you may have to take on another job to make up for the difference.

In analyzing the offer, don't avoid the tough questions. Does the bank still hold a mortgage on your house? If it does, can you still make the mortgage payments without working full time? What about health care expenses? You'll need to pay for medical coverage if it's not part of your early retirement offer. Also, do you anticipate income from other sources—an inheritance, perhaps, to up your income in your retired years?

THE MARGINAL VALUE OF CONTINUING TO WORK

If you're like most people, one key reason to hold onto your job is money. You think that you'll be better off working. Often this is true, but try calculating how much more you'll earn working full time rather than not working at all. We call this difference the *marginal value* of continuing to work—in other words, the difference that working makes in your income.

Probably, you'll take home more as a worker than as a retiree. The question is how much extra. The answer may surprise you. Look at Table 16–2. It shows how much more income a hypothetical employee—we'll call her Freida—can earn by working full time.

Table 16–2	The Marginal Value of Continuing to Work	
	Working	**Retired**
Salary	$42,000	—
Social Security taxes	(3,213)	—
Social Security benefits	—	$ 9,380
Pension plan income	—	16,800
401(k) plan income	—	3,451
Federal income tax	(4,613)	(1,350)
Commuting expenses	(1,000)	—
Other work-related expenses (clothes, meals, dry cleaning, etc.)*	(2,100)	—
After-tax income	$31,074	$28,281
Marginal income		$2,793
Marginal hourly income		$1.34

*These expenses are estimated at 5 percent of salary, a common rule of thumb.

Here we assume that Freida is 62 years old and can collect Social Security benefits. We also calculate her federal income taxes using 1995 tax rates. In figuring her taxes, we give Freida two personal exemptions and use the standard deduction rather than itemizing deductions. Also, as you'll see, we calculate only federal taxes. State taxes could take another bite.

Surprising as it may seem, Freida takes home only $2,793 more each year by continuing to work than she'd receive if she gave up her job. And the amount she earns each hour—based on a standard work year of 2,080 hours—adds up to only $1.34.

Freida should ask herself whether she needs to work full time year-round to take home $2,794 after taxes. Maybe she can earn just as much by working part-time—at a job with lower work-related expenses, less stress, and more free time to enjoy a new life style. She'd still have the benefits of working—a stimulating environment, a sense of accomplishment, social interaction, sometimes even medical benefits—without giving up her other interests.

Try your own analysis of your situation. You may be surprised at how affordable it would be for you to retire early. Just fill in the blanks in Table 16–3.

Although this analysis can give you a sense of whether continuing to work makes sense in the short term, remember that even the most generous offer may not get you to the same retirement income level in the long term. We'll now move to some specific items your severance offer may contain.

Table 16-3	Your Marginal Value of Working		
		Working	**Retired**
Salary		$_____	$_____
Social Security taxes		_____	_____
Social Security benefits		_____	_____
Pension plan income		_____	_____
IRA income		_____	_____
401(k) plan income		_____	_____
Federal income tax		_____	_____
Commuting expenses		_____	_____
Other work-related expenses (clothes, meals, dry cleaning, etc.)*		_____	_____
After-tax income		$_____	$_____
Marginal income		$_____	
Marginal hourly income		$_____	

*These expenses are estimated at 5 percent of salary, a common rule of thumb.

WHAT'S IN AN EARLY RETIREMENT OFFER?

A typical early retirement offer has four elements: severance payments, pension payments, retiree medical coverage, and life and disability coverage.

Severance Payment

Let's start with cash severance payments. In most cases, your wages and the number of years you worked for the company determine your total payment. For example, you might receive one month's salary for each year of service with the company.

You usually receive these payments in a lump sum at termination, but you might defer the payments over several years after you retire. Check your company's plan for payout options. Since most companies won't pay you interest on the amount of severance money you defer, you may be better off taking the lump sum and investing it yourself. On the other hand, taking the payments over time can be advantageous if you'll be in a lower tax bracket in those later years because your income tax liability occurs only when you receive the payments. Your severance payments will also be subject to FICA taxes if your earned income had not exceeded the annual FICA wage base (see Chapter 7) for that year.

Pension Payments

When it comes to calculating the pension you'll receive, your company may add extra years of service to determine your annual benefit. Say your company wants you to retire early and your pension plan bases its payments on your years of service times 1 percent times your average compensation during the three years when you earned the most money. If you had worked for 20 years, your early retirement package might give you another five years. So you'd multiply 25 years times 1 percent to get 25 percent of your average earnings, instead of 20 years times 1 percent.

In addition to years of service, your company may also "adjust" your age when the company figures your pension benefits for early retirement. Here's an example. Say you're 58 years old and your company offers you early retirement, but the pension plan doesn't allow workers to retire with a full pension until they reach age 62. So to make retiring early more attractive to you, your employer adds five years to your age, which brings you to 63, one year beyond the age your company requires for a full pension. If your company did not add these years to the calculation, you'd receive less than you would at the full pension age of 62.

COBRA Coverage

Note

If your company doesn't provide coverage at all, you should also know that a federal law called COBRA (Consolidated Omnibus Budget Reconciliation Act) requires that medical coverage be continued for up to 18 months from your termination date. You are responsible for paying premiums. However, they won't be more than 102 percent of the company's cost of coverage. Many companies subsidize this cost further, often for the first 12 months after you terminate.

Retiree Medical Coverage

Your retirement offer may also include continuing medical coverage during retirement, although, with rising medical insurance costs, this benefit is becoming increasingly scarce. Often, you can continue your medical coverage as part of the group until you reach Medicare eligibility at age 65. At that point, your company may cancel or reduce your health insurance.

Barring significant federal health care reform, leaving the work force before Medicare eligibility may be risky. In a 1993 survey, Buck Consultants, a national benefits consulting firm, found that of 200 corporations, 7 percent had eliminated all health coverage for early retirees and another 8 percent were considering it. And 38 percent of the remainder were planning to cut coverage or raise premiums. So, in evaluating an offer, make sure you factor in your particular company's policies. If no coverage is available, budget about $6,000 to $10,000 per year for medical coverage—more if you have health problems or preexisting conditions.

Finally, it's critical to maintain medical coverage for you and your dependents so don't overlook enrollment deadlines or miss premium payments if you elect COBRA coverage. Also, look to your spouse's employer—you might qualify for dependent's coverage under its plan. Whatever the cost, it doesn't pay to be left without coverage if you can help it. A significant illness can spell financial disaster.

Life and Disability Coverage

As a general rule, most companies eliminate or drastically reduce life and disability coverage after you leave the company. If you still have dependents at home, look into other options outside of your employer. You may also have the opportunity to convert some of your existing employer group coverage to an individual policy without evidence of insurability, but don't expect to pay the lower premiums you had while you were employed. And you'll have to make the decisions quickly— usually within 31 days of your termination date.

FINAL THOUGHTS

Accepting an early retirement offer involves answers to many complicated questions, and normally you must make your choices in a relatively short time period, say 60 to 90 days. So don't hesitate to take advantage of financial counseling help if your employer provides it, or talk to a qualified accountant, attorney, or financial planner. With the answers to these questions—plus a good cash flow and retirement sufficiency analysis—you can have a realistic idea of whether you can afford to opt for early retirement.

CHAPTER 17

HOW TO EVALUATE YOUR PENSION DISTRIBUTION OPTIONS

This is the first of several chapters concerning how to withdraw your retirement funds once you reach retirement age. This chapter discusses distributions from company-sponsored pension plans. Read on to learn about:

- What annuity distribution options are available.
- How to choose which option is right for you.
- Considerations in electing a lump sum distribution.
- Using life insurance to maximize a pension benefit.

Of course, the goal of any sound retirement distribution strategy is to maximize your income. Since a large part of that income will probably come from your company retirement plans, maximizing your income

Figure 17–1

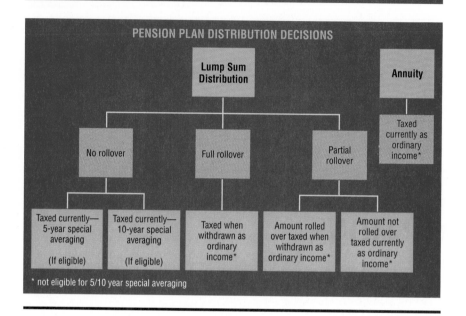

really means understanding and making the appropriate decision when it comes to your retirement plan withdrawals. As we saw in Chapter 6, making the right choices for your circumstances can have a significant impact on your retirement sufficiency analysis and your ability to reach retirement goals. In analyzing your options and getting to the right choice, you'll need to ask:

- How much income will I need and for how long?
- Do I want a guaranteed payment, or am I willing to take some investment risk in exchange for a potentially higher return?
- What are the tax consequences of my choices?
- What do I want to pass on to my heirs?

In this chapter, we cover annuity payments, which is how most pension plans pay benefits. We also talk about how to choose between an annuity and a lump sum distribution, in case your plan provides for that option. Lump sums are less common with pension plans, but almost all defined contribution plans require them. In the next chapter, we review the tax and investment complications a lump sum from your pension or savings plan can bring.

YOUR ANNUITY DISTRIBUTION OPTIONS

If your company has a defined benefit pension plan, it will provide several annuity or monthly payment distribution options. Some benefit plans also give you another choice when it comes to withdrawing your pension money. You may receive them in the form of an annuity, or you may take a lump sum distribution.

Most pension plans offer employees a choice of several annuity payments. The basic pension benefit is a single life annuity. (This is the payment option you're most likely to see on the pension estimate from your employer's benefits department.) The **single-life annuity** is a payment spread over the life of an employee—you'll receive a monthly check for as long as you live. However, after you die no further payments go to your survivors or your estate.

Many married people prefer what's known as a **joint and survivor (J&S) annuity,** which pays benefits to you and your survivor as long as *either* of you live. As shown in Table 17–1, your monthly payment will be reduced if you elect a J&S payment in exchange for a guaranteed payment to your survivor. The reduction depends on the age of your survivor. The younger the survivor, the larger the reduction.

Once you've decided to take the J&S payment, you must also decide on the dollar amount your survivor will receive. Usually the choice is between a 50 percent J&S and some other percentage—say, 75 or 100 percent. These percentages refer to the percentage of your monthly annuity payments that the survivor will receive during her lifetime after you die.

Table 17–1	Comparing Annuity Distribution Options				
		Joint and Survivor			**20-Year Term**
	Single-Life	**50%**	**75%**	**100%**	**Certain**
Monthly payment to employee	$2,000	$1,851	$1,785	$1,724	$1,792
Monthly payment to survivor	0	$926	$1,339	$1,724	$1,792 until expiration

Note: Table assumes employee and spouse are of equal age. Rounded for consistency.

For example, if your single-life annuity is $2,000 per month, your surviving spouse or other beneficiary will receive nothing when you die. With a 50 percent J&S option, your annuity is reduced from $2,000 to $1,851 per month, which you will receive as long as both of you are alive. Your beneficiary will receive $925.50 per month (50 percent of $1,851) after you die. With a 100 percent J&S, your annuity is reduced further to account for the extra amount your beneficiary will receive after you die. Therefore, you will receive $1,724 per month when you are both alive, and your beneficiary will continue to receive the $1,724 per month for as long as he lives. The actual reductions will depend on the terms of the plan and the difference between your age and your beneficiary's age.

A less common distribution option is an annuity that pays benefits for your life, with a set number of payments guaranteed. This is often called a *term certain option*. For example, your plan might offer an annuity that pays a benefit for your life with 20 years of payments guaranteed. If you die before the 20 years are complete, the plan continues to make payments to your designated survivor until the end of the 20-year period.

One last option is a level income payment, which can be offered to people who retire before they become eligible to collect Social Security. With this option, the plan pays a set dollar amount from your retirement date until you turn age 62, and then reduces its payment once you begin to receive Social Security payments. After age 62, the combination of your post–age-62 pension and Social Security payment equals what you were receiving before age 62 so you receive the same amount of money, just from different sources.

WHAT TYPE OF ANNUITY IS BEST?

There are many financial levers driving this decision: your marital status; the health and age of you and your spouse (or whomever you designate as beneficiary) at the time you retire; the financial resources available to your surviving spouse; and whether you have any other beneficiaries you want to provide for. Furthermore, federal law requires that both you and your spouse decide. If you're married and opt for anything other than a 50 percent or higher J&S with your spouse, then under the law, your spouse has to give consent. This consent must be in the form of a notarized waiver that both you and your spouse have signed.

For most people the main decision is between the higher monthly income from the single-life annuity and the added security of the joint and survivor payment. As we discussed before, you'll receive less money each month with a J&S annuity than you would with a single-life annuity.

Still, if you and your spouse die when the actuaries say you're supposed to, the *total* dollar amount is the same for both choices. In other words, single-life and joint and survivor annuities are designed to be actuarially equivalent.

So should you choose a single-life or a joint and survivor? A primary consideration is your health and the health of your beneficiary. If you think you're likely to die first, a J&S annuity is probably your best bet. If your beneficiary is likely to die before you, you may want to opt for a single-life annuity. And don't expect your J&S payment to automatically increase to a single-life pension if your beneficiary dies first. Very few company pensions provide that option.

Another important consideration is whether your survivor has a pension or other retirement income of his own. If he doesn't need income from your annuity, choose a single-life. You may also have life insurance or other assets to provide income to your survivor, which, again, makes a single-life annuity attractive. In these cases, a term certain option, if offered, may be a good compromise. The guarantee would provide additional security compared to a single-life payment should you die prematurely.

PENSION MAX—DOES IT MAKE SENSE?

It is sometimes recommended that retiring employees elect a single-life option rather than a joint and survivor option, and invest the annual difference between the two pensions in a life insurance policy on the employee's life. This is commonly called the *pension maximization strategy* or *pension max* for short. Table 17–2 shows a hypothetical proposal. The basis for the proposal is that the insurance policy pays a death benefit at the death of the employee, which, when invested by the survivor produces an annual income stream that is equal to or greater than the survivor annuity. In the event that the spouse dies first, the

Table 17–2	Pension Max Illustration for a 55-Year-Old Male in Good Health
Monthly single-life benefit	$2,000
50% joint and survivor benefit	$1,851
Monthly Difference	$ 149
Monthly survivor benefit under 50% joint and survivor option	$925.50 (a)
Approximate amount of whole life insurance that could be purchased at age 55 assuming $149 monthly premium = $85,000.	
Monthly income available to survivor assuming she annutizes the proceeds at 8 percent investment return from age 70 to age 90 = $721.45 (b)	
Difference (b)−(a) ⟨$204.05⟩	

employee could either cancel the policy and spend the premium, or leave it in force and have the death benefit avail able to heirs.

Sounds like a much better deal, except that several levers drive the success of this strategy, none of which you probably have much control over. So before you jump at what may seem to be a sure thing, consider the following:

- If your spouse couldn't get the investment return needed with reasonable risk, take the annuity. The ultimate success of this strategy depends heavily on investment returns. In Table 17–2, the spouse would need an investment return of around 12 percent for the annuitized value of the $85,000 death benefit to equal the $925.50/month survivor annuity payment.

- If the annual cost of insurance is more than the after-tax difference between the single-life and joint and survivor benefit, the pension makes more sense. You probably couldn't get enough death benefit to provide the necessary income.

- Consider your insurability. Sometimes these proposals are illustrated using select or preferred ratings that you might not qualify for when medical records are checked and the policy is actually written. DO NOT elect to give up the survivor payment until you have a signed commitment (called a *binder*) from the company to write the policy on the terms illustrated. Once you sign the election to take single-life, you might not be able to change your mind.

- Carefully examine the actual policy you are offered. If it contains a combination of whole life and term insurance (called a *term rider*), a portion of the death benefit may depend on the long-term policy dividend performance. If the dividend performance isn't there, you could be forced to pay in more premiums or accept a reduced death benefit.

- If your pension may be indexed for inflation, consider those potential cost-of-living increases in evaluating the option. See Chapter 6 for an illustration of the value of cost-of-living adjustments to your pension during retirement.

CHOOSING AN ANNUITY VERSUS A LUMP SUM

If your pension plan provides both types of payments, you have a difficult choice to make. You should first know that annuities and lump sum distributions are also designed to be "actuarially equivalent"—either way, you're supposed to get the same amount of money in the end.

However, annuities and lump sums are not equivalent if you die before or after the actuaries say you should. If you die sooner than your actuarial life expectancy, you're usually better off with a lump sum. If you die later, you're better off with an annuity. Obviously, if you take the lump sum and don't spend it down, you can pass it on to your children or other beneficiaries. Furthermore, as shown in Table 17-3, the assumptions used by your plan can significantly affect the amount of money you actually receive as a lump sum.

Another consideration is the rate of return you'll get on your money. When you take an annuity, your company retirement plan takes responsibility for investing the money and the annuity payments are calculated assuming a particular investment rate of return. For most plans, these assumed rates range somewhere between 5 and 8 percent. If you think you can beat this assumed rate of return, you may opt for a lump sum payment. Also, if you

Table 17–3	The Lump Sum versus Annuity Decision	
	Annuity	**Lump Sum**
Payment period	Guaranteed for life	One-time payment
Investment risk	Pension plan	You
Life expectancy risk	Pension plan	You
Benefits available to heirs	No	Yes
Tax considerations	Simple	Can be complex
Inflation protection	Generally not	Yes, if invested well
Investment flexibility	N/A	Yes

choose the annuity, you get essentially a guaranteed payment for life. The investment risk is the company's, not yours. When you take a lump sum distribution, though, you assume responsibility for investing your retirement dollars, and you bear the investment risk. On the other hand, since most annuities aren't indexed for inflation (see Chapter 7), investing the lump sum allows for more inflation protection.

Finally, convenience may be an issue for you. Taking an annuity means you'll automatically receive a check each month and, if you like, have the income taxes withdrawn by your company. With a lump sum withdrawal, you'll have to arrange the amount and timing of your payments and make estimated tax payments. (See Chapter 19.)

In summary, here are some thoughts on how to evaluate your distribution options:

- If your health is poor, consider the lump sum. Your spouse will have the full lump sum instead of a reduced monthly pension over his lifetime. (Note: For this reason, some plans require a physical examination to get a lump sum.)

- If simplicity and peace of mind are your goals, take the annuity. Your tax and investment decisions are much less complicated and you know your pension payment will be there even if investment markets go sour.

- If you simply can't handle money or are heavily in debt, take the annuity. The monthly payments provide lifetime security, whereas once the lump sum is gone, it's gone. Furthermore, using the lump sum to pay down large debts eliminates the debt but also eliminates your future security.

- If you don't need the income right now, take the lump sum and invest it tax-deferred through an IRA. You can allow it to grow, begin drawing the minimum needed to satisfy the IRS requirements at age 70½, and perhaps pass on an inheritance to your children.

- Don't forget about inflation. Wise investment decisions can help offset inflation's future toll, but the annuity simply continues to lose purchasing power.

- Get some help! Hire an advisor and formulate a plan before you choose. Generally speaking, an experienced accountant or tax advisor will give you the most objective assistance. Investment advisors are often biased toward lump sums, but by all means contact one if you take the lump sum to develop your long-term investment strategy. A compromise strategy may be to take a lump sum, but use some of it to buy an annuity contract from an insurance company.

- Lastly, remember that it's as much your spouse's decision as yours. Remember the rule: If you're married and choose anything other than a 50 percent or greater joint and survivor annuity, your spouse must consent to the decision.

As mentioned above, if you decide on the lump sum, your financial life becomes much more complicated, thanks primarily to Uncle Sam. The next chapter discusses the tax and financial consequences of lump sum distributions.

CHAPTER 18

WHAT YOU NEED TO KNOW ABOUT LUMP SUM DISTRIBUTIONS

In this chapter, we take a closer look at the tax and financial implications of lump sum distributions. Read on to learn:

- The benefits of an IRA rollover.
- Whether forward averaging makes sense.
- How the excess distributions tax works.

As we saw in the last chapter, certain pension plans provide for lump sum withdrawals, but all 401(k) plans eventually require them. Thus, you're likely to have at least one lump sum distribution to deal with at the time you retire. Lump sum withdrawals have important tax and investment consequences which we will cover in this chapter.

Figure 18–1

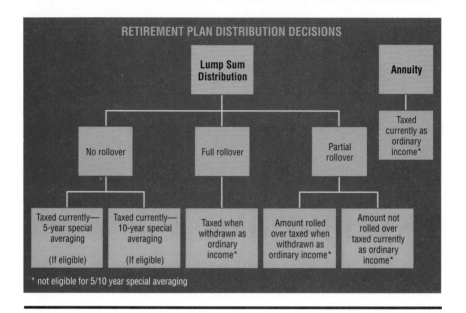

WHAT CAN YOU DO WITH A LUMP SUM?

With lump sum distributions, your main advantage is flexibility. A lump sum gives you many choices related to how you invest your money and pay your taxes. You also have an opportunity to leave your heirs a lump sum of money that isn't available with a pension annuity. Maximizing your retirement income means making the best choice among these investment and tax options relative to your own personal situation.

PAYING YOUR TAXES

As illustrated in Figure 18–1, when it comes to income taxes, you can pay them up front when you receive the distribution, and you may get a significant tax break if you qualify for forward averaging (see discussion below). Or you can roll over your funds into a rollover IRA and postpone paying taxes until you take the money out of the IRA. You can also combine your choices—roll over part of your distribution to an IRA, deferring taxes on that portion, and pay taxes on the portion you don't roll over. Finally, if you aren't retiring, but are merely changing employers, you might be able to simply transfer the lump sum to your new employer's plan. All of these choices have important tax and financial consequences.

THE ROLLOVER IRA

A rollover IRA is similar to an ordinary IRA in that the annual earnings accumulate tax-deferred; they aren't taxed until the money is taken out. But a rollover IRA does not give you a possible tax deduction on your tax return like an ordinary IRA, as discussed in Chapter 9.

More importantly, there is no dollar limit on the amount you can contribute to a rollover IRA. If you were lucky enough to have $500,000 in your 401(k) plan, you could take it out of the plan, roll the whole amount over to the IRA, and not pay any tax until you begin taking the IRA money out. And what's more, the money will continue to grow tax-deferred.

As we will see, a rollover IRA is the option of choice for most people taking a lump sum distribution. The entire next chapter is devoted to this valuable tax planning tool.

Meet the Deadline

 Caution If you take the money yourself and do not use a direct rollover, **do not miss the 60-day deadline.** If you do, the right to roll your distribution into an IRA is gone forever. The clock starts ticking from the day you receive the check so make copies of the check and postmarked envelope for proof.

THE 20 PERCENT WITHHOLDING TAX TRAP

If you choose an IRA rollover, the law gives you 60 days from the date you receive your distribution to get it into the IRA or other tax-favored retirement account. However, the way that you roll over the distribution can have a dramatic impact on your tax situation.

There are two ways that you can roll over a distribution into an IRA. The first way is to actually receive the money and within 60 days deposit that

Figure 18–2

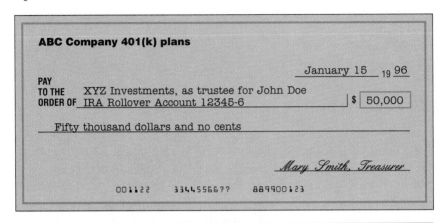

money into an IRA. The second way is a direct rollover, where your company plan trustee sends the money directly to your IRA and you never get your hands on the money.

If you choose to receive the funds yourself, the law requires your employer to withhold 20 percent of your distribution for federal taxes. So if you have a $50,000 lump sum distribution, you will only receive $40,000 ($50,000 less the 20 percent withholding of $10,000, which will be sent to the IRS). Thus, you'll only have $40,000 to roll over. If you don't come up with the additional $10,000 out of your pocket and put it into the IRA to roll over, then that $10,000 will be considered a taxable distribution. And it might also be subject to a 10 percent penalty if you receive the distribution before you are 59½. The only way to avoid this trap is to have the money transferred directly to your IRA (usually by wire transfer) or to have the check made out directly to the name of your IRA rollover account. If you do receive a check, the payee description must reflect the trustee's name, as in Figure 18–2.

PAYING YOUR TAXES NOW

If you withdraw all the money out of your company retirement plan in one lump sum and don't roll it over, you may be eligible for a tax break known as *forward averaging*. Forward averaging allows you to pay tax at a rate that may be less than your current tax rate as long as you don't mind paying the taxes up front when you get your distribution. For some people, forward averaging can be a significant advantage.

Table 18–1	Approximate Effective Tax Rates—Lump Sum Distributions	
Taxable Distribution	**Ten-Year Averaging**	**Five-Year Averaging**
$ 25,000	7.2%	9.6%
50,000	11.7	13.8
100,000	14.5	15.0
200,000	18.5	21.7
300,000	22.1	23.3
400,000	25.7	25.2
500,000	28.7	28.0

Why? You pay less total tax, as shown in Table 18–1. Although you receive the total amount of your distribution in one year, you calculate your tax as if you had withdrawn the money over 5 or 10 years. Furthermore, you calculate your forward averaging tax separately from your other income. The result is that you pay all the tax in the year you receive your distribution, but you may pay it at lower marginal rates.

Where it gets confusing is that there are actually two types of averaging (5-year and 10-year) and your choice depends on your age. When Congress enacted the 5-year averaging rules in 1986, it gave taxpayers whose birthdays fell on December 31, 1935, or earlier a choice—they can use either 5-year averaging or 10-year averaging.

Qualifying Lump Sum Distributions

Caution

To use either 5- or 10-year averaging, you must have a "qualifying" lump sum distribution. If you don't meet these tests, you can't use averaging although you may still be able to roll your distribution into an IRA.

Under the rules, the distribution must be from a qualified retirement plan, such as a pension, 401(k), or profit-sharing plan, in which you participated for at least five tax years. (The IRS will waive this latter rule, though, if the distribution is made because of your death.) YOU CANNOT USE AVERAGING ON A DISTRIBUTION FROM AN IRA. Also, you must have separated from service with your employer or have attained age 59½.

Also, the amount you receive must equal the full amount due you from all plans of the same type—for example, all profit-sharing–type plans, pension-type plans, and stock bonus–type plans. To use averaging, you must receive the lump sum(s) in a single tax year.

Tip

Another Break, If You Qualify

Another benefit is available if you or your employer made contributions prior to 1974 and you qualify for 10-year averaging. A part of your distribution will be capital gain that will qualify for a special 20 percent tax rate. The remaining post-1973 portion is taxed under 5- or 10-year averaging. This benefit is only available if you were born before 1936.

Regardless of which version you use, you're entitled to use averaging only once in your life. (If you used 10-year averaging before 1986, special rules apply; consult your tax advisor.) As you can see from Table 18–1, 10-year averaging is slightly better if your distribution is below $400,000. You pay less tax with 10-year averaging if your 1995 distribution comes to less than $376,365.

To use 10-year averaging, you must have been born before 1936 and the distribution must be made either because of your death, because you reached age 59½, because you terminated your employment, or because you were self-employed *and* became disabled.

If you were born after 1935, then you can only use 5-year averaging, and must be at least 59½ when you receive your distribution. Thus, the earliest someone born after 1935 can begin using 5-year averaging is in 1995. But if you were born before 1936, you're entitled to use 10-year averaging even if you take a lump sum withdrawal prior to age 59½.

SHOULD I ELECT AVERAGING OR ROLL OVER INTO AN IRA?

With all of these confusing rules, how do you know which way is best for you? The decision on when to withdraw your money and how to pay taxes on the funds depends on the size of the distribution, when you need the funds, and your personal financial situation. So you need to ask yourself three basic questions before making a decision.

- First, are you going to need your retirement dollars in the near future? Say, for example, you need your lump sum to make a down payment on a piece of real estate. Then taking your lump sum distribution, electing special averaging, and not rolling it over to an IRA is the better choice. If you have to pay the tax now to get access to a large portion of the funds, you might as well pay it at the lower rates available with averaging.

- Second, do you plan to invest your lump sum to provide you with a long, steady stream of income beginning at retirement or at some future date after you retire? In this case, an IRA rollover usually makes the most sense even though you pay tax at a higher overall rate.

- Third, do you need your lump sum at some future date to make a major purchase (again, buying real estate, say)? In this case, your choice depends on when you need the funds. If you need them later rather than sooner, you may want to roll them over to an IRA for now. Then you can withdraw the money from your IRA when you need it. The tax-deferred compounding may outweigh the taxes saved using averaging.

Let's take a closer look at each of these situations.

Near-Term Need

If you have a near-term need for *all* the funds, taking your lump sum distribution and electing 5- or 10-year averaging is your best bet. If you place the funds in an IRA, you would pay taxes on any amounts you withdraw at regular tax rates. Remember, you cannot use special averaging on IRA distributions.

Also, as discussed later, if your IRA (or other qualified plan) distribution would top $150,000, the excess is subject to a 15 percent excise tax. However, if you elect 5- or 10-year averaging, then you are talking about a lump sum and the ceiling for lump sum distributions is $750,000 a year. (Beginning in 1995, the $150,000 will be increased annually for inflation. Consequently the lump sum amount will also increase as it is five times the annual limit amount.)

Table 18–2 gives an example that compares 10-year averaging with rolling over money to an IRA. We'll assume that the total distribution comes to $250,000. You subtract your after-tax contributions to the plan to get your total *taxable* distribution of $200,000. Your tax bracket is 31 percent, and you're investing the money for one year. You would get an 8 percent return on your money if you placed it in an IRA. You would earn an after-tax return of 5.52 percent $(8 - (8 \times .31))$ investing

Table 18–2 Short Term Need	10-Year Averaging	IRA Rollover
Total distribution	$250,000	$250,000
After-tax contributions	(50,000)	(50,000)
Taxable distribution	200,000	200,000
Tax (10-year averaging)	(36,922)	(0)
Amount available to invest	$163,078	$200,000
Invested at 5.52%/8% for one year	$172,080	$216,000
Less taxes payable on distribution	(0)	(76,860)*
Net amount available	$172,080	$139,140

*Includes a 15% excise tax on the excess over $150,000.

outside of the IRA. As you can see, if you use special averaging, you're better off by almost $33,000.

Longer-Term Need

On the other hand, if you want your retirement dollars to generate a stream of income for you throughout retirement, you're almost always better off rolling the funds over into an IRA. Your money isn't taxed currently and your investment earnings continue to grow on a tax-deferred basis. The tax-deferred compounding you get with the IRA will usually offset the reduced tax rates of special averaging.

Table 18–3 Longer Term Need	10-Year Averaging	IRA Rollover
Total distribution	$250,000	$250,000
After-tax contributions	(50,000)	(50,000)
Taxable distribution	200,000	200,000
Tax (10-year averaging)	(36,922)	(0)
Amount available to invest	$163,078	$200,000
Monthly annuity paid out for 25 years (5.52%/8%)	$ 1,004	$ 1,544
Less taxes due on each distribution	(0)	(479)
Net monthly annuity	$ 1,004	$ 1,065
Total distribution after 25 years	$301,200	$319,500

The example in Table 18–3 illustrates a stream of income over 25 years. Again, we'll assume a taxable distribution of $200,000, an 8 percent return on the IRA funds, and an after-tax return of 5.52 percent on the non-IRA funds. As you can see, if you need a steady stream of income, you are better off rolling over your dollars to an IRA. While $18,000 may not seem like a huge difference, the benefit of the IRA becomes much more pronounced the higher your tax rate and the larger the distribution.

Uncertain Needs

Your decision may not be as cut and dried as the two scenarios illustrated above, although you know you'll need your retirement funds sometime in the future. Initially, as we just saw, electing special averaging may be more advantageous. However, the longer you invest the funds, the smaller the advantage of forward averaging. At some point, rolling over the funds into an IRA becomes more beneficial. The deciding factors include

- The length of time you'll leave the funds invested before you withdraw them.
- The rate of return you'll earn on the dollars you've invested.
- Your marginal federal and state income tax brackets at the time you ultimately withdraw your funds.

Let's again look at the same facts: Your distribution adds up to $200,000, your marginal tax rate is 31 percent, and you could earn 8 percent in an IRA and an equivalent after-tax rate of 5.52 percent outside of an IRA.

Figure 18–3   Crossover Point

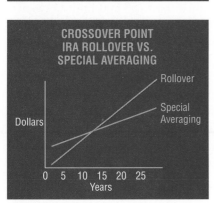

CROSSOVER POINT
IRA ROLLOVER VS.
SPECIAL AVERAGING

Rollover

Special
Averaging

Dollars

0   5   10   15   20   25
Years

As you can see in Figure 18–3, your "crossover" point is about 13 years for this $200,000 distribution using the assumptions described. If you needed all your dollars in fewer than 13 years, you would elect special averaging when you received the $200,000 distribution. If you planned to invest the funds for more than 13 years, you'd be better off rolling over the $200,000 to an IRA.

Furthermore, if you want a lump sum of money (for that retirement home, for example) as well as a stream of income, you have to analyze your situation closely to determine which choice you should make. One solution may be to do a partial rollover. The amount rolled over is not currently taxed. However, you would have to pay taxes on the amount you did not roll over, and you would not be eligible to use special averaging. Another option might be to take the lump sum, pay the tax, and invest a part of the proceeds in an annuity contract. Remember again that unless you know you will need to spend your funds almost immediately, the IRA is generally preferable. If you aren't comfortable analyzing these choices, we recommend getting assistance from an experienced tax accountant or financial planner.

THE EXCESS DISTRIBUTION TAX

As if these choices weren't complex enough, the IRS has another wrinkle for wealthy taxpayers in the form of the 15 percent additional tax on excess distributions. To know if you're subject to the tax, add up all of your distributions from pensions and tax-deferred retirement accounts, such as your 401(k), Keogh, IRA, or ESOP. Exclude Social Security benefits and any money that represents after-tax contributions you made to a plan. Then, from this amount, subtract $150,000. The amount that tops $150,000 is your excess distribution unless you've withdrawn a lump sum this year. In that case, your excess distribution is the amount that exceeds $750,000. One piece of good news: Starting in 1995, the IRS is adjusting the $150,000 and $750,000 limits annually for inflation.

If you roll your distribution into an IRA or other qualified plan, then that distribution is not counted against the $750,000 limit in calculating your excess distribution. But when you later take the money out of the IRA or plan, it may be subject to the $150,000 annual distributions limit. Furthermore, this tax may also apply at your death! (See Chapter 23.) The bottom line: If you have retirement plan assets in excess of $750,000, your best bet is probably the IRA rollover since at least you can defer the tax until you start taking money out of the IRA and possibly avoid the tax altogether if those distributions do not exceed $150,000 indexed for inflation. The long-term implications of the excess distributions tax are covered more fully in the next chapter.

CHAPTER 19

MANAGING YOUR IRA DISTRIBUTIONS

In this chapter, we review the tax and financial consequences of taking distributions from IRAs, including:

- How should you plan to withdraw funds from your IRA?
- How does your age determine your tax consequences?
- What is your regular tax liability?
- What penalty taxes could apply?
- What are the minimum distribution rules?
- What are the tax consequences to your survivors?

Sooner or later, the majority of retirement lump sum distributions will probably end up in IRAs. We've discussed the benefits of IRAs and tax deferral in several prior chapters. However, because of these benefits, Internal Revenue Service rules impose some special restrictions on IRA withdrawals. In this chapter, we review the rules and suggest some strategies for getting money out of your IRAs.

IRA WITHDRAWALS AND INCOME TAXES

In reviewing the tax consequences of IRA withdrawals, it's important
to understand that an IRA withdrawal is treated as ordinary taxable
income. No matter what investments are in your IRA, any withdrawal
will be considered income taxable at your current marginal tax rate.
Thus, you get no capital gain break even if your entire IRA is invested
in appreciated stock, for example. Likewise, you can't deduct a loss if
the investments haven't performed well. Furthermore, the IRS won't
allow you to ease your tax burden by using 5-year or 10-year averaging
when you take out money from your IRA.

This isn't all bad, however, due to the value of interest that com-
pounds on a tax-deferred basis. The longer your funds stay in your
IRA, the more you can accumulate tax-deferred. Once again, maximizing your income from IRAs depends to a large extent on your age and
the amount of time you can let the IRA funds grow.

PENALTY TAXES AND YOUR IRA WITHDRAWALS

The tax rules that catch most people are those involving early withdrawal penalties. Once you reach age 59½, you may pull out your
money—in any amount and at any time—without any early withdrawal
penalty. But prior to age 59½, the IRS imposes a 10 percent penalty (in
addition to any regular tax liability) unless your withdrawals meet some
very specific exceptions. This early withdrawal penalty also applies to
distributions from company-
sponsored qualified plans. If you
retire from your company in the
calendar year that you turn 55, or
later, then the 10 percent penalty
will not apply to distributions from
your company-sponsored qualified
plans.

Figure 19–1   What Are the Penalty
Taxes?

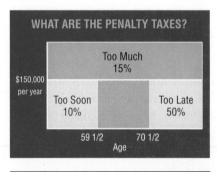

Also, at age 70½ you must pull
out at least a minimum amount
each year (regardless of what you
have withdrawn prior to turning
70½) to avoid a 50 percent penalty.
And if you ever withdraw too

much (that is, over $150,000 in any one year), you must pay a 15 percent excise tax on the excess over that amount. We'll discuss each of these penalty rules in turn, starting with the 10 percent penalty for premature IRA withdrawals.

Rule 1: Under Age 59½

If you're under age 59½, you'll pay regular income plus a 10 percent penalty tax on the taxable portion of funds withdrawn from your IRA. However, while regular income tax will be due (except on your after-tax contributions), you would avoid the penalty tax if your distribution occurred because:

- You become totally and permanently disabled or
- You die and your IRA balance is distributed to your beneficiary or estate.

Assuming neither of these exceptions apply, you can avoid the 10 percent early withdrawal penalty only if you withdraw your money in the form of an annuity, that is, in payments that would stretch over your lifetime. The tax law calls them *substantially equal periodic payments.*

According to the IRS, the payments must be of approximately equal amounts and must be made at least annually. However, although the payments are calculated based on your life expectancy, you don't have to take payments for the rest of your life. Once you start the payments, you must continue to receive them for at least five years or until you reach age 59½, whichever is longer. Otherwise, your distributions don't escape the early withdrawal penalty. For example, if you start payments when you are age 53, you must continue until age 59½, because age 59½ is farther off than five years. On the other hand, if you start taking payments at age 57, you must continue until age 62 because age 62 (or five years) is farther off than age 59½.

You can use any one of three methods to calculate your payment, but once you decide on a method, you can't change it. Each of

Figure 19–2   Substantially Equal Payments
Acceptable Payment Methods

- Payments must be determined by using one of three IRS-approved methods:
    Straight Life Expectancy
    Amortization
    Annuity Method
- Payment must be made at least annually

these methods base payments on your life expectancy or the joint life expectancies of you and the beneficiary of your account. They are

- **Straight life expectancy.** With this method, you simply divide the total balance in your account by either your individual life expectancy or the combined life expectancies of you and your beneficiary. This method will usually give you the lowest annual payment.

- **Amortization.** This method allows you to determine your payment by amortizing your account balance over your life expectancy (or the joint life expectancies of you and your spouse) at a reasonable interest rate. There is some leeway allowed in the interest rate you use, as long as it is "reasonable" at the time you start your payments and you don't change it throughout your required payment period. Generally, you can get larger payments by assuming a higher interest rate. But beware—you need to establish with the IRS (if asked) that you used a reasonable rate. For example, if the prime rate is 6 percent and you used a 15 percent interest assumption in your calculations, it might be a challenge to convince the IRS that your 15 percent rate was reasonable!

- **Annuity.** This method is similar to amortization, except that instead of using IRS life expectancy tables, you can use any generally accepted mortality table, such as those published by an insurance company. This method will generally give you the highest payment.

The tables that you use to determine your life expectancy are in IRS Publication 590, which is available in most public libraries or from the IRS. Also, IRS Notice 89-25 describes these three methods in detail; ask a tax accountant or financial planner for a copy.

Here's an example of how it works. At age 53, according to the IRS tables, you have a life expectancy of 30.4 years. In your IRA, you've accumulated $100,000. So you may withdraw $6,635

Figure 19–3	What Is a Substantially Equal Payment?	
Assumptions:		
$100,000 balance; employee age 53, spouse age 51		
Straight Life Expectancy		
Single life		$3,290
Joint life		$2,681
Amortization		
Single—5% rate of interest		$6,635
Joint—5% rate of interest		$6,073

How Much Can You Take?

Tip

If you have multiple IRAs and you want to receive money from any one or more of them using these rules to escape early withdrawal penalties, the IRS has privately ruled (Private Letter Ruling 8946045) that you do not need to look at the total IRA account balances to determine the amount of required withdrawal. The required withdrawal amount may be determined on an individual IRA-by-IRA basis. However, Private Letter Rulings have limited authority, so check with your tax advisor before relying on them.

annually (assuming a 5 percent interest rate) from the account without paying a penalty. Because you're 53, you would have to continue taking an annual withdrawal until you turn 59½ (the greater of five years or age 59½). After you turn 59½, you can withdraw as little or as much as you want, or none at all!

If, on the other hand, you wanted the minimum possible payment, you could use life expectancy only without an assumed interest rate. You can use a single-life expectancy or the combined life expectancies of you and your IRA beneficiary. So you do have some flexibility in determining your payments using any of the IRS-approved methods, but once you pick a method, you must stick with it.

There is one other exception to the 10 percent penalty. Uncle Sam says you will not be subject to the 10 percent penalty if you take a distribution from a qualified company retirement plan—*not from an IRA*—because you have separated service with the company in or after the year of reaching age 55. (Unfortunately, if you then roll the distribution into an IRA, and then withdraw from the IRA before age 59½, the 10 percent penalty again applies.)

Let's say you leave your company in March when you're 54 years old and celebrate your 55th birthday in May. You have $100,000 in your 401(k) account and decide to roll over $80,000 into an IRA and use the remaining $20,000 to buy a new car. The $20,000 would be subject to ordinary income tax but not to the 10 percent penalty because you took a distribution from a company plan in the year you turned 55 (or older). The $80,000 would not be subject to any tax until you withdrew it from the IRA. And you can avoid the 10 percent penalty on the $80,000 if you do not withdraw any money *from the IRA* until you're at least 59½.

Rule 2: Between Ages 59½ and 70½

Once you reach age 59½, you may pull out your money—in almost any amount and at any time—without any early withdrawal penalty. If you're between these ages, the only penalty tax you might need to consider is the 15 percent excess distributions tax, which we'll cover a bit later.

Rule 3: After Age 70½

As we've mentioned, the IRS doesn't like late IRA withdrawals any more than early withdrawals. According to the rules, you must begin withdrawing at least a minimum amount of your accumulated IRA funds before April 1 of the year following the year you reach age 70½.

If you fail to take out the required amount, your mistake will cost you. You'll pay a penalty that comes to 50 percent of the difference between the amount you pulled out and the amount IRS says you should take out. Consider this example. You're age 70½, and the IRS tables say that, based on your life expectancy, you must withdraw at least $20,000 annually from your IRA. But, in 1995, you only take out $5,000. The IRS says you must pay 50 percent of the difference between the amount you withdrew—$5,000—and the amount you were required to withdraw—$20,000. So you'll pay a penalty of $7,500—that is, 50 percent times $15,000—plus the regular income tax on the $20,000 you should have taken out. As you can see, the penalty for ignoring the rules (or not knowing about them) can be substantial. Your IRA administrator (a bank or mutual fund company, for example) should be able to help you understand these rules, but failing to comply with them is your responsibility, not theirs.

The amount you're required to take out each year depends on either your own life expectancy or—if you prefer—the joint life expectancies of you and your beneficiary. You can also take out more than the minimum if you want to. There are two methods that you can use: the *term certain method* and the *annual recalculation method*. With each method, you divide your account value at December 31 of the prior year by a life expectancy factor to arrive at the required annual payment; the difference is in how you arrive at the life expectancy factor. You can use either method, but once you elect it, you can't change to a different method during your lifetime.

- **Term certain method.** Here, you look up your life expectancy in the IRS tables and subtract one from that number every year to get the life expectancy factor. If you're 70½, your single life expectancy is 16 years, so in year one you divide by 16, in year 2 by 15, and so on.
- **Annual recalculation method.** With this method, you go to the life expectancy tables each year to determine the life expectancy factor. For example, in the first year your single life expectancy would be the same (16 years), but in year 2 you would divide by 15.3, in year 3 by 14.6, and so on.

The annual recalculation method gives a slightly smaller payment because you never "run out" of life expectancy. With the term certain method, of course, by year 16 (when you're age 86) you would divide your account balance by 1 and withdraw the entire account balance, whereas with annual recalculation you would still have a life expectancy of 6.5 years.

You may also reduce the amount of required withdrawals from your IRA by naming a younger person—your child, for example—as your beneficiary. If you do, your joint life expectancy will be longer. But, if you name a younger person other than your spouse as your beneficiary, the IRS only lets you use a life expectancy that is 10 years less than your own.

The distribution and taxation of your remaining account balance at death will depend on (1) whether you selected the term certain method or the recalculation method and (2) whether your beneficiary is your spouse. Consult a professional tax advisor to learn all the nuances of the minimum distribution rules.

15 PERCENT EXCISE TAX ON EXCESS RETIREMENT DISTRIBUTIONS

If your lifestyle, needs, and other retirement resources will allow it, a general rule of thumb is to not begin withdrawing money from your IRA until you reach age 70½. That way, earnings on your retirement dollars continue to compound tax-deferred as long as possible.

But this rule of thumb doesn't always hold true if you have very large account balances. You need to take into account not only the amount that's deposited in your IRA now, but how much your balance

Table 19–1	Breakeven IRA Balances at Various Ages Where No Excise Tax Will Be Generated				
	Current IRA Balance at Various Investment Returns				
Current Age	**6%**	**7%**	**8%**	**9%**	**10%**
50	$1,162,430	$829,010	$593,090	$425,620	$306,360
55	1,278,590	955,690	716,270	538,250	406,540
60	1,406,360	1,101,720	865,030	680,700	536,830
65	1,546,880	1,270,050	1,044,660	860,840	710,610

Assumptions: Distributions beginning at age 70½ with 16-year single life expectancy. Inflation rate for distribution threshold is 4 percent per year.

will grow. Say, for example, that when you were 60 years old you rolled over $1,500,000 from all your company retirement plans into an IRA and it grows at the rate of 8 percent a year. Now you're 70½ and your account is worth nearly $3.5 million. Then you begin to withdraw the funds using the term certain method with a life expectancy of 16 years. Your 1995 required withdrawal—based on your life expectancy—is at least $218,750. This amount tops the excise tax limit, which in 1995 is $150,000. (It will increase each year by inflation.)

That means you're subject to the 15 percent excise tax. In this case, you'd be better off withdrawing *some* of your money earlier so that your required minimum withdrawal at age 70½ will be less than the excise limit. How much depends on your account balance and your current age. Table 19–1 can give you a sense of the approximate current IRA balances that could produce the excise tax at various ages.

Table 19–2	States That Currently Exclude IRA Withdrawals from Income Tax
Illinois	
Mississippi	
New Jersey	
New York ($20,000 exclusion)	
North Carolina ($2,000 exclusion, $4,000 for joint filers)	
Pennsylvania	

STATE TAXES ON IRA WITHDRAWALS

Depending on where you decide to retire, state income taxes can be a significant additional tax burden. Some states allow full or partial

Table 19–3	States That Currently Impose No Income Tax
Alaska	
Florida	
Nevada	
New Hampshire	
South Dakota	
Tennessee	
Texas	
Washington	
Wyoming	

exclusion of IRA withdrawals from income tax. Some others impose no income tax at all. (See Tables 19–2 and 19–3.) Some states (Arkansas, California, Maine, Nebraska, Pennsylvania, and Wisconsin) also impose premature withdrawal penalties. When deciding where you'll retire, you should always factor in your overall state taxes on IRA distributions.

IRA WITHDRAWALS—INCOME, PRINCIPAL, OR BOTH?

Although most people would like to live off of the income from their IRA account only and preserve the principal for their heirs, the IRS tables in effect force you to begin withdrawing principal in order to spend down your account over your life expectancy. Nonetheless, you can certainly withdraw income only between ages 59½ and 70½. Then, once you reach age 70½, you could choose the minimum distribution method that gets you as close as possible to the annual income from the account. For example, if you and your beneficiary are about the same age, you could live off the income only from an IRA earning 8 percent per year until about age 78. But keep in mind our discussion in Chapters 4 through 6 about the need to possibly dip into principal because of inflation's effects on the purchasing power of your retirement income. You may end up taking more than the minimum distribution necessary just to keep pace with inflation. In managing your IRA distributions, a professional advisor is important both to avoid penalties and effectively plan your distributions to meet your overall retirement objectives.

WATCH YOUR TAX PAYMENTS!

During our working years, most of us pay taxes the easy way—through payroll withholding. And unless you report substantial unearned income (dividends, interest, capital gains, and so on), you aren't required to make estimated income tax payments to the government.

But that situation is likely to change once you retire because there will be no withholding on your IRA distributions. So, like your self-employed friends, you'll face not one tax due date (April 15), but four: April 15, June 15, and September 15 of the current year and January 15 of the following year. On these days, you'll have to make quarterly estimated tax payments to the federal government—and probably to your state government as well. If you underpay your estimated taxes, IRS will slap you with an underpayment penalty on the amount you fall short. The amount of the penalty rises or falls with current interest rates. Technically speaking, the interest rate is the federal short-term rate plus three percentage points, which in 1994 averaged about 8 percent. So if you plan to retire soon, it's important that you know the estimated tax rules.

How Much Do You Pay?

The IRS doesn't care if it gets its tax money through payroll withholding, pension withholding, withholding on IRA distributions, estimated taxes, or some combination of each of them. But, as you might expect, you must make your payments on time. If you or your spouse don't have enough taxes withheld from your paychecks, or aren't collecting a salary, you'll pay the difference in the form of estimated tax payments.

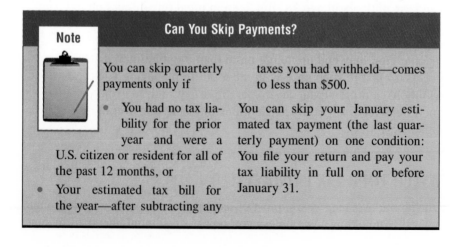

Note

Can You Skip Payments?

You can skip quarterly payments only if

- You had no tax liability for the prior year and were a U.S. citizen or resident for all of the past 12 months, or
- Your estimated tax bill for the year—after subtracting any

taxes you had withheld—comes to less than $500.

You can skip your January estimated tax payment (the last quarterly payment) on one condition: You file your return and pay your tax liability in full on or before January 31.

Managing Your Payments

Remember, the law says that your four quarterly payments must equal the lesser of 90 percent of your current year's tax liability (total tax you pay for the year) or 100 percent of the total tax you paid the previous year—that is, the "total tax" (not just the balance due) shown on your last year's return. But if your prior year's adjusted gross income (AGI) exceeded $150,000, you choose between 90 percent of your current year's tax liability and 110 percent of your prior year's tax liability. AGI is the total of all your taxable income before your deductions and exemptions—it's the last number of the first page of your Form 1040.

Here is an example. Let's say your federal tax liability last year was $15,000 and that your AGI was $100,000. This year, you expect to have more investment income than you did last year and estimate that your tax will come to $20,000. So how much should you pay to the IRS in quarterly payments this year?

Under the rules, you may send either $15,000 (the amount you paid last year) or $18,000 (which is 90 percent of the $20,000 you estimate you'll owe this year). Naturally, you choose the $15,000 option. But, of course, when you actually file your return, you'll still owe the remaining $5,000, but there won't be any underpayment penalty. And *you* had use of the $5,000 for the whole year.

If your prior year's AGI had exceeded $150,000, your choice would have been between $16,500, which is 110 percent of the prior year's liability, and $18,000. Again, you would choose the smaller amount, $16,500.

If your retirement income is going to be fairly constant from year to year, then it is probably easier to base your estimated tax payments on last year's tax liability than to try and project what your tax liability for this year will be. Simply divide the *total tax* shown on your last year's tax return by 4 and you have the amount you need to pay each quarter.

Now you know how to take your money out of retirement plans. In the next section, we look at how you can protect yourself financially should you become ill.

MEDICAL ISSUES

CHAPTER 20   Medical Coverage during Retirement   263

CHAPTER 21   Long Term Care and How to Pay for It   273

MEDICAL COVERAGE DURING RETIREMENT

This chapter covers the basics of postretirement medical care and the effect it can have on your retirement spending plan. Read on to understand:

- The Medicare system.
- What isn't covered by Medicare.
- If Medigap policies make sense.
- How much medical coverage will cost if you're not old enough for Medicare.

When you're an employee, a company-provided health insurance program probably covers most of your needs. But when you retire, what options are available? As we all know, the face of health care in the United States is changing rapidly. In times past, a combination of company-sponsored lifetime medical coverage (often at no cost to the retiree) and Medicare (heavily subsidized by the government) provided adequate coverage for many retired Americans.

These days, if retiree medical coverage is available at all, you're likely to pay handsomely for it. Companies are increasingly wary of providing this coverage due to escalating health care costs, new accounting rules for medical costs, and the growing life expectancies of retirees. Retiree cost shifting has become a common solution—witness the 84,000 retirees of a Fortune 100 company who saw their annual medical insurance cost recently go from zero to $780 per year. Of course, Medicare reform looms on the Washington horizon, so your medical coverage 10 years from now is unlikely to look the same as it does today.

As we saw in Chapter 5, the cost of medical coverage should be considered in developing your long-term retirement spending plan since it's unlikely that this retirement expense will get smaller as time passes. The question isn't whether you'll pay for medical coverage, but more likely how much you'll pay!

THE HIERARCHY OF RETIREE MEDICAL COVERAGE

In the United States, most retirees obtain medical coverage through one or more of three primary sources. Medicare—a federally sponsored, national health insurance program—is your first line of defense. Next comes your company postretirement medical insurance plan—if you're lucky enough to have one—or a health insurance policy that you've purchased yourself. The payor of last resort is Medicaid, the government medical insurance program for those who, after having exhausted their financial resources, are unable to pay for health care.

Sharing the Cost

Note

A recent Wyatt company survey indicated that the average cost of health benefits for a pre–age-65 retiree and spouse in 1993 was $4,596, of which retirees picked up about $2,000. A full 85 percent of large employers now require some form of retiree contribution to the cost of medical care. And the trend will continue. A survey in *Business and Health* (April 1990) indicated that 81 percent of corporate executives will use employee cost-sharing and higher deductibles to control medical costs.

UNDER AGE 65— YOUR OPTIONS

While much of this chapter discusses post–age-65 medical cov-

| Figure 20-1 | Health Care Resources During Retirement | | | |

		Long-Term Health Care		
Resources	Acute Care Hospitalization	Skilled Nursing Care	Intermediate/ Custodial Care	Assisted Living Facilities
Medicaid	Welfare system only	May cover	May cover	Does not cover
Medicare	Primary coverage starting at age 65	Covers some	Does not cover	Does not cover
Company medical plan	Coverage up to age 65. Then plan becomes secondary.	Covers some	Does not cover	Does not cover
MediGap policy	Covers "gaps" between Medicare and retiree medical plan	May cover	Does not cover	Does not cover
LTHC policy	Does not cover	May cover	May cover	May cover

erage, "early" retirees should recognize adequate medical coverage as central to their financial security. After all, a catastrophic illness can quickly wipe out even the best laid retirement plans. If you're under age 65 and retired, you may have access to company-sponsored medical coverage or COBRA continuation coverage. If your spouse works, you may be able to obtain coverage as a dependent on her policy.

If not, as Table 20–1 indicates, expect to include upwards of $5,000 per year in your retirement spending plan for adequate individual medical coverage until Medicare begins at age 65. You may be able to

| Table 20–1 | Comparative Costs of Medical Coverage for Age-55 Early Retiree in Good Health | | |

	COBRA (18 Months from Termination)	Personal Medical Policy to Age 65	Medicare plus Medigap after Age 65
Approximate Cost	$3,000–$4,000	$4,500–$6,000	$2,000–$2,500

convert your pre–age-65 coverage to an individual Medigap policy once you turn 65.

POST–AGE-65 COVERAGE—MEDICARE

Once you turn age 65, you become eligible for Medicare. First enacted in 1965, Medicare—the federal health insurance program for people 65 or older— is run by the Health Care Financing Administration of the U.S. Department of Health and Human Services (HHS). Social Security Administration offices across the country take applications for Medicare and provide general information about the program.

Medicare is actually two programs. Medicare Part A (Hospital Insurance) helps pay when you're hospitalized or in a skilled nursing home. This coverage is free to you; it's paid for by part of the Social Security taxes you've already paid over the years on your wages. Medicare Part B (Medical Insurance) helps cover your doctor bills and the expense of most other outpatient services. If you choose to enroll for this coverage, you will pay a monthly premium, which is deducted from your Social Security benefits. (For 1995, the premium is $46.10 per month.)

Applying for Medicare

Almost anyone who's 65 years of age or older and entitled to Social Security benefits is automatically eligible for Medicare. However, if you don't receive Social Security benefits and you're 65 or older, you can choose to buy the coverage, much like you buy private insurance, for a monthly premium.

If you're already drawing Social Security retirement benefits when you turn 65, you're automatically enrolled in both Part A and Part B. Two or three months before you turn 65, you'll get a package in the mail containing your Medicare card. At that time, you can choose not to enroll in Part B, the part that requires a monthly premium. If you don't enroll in Part B when you become eligible, you'll pay higher premiums. The premiums go up 10 percent for each full 12-month period that you defer enrollment.

If you plan to retire when you turn 65, you can sign up for Medicare at the same time you apply for your retirement benefits. Simply contact Social Security about three months before your 65th birthday. If you plan to work past age 65, you are still eligible for Medicare at 65. Contact Social Security about three months before your 65th birthday so they can help you decide if you should sign up for Medicare.

Medicare Part A Coverage

Medicare hospital insurance can help pay for inpatient hospital care in a hospital, skilled nursing facility, or psychiatric hospital. In addition, it pays for hospice care, pays the full cost of medically necessary home health care, and pays 80 percent of the approved cost for wheelchairs, hospital beds, and other durable medical equipment supplied under the home health care benefit.

There are of course limits on coverage. For the first 60 days, Medicare usually pays all your hospital charges—as long as they don't top the approved amounts—after you pay an initial deductible in 1995 of $716, but no more than the actual charges. For the next 30 days, you pay $179 a day and Medicare covers the rest. After 90 days, you can either pay $358 per day for up to 60 "lifetime reserve" days or pay the full cost yourself. Your benefit period ends 60 days after you are discharged from the hospital or skilled nursing facility. If you are admitted to a hospital again, you will have to pay another deductible as well as the other cost-sharing amounts.

If you are admitted to a skilled nursing facility, you pay nothing for the first 20 days, except for charges that Medicare does not cover. For the next 80 days, you pay charges up to $89.50 per day, and Medicare pays the rest. No benefits are available after 100 days of care in a "benefit period."

Medicare Part B Coverage

Medicare Part B pays for doctors' services; outpatient hospital services; home health visits; diagnostic X-ray, laboratory, and other tests; necessary ambulance services; and other medical services and supplies not covered by Part A. You pay a $100 deductible per year; after that, Part B will pay 80 percent of covered expenses, which may not exceed the charges allowed by Medicare.

Medicare and Your Doctor

Keep in mind that not all doctors participate in Medicare. For non-participating doctors, patients pay the bill and submit forms to Medicare for allowed reimbursement. To learn the names of doctors in your area who participate in Medicare, consult your local *Medicare Participating Physicians/Suppliers Directory*, a government publication available at your local Social Security office. It will tell you which doctors in your area accept "assignments" on Medicare claims. Assignment is an arrangement whereby a physician or medical supplier agrees to accept the Medicare-approved amount as the total charge for services and supplies covered under Part B. Medicare pays the provider directly, except for the deductible and coinsurance amounts that you must pay.

While physicians who do not accept assignment of a Medicare claim can charge more than physicians who do, there is a limit as to the amount they can charge you for service covered by Medicare. Under the law, they cannot charge more than 115 percent of the Medicare-approved amount for the service. *You do not have to pay charges that exceed the legal limit.*

Physicians who knowingly, willfully, and repeatedly charge more than the legal limit are subject to sanctions. If you think you're overcharged, or you want to know what the limiting charge is for a particular service, contact the Medicare carrier for your area. The names and addresses of the carriers and areas they serve are listed in the back of *The Medicare Handbook*, which is available from any Social Security Administration office or from Medicare.

What Is an Approved Amount?

Note

It's the price for services that Medicare deems reasonable and customary in your city, town, or other geographic area—for example, $40 for a doctor visit. If your doctor charges more than the approved amount, you or your insurance carrier may have to pay any excess charges over the approved amount. Let's say that in the city you live the approved amount for an office visit with a doctor is $40, but your physician charges $45.00. You or your private insurance carrier will pay $13—that is, 20 percent of the approved amount or $8, plus $5 (the difference between $40 and $45).

FILLING THE GAPS IN MEDICARE COVERAGE

Not all health services are covered by Medicare. For example, Medicare does not pay for custodial care; nursing home care (except skilled nursing care); dental care and dentures; routine physical checkups and related tests; eyeglasses, hearing aids, and examinations to prescribe and fit them; and prescription drugs. Most people with long-term health problems, such as Alzheimer's disease, need custodial—not skilled—care, and Medicare doesn't pay for custodial care at all. (Custodial care is care given by someone who is not medically skilled. Examples are help with dressing, walking, and eating.) Nursing home care is discussed in the next chapter.

Besides long-term care, which isn't covered by Medicare or Medigap policies, you may still want to cover the expenses that Medicare doesn't pay by purchasing Medicare Supplement Insurance, commonly called Medigap. Medigap policies are plans that you buy from private insurance carriers, which fill in the *gaps* in Medicare coverage. Due in part to decreases in the level of employer-provided health care coverage, Medigap policies are becoming much more popular.

Medigap policies range from $400 for a basic policy to $2,000 a year, but a higher price tag doesn't always translate into better coverage. To make it easier for consumers to comparison shop for Medigap insurance, in 1990 the federal government required insurers to offer Medigap policies in 10 standard formats. These plans, which have letter designations ranging from A through J, were developed by the National Association of Insurance Commissioners and incorporated into state and federal laws. Table 20–2 shows each plan's features. Each policy must provide a core package of benefits that plugs the biggest gaps: co-insurance provisions and the cost of a long hospital stay. Other policies offer varying degrees of coverage, up to plan J, which is the most comprehensive. To make it easier for consumers to compare plans and premiums, the same format, language, and definitions must be used in describing the benefits of each of the plans. A uniform chart and outline of coverage also must be used by the insurer to summarize those benefits for you.

After 1990, federal law requires insurers to issue a Medigap policy to anyone, regardless of medical condition, who applies within six months of their 65th birthday. These policies must also be guaranteed renewable, unless the insured doesn't pay premiums.

If you'd like more information on Medigap plans, write to the Consumer Information Center (Department 87, Pueblo, Colorado 81009)

Table 20–2	The 10 Standard Medigap Policies									
	A	**B**	**C**	**D**	**E**	**F**	**G**	**H**	**I**	**J**
Basic Benefits	√	√	√	√	√	√	√	√	√	√
Part A deductible		√	√	√	√	√	√	√	√	√
Part B deductible			√			√				
Part B—excess doctor bills						100%	80%		100%	100%
Skilled nursing co-insurance			√	√	√	√	√	√	√	√
At-home care			√			√			√	√
Prescription drugs								√	√	√
Preventive medical care					√					√
Health care abroad			√	√	√	√	√	√	√	√

√ = Policy offers this benefit.

and ask for a copy of *Guide to Health Insurance for People with Medicare*. It's free for the asking.

IF YOU'RE STILL EMPLOYED

If you're working past age 65 and remain covered under an employer group health plan, you can wait to enroll in Medicare medical insurance (Part B) during a seven-month "special enrollment period." This period begins with the month the group health coverage ends or the month employment ends—whichever comes first. If you meet certain requirements, you won't have to pay the 10 percent surcharge.

If you enroll in Medicare and accept your employer's health insurance plan, Medicare will be the *secondary payor*. This means that your employer's plan pays first on your hospital and medical bills. If the employer's plan does not pay all of your expenses, Medicare may pay secondary benefits. On the other hand, if you reject the employer's health plan, Medicare will be the primary health insurance payor.

WHERE CAN YOU LEARN MORE?

If you'd like more information on Medicare, you may call Medicare (the toll-free number is 1-800-638-6833) or write to the Consumer Information Center, Department 87, Pueblo, Colorado 81009, and ask for copies of some of these booklets: *Your Medicare Handbook; Medicare: Hospice Benefits; Medicare and Coordinated Care Plans; Medicare and Other Health Benefits;* and *Medicare and Your Physician's Bill.*

The American Association of Retired Persons (AARP) also has some good publications on Medicare and Medigap: *Medicare: What It Covers, What It Doesn't* (#D13133); *Knowing Your Rights* (#D12330); and *Medigap: Medicare Supplemental Insurance—A Consumer's Guide* (#D14042). To request these free publications, write to AARP Fulfillment, 601 E Street NW, Washington, D.C. 20049.

The next chapter discusses the biggest potential gap in your retiree medical coverage, the cost of nursing home care.

CHAPTER 21

LONG-TERM CARE AND HOW TO PAY FOR IT

This chapter examines one of the greater risks to your financial security during retirement: the chance that you will need custodial long-term care at some point during your retirement years. Read on to understand:

- Why increasing life expectancies are a cause for concern.
- How the federal government might help.
- Long-term care insurance.
- Other alternatives for care.

The longer you live, the greater the chance that you'll need long-term care insurance. And most of us are living longer. Since 1940, the odds of living to age 85 have doubled—from one-in-five to two-in-five—and they're expected to jump to three-in-five by the year 2030.

With that increased life span has come a new set of concerns related to long-term health care for the elderly. In fact, some 30 percent of Americans who are 85 years of age or older now reside in nursing

Figure 21–1

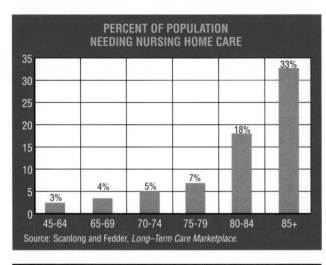

PERCENT OF POPULATION
NEEDING NURSING HOME CARE

Source: Scanlong and Fedder, *Long–Term Care Marketplace.*

homes. Another 20 percent or so require home care—that is, they receive regular assistance from nurses, housekeepers, or meal delivery services. By the year 2000, almost 9 million older Americans will need long-term care services, up from about 7 million in 1988.

Where the inability to care for oneself once resulted primarily from acute diseases, it's now more likely to come gradually as part of the aging process. People live for years with Alzheimer's disease and other chronic ailments that don't require long hospital stays, but leave their victims increasingly helpless.

In prior days, long-term care was the responsibility of offspring, but these days the caregivers are likely to be paid professionals. Clearly, in doing your retirement spending plan to determine your income needs and goals, this is a cost you should count on in the later phases of retirement!

THE COST OF LONG-TERM CARE

Incurring long-term care can leave you financially crippled. And normally Medicare doesn't help. Many people think Medicare will pick up their nursing home bills, but it pays only for the first 100 days in so-called skilled nursing facilities—and then only if admission follows a hospital stay. According to the American Health Care Association, Medicare pays less than 2 percent of all long-term care-related expenses.

Nursing home costs range from $35,000 to more than $60,000 a year—per person. The amount varies considerably depending on the quality of services and geographic location—and fees are rising at a rate that's higher than inflation! The Health Insurance Association of America estimates the average nursing home stay at about 2.5 years. And home care services (which can include physical therapy, administration of drugs, and food preparation) are no bargain either.

With these cost levels, planning for long-term care becomes a necessity if you want to provide for quality care and conserve even a modest estate for your heirs. Evaluating your long-term care options in today's environment comes down to three basic choices:

- Do nothing. That is, assume the risk that you won't need long-term care, or if you do need it, then pay the cost out of current income and investment assets. To the extent that either is insufficient, look to Medicaid for assistance.
- Transfer the risk to an insurance company by purchasing a long-term care insurance policy. Like any insurance policy, this involves paying annual premiums to obtain the company's guarantee of some level of coverage.
- Combine the two preceding options by choosing a long-term care policy with coverage exclusions, with lower daily benefits, or that pays benefits only after certain waiting periods have expired.

MEDICAID AS AN OPTION

Medicaid is a state-run program designed primarily to help those with low income and few or no resources. It provides a safety net of sorts for retirees—but only those in the most dire situations. Yet, approximately 61 percent of retirees rely on Medicaid to cover at least a portion of the cost of custodial care.

While the federal government helps pay for Medicaid, each state has its own rules about who is eligible and what is covered. You're eligible for Medicaid if your health care costs absorb almost all of your income, and you've used up all but $1,000 to $4,000 of your assets excluding your home—the exact amount varies by state. Exempt assets typically include personal property, one automobile, and life insurance of less than $1,500. If you would like to know more about the Medicaid program, contact your local social services or welfare office. Your financial advisor should also know the rules in your state.

Estate Planning and Medicaid

Generally, the goal of Medicaid planning is to preserve family assets by transferring them to family members or trusts so that a family member can qualify for Medicaid. For example, many people attempt to preserve their assets while qualifying for Medicaid by transferring assets to family members. In order for these gifts to remove assets from Medicaid, you must make the transfers more than 36 months before the Medicaid application (30 months for transfers prior to August 10, 1993), or the assets are attributed back to the family member.

Similarly, many people attempt to shelter assets from Medicaid consideration by using a Medicaid Qualifying Trust (MQT), which is a type of irrevocable living trust. If you were to set up such a trust, buy enough long-term care insurance to cover the first 60 months of care because a 60-months rule applies to transfers in trust. In addition, these trusts' viability is currently in question due to recent federal regulations and state statutes that require use of trust principal by potential Medicaid recipients under certain circumstances. These revisions (enacted in 1993) make it much more difficult to use trusts in Medicaid planning.

This type of planning is currently quite controversial as it raises moral and ethical questions surrounding the use of public funds for those who aren't truly poor. Opponents of Medicaid planning argue that scarce public funds should not be available to families who have sufficient resources to pay for nursing home care, but are merely taking advantage of loopholes in the system. Because the legal aspects of Medicaid planning are currently in flux and the tax and financial implications are highly complex, we suggest the services of a competent attorney if you are interested in Medicaid planning.

LONG-TERM CARE INSURANCE

Given the complexities of Medicaid planning and the risks to financial security that long-term care poses, buying long-term care insurance may be the easiest alternative for most people. But whether you should sign up for long-term care insurance now depends largely on your age.

Figure 21–2

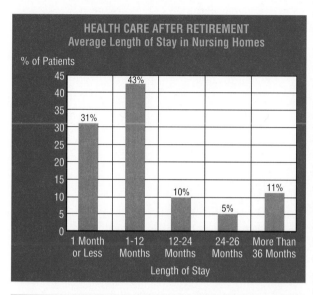

People under age 50 are best advised to do nothing because many retirement planning experts believe broader and better solutions, public or private, probably lie ahead. However, others argue that buying policies when you're under age 50 and locking in lower rates makes good sense. (Depending on the policy, current pre-mium rates for a 65-year-old can be as much as four times that for a 55-year-old.)

It's becoming more common for large companies to offer group long-term care policies to employees, so check out your company bene-fit plans. Some professional associations also offer policies. You can often purchase coverage for relatives, such as aging parents, as well as for you and your spouse.

What to Look for in a Long-Term Care Policy

Ideally, a long-term care policy should offer the widest possible options, including nursing homes in three categories of medical care: skilled homes; intermediate homes, which provide rehabilitative therapy; and custodial homes, which offer little more than practical nursing. The best policies also pay for care at home, adult day care centers, and brief intermittent care at a nursing home, also known as respite care.

The policy should offer those benefits in nearly equal amounts. A policy that covers nursing home care for years but home care for only a month or so forces you to opt for institutionalization or to skip benefits.

Table 21–1   Evaluating Long-Term Care Policies

Feature	Recommended	Comment
Monthly premium	It varies	
Daily nursing home benefit	$80.00 and up	(Will depend upon the local cost of a nursing home.)
How long until benefits begin?	Within 20 days	
Maximum benefit period— one stay	30 months and up	(The chances of staying in a nursing home for more than 3
Maximum benefit period— all stays	30 months and up	years is only 3.2% of men and 5.9% for women.)
Does it pay full benefits in a:		
Skilled nursing facility?	Yes	
Intermediate facility?	Yes	
Custodial facility?	Yes	
Is hospitalization required?	Yes	(73% of admissions into nursing homes come from homes, not hospitals.)
Can I enter any level of care?	Yes	(Many policies require skilled care at the "entry point" for coverage if intermediate or custodial care is available. With this restriction there is a 45% chance of not collecting benefits.)
Does it pay for home care?	Yes	Home care is the fastest growing kind of care in the country.
Does it pay for adult day care?	Yes	
Are benefits increased for inflation?	Yes	(At least 5%)
Does it have waiver of premium?	Yes	No premiums due when receiving benefits.
Is it guaranteed renewable?	Yes	
Does the premium stay level?	Yes	
Does it cover mental disorders (e.g., dementia and Alzheimer's)?	Yes	
Does it cover nerve and muscular disorders?	Yes	
What is the company's Best rating?	A or A+	

Prepared with contribution from HICAP

Table 21–2	Comparative Costs of Long-Term Care Coverage at Various Ages
Age	**Level Premium per Year**
30s	$ 100
40s	200
50s	800
60s	1,500
70s	3,000
80s	4,000

Most companies now cover home care, but some charge extra for it or reduce payments over time. Some plans pay for home care only after you've been in a nursing home for a period of time and then only for as many days as you were there. Some policies require hospitalization for three days before benefits begin, yet the need for care is often the result of a deteriorating condition such as arthritis, which may not put you in the hospital at all. The best policies require only that a doctor certify the need for care.

Always look for a guaranteed renewable policy. Certain states forbid insurance carriers from canceling your long-term care policy because of either your age or deteriorating health. Make sure your coverage will continue for as long as you want it to and that your premiums can't be increased unless the company increases them across the board.

WHAT ARE THE DRAWBACKS OF THESE POLICIES?

Almost all policies have one major drawback—they indemnify you a fixed-dollar amount per day, generally $30 to $200 per day, no matter how much you're paying for services. In contrast, hospital and major-medical insurance pays all or a high percentage of each bill. Long-term care policies also include deductibles in the form of a waiting period. The number of days you pay before your benefits begin and how long the benefits continue will greatly influence the premium you pay. Most insurers offer at least two choices of waiting periods—typically, any-where from 20 to 100 days. Selecting a 100-day waiting period can reduce your premium by as much as 30 percent. So you probably want to choose as long a waiting period as you can afford.

At the other end, though, more is worth paying for. Since the major-ity of policyholders will need care for less than a year, benefits that quit after one year or so may cost only half as much as those continuing for the six-year maximum many policies currently offer. The extra cover-age, however, can mean the difference between solvency and bank-ruptcy for the minority whose confinement continues for years.

Table 21–3	How to Check Out an Insurer	
Rating Service	**Top Two Ratings**	**Telephone Number**
AM Best*	A+, Contingent A+	(908) 439-2200
Duff & Phelps	AAA, AA+	(312) 368-3157
Moody's Investors Service	Aaa, Aa1	(212) 553-0377
Standard & Poor's	AAA, AA+	(212) 208-1527
Weiss Research*	A+, A	1-800-289-9222

*Fee for an over-the-phone rating.

WHO SELLS LONG-TERM CARE INSURANCE?

Over 100 commercial insurers and a number of Blue Cross plans now offer coverage for long-term care in either a nursing home or the patient's own dwelling. Be certain to check on the financial strength of the insurance company before you buy the policy. Table 21–3 lists major organizations that rate insurance companies. Be particularly careful with long-term care coverage. Because it's fairly new, insurers are wary of assuming too much risk.

For more information about long-term care insurance, request a copy of *A Shopper's Guide to Long-Term Care Insurance* from either your state insurance department or the National Association of Insurance Commissioners, 120 W. 12th Street, Suite 1100, Kansas City, Missouri 64105-1925. You may also obtain a copy of the *Guide to Choosing a Nursing Home* by writing to Medicare Publications, Health Care Financing Administration, 6325 Security Boulevard, Baltimore, Maryland 21207.

The American Association of Retired Persons also offers useful free publications: *Making Wise Decisions for Long-Term Care* (#D12435), *Before You Buy—A Guide to Long-Term Care Insurance* (#D12893), and *Nursing Home Life: A Guide for Residents and Families* (#D13063). You can request these publications by writing to AARP Fulfillment, 601 E Street NW, Washington, D.C. 20049.

OTHER OPTIONS FOR CARE

If you're 60 years of age or older and in good health, one viable way to cover your current and future health care needs is to enroll in one of the nation's so-called continuing care retirement communities (CCRCs).

Using Life Insurance Benefits During Your Lifetime

Tip

Some insurance companies have recently begun to offer policyholders an option to receive part of the proceeds of their policies during life if a catastrophic illness or permanent confinement to a long-term care facility occurs. These "living benefits" riders can be added to existing policies or included with new ones. Today, approximately 200 companies offer this option.

Under these riders, you can receive from 25 percent to 100 percent of the policy death benefit; the exact amount depends on life expectancy (usually 12 months or less) and state regulations. Some good news? According to interim IRS regulations, the proceeds will not be considered income for federal tax purposes.

In 1992, approximately 700 CCRCs provided health and housing services to about 220,000 residents nationwide. The typical resident is age 70 and, although reasonably healthy, has perhaps a heart condition or other medical problem. Residents of these communities get private apartments plus services such as housekeeping, meals, and medical care, including nursing home care, on an as-needed basis.

Some communities charge a flat fee for entrance—usually $50,000 to $200,000 depending on the size of your apartment—and $800 to $2,000 a month for maintenance, meals, and health care. You then get whatever services you require at no additional cost. Most CCRCs return a portion of entrance fees to your estate at death, depending on how long you lived at the CCRC. CCRCs also differ in the amount of nursing care provided so you should select one according to your health.

Other communities charge less but residents must pay extra for services beyond the minimum specified in their contracts, so read the fine print before you sign on the dotted line. For instance, a contract might limit home health care to 60 days or require residents to pay 80 percent of the cost of care in the community's nursing home.

Many fees are all-inclusive, but if you move to a community with separate fees for all or some services, you may still need Medigap and long-term care insurance. These policies are sometimes offered at

Table 21–4	Levels of CCRC Care		
Level of Care	**Nursing Services Included***	**Approximate Entrance Cost**	**Approximate Monthly Fee**
Extensive care	Unlimited care	$50,000–$200,000	$1,000
Modified care	15–20 days nursing care per year plus daily fee for additional days	$40,000–$60,000	$800
Fee for service	Same as under extensive care, but all services are at a daily fee	$35,000–$40,000	$700, not including nursing care

*All provide guaranteed access to nursing care.

group rates to residents, for which you can save as much as 15 percent to 25 percent. Also, entrance fees at continuing care communities are at least partially refundable if you change your mind at any time after you sign your contract.

It's wise to check the reputation of a facility you're considering. You can do so by writing the attorney general of the state where the community is located and visit the facility, talk to residents and their relatives about the level of care provided. Another indicator of sound management is accreditation by the American Association of Homes for the Aging (AAHA), a trade group. But accreditation is voluntary, and just over 150 communities have met AAHA standards so far. For a free list of accredited facilities, write the American Association of Homes for the Aging, 901 E Street NW, Suite 500, Washington, D.C. 20004-2037. The group also publishes a guide on how to choose a continuing care community. If you would like complete profiles on more than 300 continuing care retirement communities, send $24.95 to the same address for a copy of *The Consumers' Continuing Care Retirement Directory*.

Long-term care is as much about estate planning (conserving your assets), as it is about taking care of you and your spouse. The next three chapters discuss the fundamentals of estate planning in detail.

ESTATE PLANNING

CHAPTER 22   Fundamentals of Estate Planning   285

CHAPTER 23   Making Sense of Estate Taxes   301

CHAPTER 24   Understanding Estate Administration
and Probate   317

283

FUNDAMENTALS OF ESTATE PLANNING

In the next three chapters, we discuss the fundamentals of estate planning. This chapter reviews:

- Setting your estate planning goals and objectives.
- Basic estate planning documents: wills, living wills, and powers of attorney.
- Property ownership and how property passes to your heirs.
- Using trusts in your estate plan.
- Whether you need life insurance as a retiree.

   Throughout this book, we have tried to present a balanced view that retirement planning encompasses a variety of financial and nonfinancial matters. Both aspects must be present for you to effectively define and achieve your retirement goals. Not surprisingly, planning your estate involves both financial and nonfinancial objectives. On the financial side, you want to minimize or eliminate expenses such as taxes on the transfer of your assets at death. And the nonfinancial goals? Most people want to make sure they provide properly for those who are financially dependent on them and perhaps leave something to people or organizations about whom they care.

Estate planning can be difficult—not only because of the financial complexities but because the process brings you face to face with your own mortality. Moreover, estate planning is a big responsibility as you try to foresee the time when you'll no longer be around to make decisions. Other people—particularly people you love—will be affected by the plans you make now, and they'll be expected to exercise their judgment once you're gone.

To develop an effective estate plan, you can generally follow five basic steps:

- Determine your objectives.
- Prepare an inventory of current assets and liabilities.
- Determine the current form of ownership of these assets and, under your current plan, who will receive them.
- Calculate the potential estate tax.
- Use planning techniques to reach your financial and personal objectives and minimize taxes.

In this chapter we discuss the first three steps. In addition, we also discuss the need for life insurance as a means to accomplish short- and long-term estate planning goals.

DETERMINING YOUR OBJECTIVES

Determining your objectives in estate planning is another way of saying who will get what and when they will get it. This decision is, of course, very personal. Most people want to plan for their spouse, a significant other, children, and close relatives first. They might also want to leave a legacy to their alma mater or to a favorite charity.

Keep in mind, however, that practicality alone doesn't dictate what you leave and to whom. Your personal philosophy also plays a part and affects what you do with your money while you're alive. For instance, you may consider it your responsibility to leave a legacy for your children. Or you may think that your only responsibility to your

Figure 22-1   What Do You Think?

Give your children enough money so that they feel they could do anything, but not so much that they could do nothing.
—Warren Buffett, multibillionaire chairman of Berkshire-Hathaway

offspring is to provide them with a good education. In this case, you may decide to dispose of much of your estate while you're still living.

You also need to consider what effect large bequests might have on your children. Will they use their inheritances wisely? Would inheriting a large sum stifle their ambition?

What about a family business? Do your children want to run the business and do they have the skills and talent to do so? Or are you trying to live your dreams through them?

COMMUNICATION IS THE KEY

In estate planning, the best idea is often to just talk it over. Discuss your estate plan with your heirs. Share information on the value of your estate, the location of information, and what funeral and religious arrangements you would like. Open communication will help your family implement your wishes, prevent costly family litigation, and give you peace of mind.

When your children are old enough, discuss with them the general size of your estate and what you plan to do with it. It also makes sense to observe how your children have handled money over the years. Are they responsible with their own funds? Have they earned money on their own? What have they done with their earnings?

Maybe you think your children won't be mature enough to handle a sudden financial windfall. Many parents don't, and their solution is to tie up the money they leave as long as they think is necessary. While most states consider 18 or 21 the legal age of majority, you can state in your will that your children can't collect their inheritance until they reach, say, age 30 or 35. Or you can structure a trust that gives them access to income, but prevents them from touching principal. Some people allow the trustee to distribute principal only for specific purposes, such as health or education. Other people design trusts that don't pay out until the child gets her college degree or shows proof of earning a salary.

Once you decide who will get your property, the next question is how should you express those wishes so that they will be carried out by heirs and caregivers. Directions on your wishes in the event of permanent incapacitation or death can bring forward important medical, ethical, and religious issues. Fortunately, it is relatively easy to express these wishes in a variety of estate-planning documents, as explained below.

LIVING WILLS

Living wills are legal documents that state your wishes concerning when you want life-sustaining treatment continued or withdrawn if you are unable to communicate your wishes due to incapacity. A living will states that you don't want to be kept alive by "heroic" or "extraordinary" means—life support machines, for example. The living will is followed if you are unable to provide guidance at the time a medical decision is needed.

Most states have laws that define people's right to refuse medical treatment and the right to express their wishes in advance directives or living wills. These documents aren't legally binding in some states. Nonetheless, you can formally let your family and friends know how you feel about these heroic measures.

These days, you don't necessarily need an attorney to prepare a living will. Many states have statutory living will forms that meet state law requirements, and are available in many banks, libraries, and legal supply stores. Also, don't be surprised if on entering a hospital, you are asked whether you want to have a living will prepared prior to surgery or inpatient care. (See the accompanying tip.) Lastly, keep in mind that if you move, your living will may not be valid in the new state, and

Want More Information?

Tip

To obtain more information about living wills and powers of attorney for health care, request the free brochure *Medicare and Advance Directives* from the Consumer Information Center (Department 87, Pueblo, Colorado 81009). To get information on your particular state's rules, as well as statutory forms if they exist for your state, write Concern for Dying/Society for the Right to Die, 250 West 57th Street, New York, New York 10107.

some states only treat living wills as valid for a certain period of time—say, five years after you sign it.

POWER OF ATTORNEY FOR HEALTH CARE

A related document is a *durable power of attorney for health care*, sometimes called a *health care proxy*. This document names another person, such as spouse, child, or close friend, as your authorized spokesperson in making medical decisions if you should become unable to make them for yourself. The word *durable* means that the authority in this document continues throughout your incapacity or disability. You can also include instructions about any treatment you want to avoid. Again, every state has different rules, so be sure to abide by the rules of your state.

The health care power of attorney is somewhat more flexible than the living will in that it names a particular person to act as your agent to make decisions for you. Also, it applies to all medical decisions, whereas a living will typically only covers life-sustaining measures in the event of an illness or injury that is likely to cause death. Because these documents cover different situations, most people should use both as a part of their estate plan.

ANATOMICAL GIFTS

Any person who is at least 18 years old can give all or any part of his body to a hospital, a medical or dental school, an organ bank, or a specific individual. These gifts are increasingly valuable since the demand for hearts, eyes, and other transplantable organs far exceeds the supply.

Most often, these gifts are made by will, but it is important that family members also be notified so that the donation may be made immediately at death. Otherwise, by the time the will is located and read, the time for making the donation may well have passed.

You can make an anatomical gift using a card or form obtained from a hospital, medical school, or gift society. In some states, there is also a form for an anatomical gift on the back of each driver's license. Each state has its own laws so check your particular state's rules regarding these gifts.

GENERAL POWER OF ATTORNEY

A durable general power of attorney is similar to the power of attorney for health care in that you authorize someone to make decisions for you if you should become unable to make them yourself. The difference is that you're giving someone the ability to make financial decisions on your behalf. If these directions aren't contained in other estate planning documents, such as your living trust, this document should be a part of your estate plan.

WILLS AND WHY YOU NEED ONE

People who fail to make wills don't suffer; their heirs do. In fact, if you neglect to make one, those whom you want to provide for the most may inherit the least—or even nothing at all. So if you're one of the 7 out of 10 Americans who don't have a will, we hope that you'll make one. And if you have made a will, we hope that you'll review it periodically to make sure it represents your current wishes.

A will is the most important estate planning document you can have. If you die without having made a will, you've died *intestate*. Under the intestacy laws, your home state has already decided how some of your property gets divided between your heirs. Most states

Figure 22–2

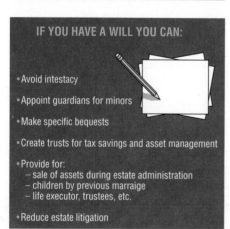

IF YOU HAVE A WILL YOU CAN:

• Avoid intestacy

• Appoint guardians for minors

• Make specific bequests

• Create trusts for tax savings and asset management

• Provide for:
  – sale of assets during estate administration
  – children by previous marraige
  – life executor, trustees, etc.

• Reduce estate litigation

divide the property between the spouse and children, often 50/50. While that may not seem bad, any share that goes to minor children will probably have to be managed and supervised through a court-supervised conservatorship. In most states, the children receive their shares when they turn age 18.

Even if you don't face any of these problems, not having a will could prove expensive. The intestacy process is time-consuming and expensive, involving attorney's fees, court costs, and the posting of bonds. Many state courts require estate administrators to post a bond of $1,000 or more, which will come from the assets of your estate. So if you think a will is too expensive, start adding up the costs of not having one!

Aside from simply preparing a will and designating the beneficiaries of your estate, the two most important decisions you will need to make are (1) who will act as guardian if you have any minor children and (2) who will be your executor. We discuss each of these in more detail in Chapter 24 on estate administration.

Who Should Prepare Your Will?

You should first know that the two chief types of wills are *witnessed wills* and *holographic* or *handwritten wills*. All states recognize the validity of witnessed wills, but only a handful recognize holographic wills.

Even in those states that recognize them, holographic wills must be written, dated, and signed in your hand and have no other printed or typed material on them, to be considered valid. If you have a witnessed will, it doesn't matter if it's typed or handwritten. However, it's only valid and legal if witnesses have signed it.

So you could write out or type your will, have two or three people—none of whom will benefit under the will—witness it, and feel reasonably confident that the document could stand up against any court challenges. The number of witnesses required varies from state to state. Most states require that you have at least two witnesses to your signature.

These days, there are many alternatives to having an attorney prepare a will, although the cost of professional advice may be lower than you think—anywhere from $75 to $500 for a simple will, depending on where you live. The cost can be even lower if your company benefit package includes a group legal plan. Under many of these plans, you

In a typical will, you are the **testator,** and the first paragraph of a will states your name and address. It also says that you're making your will knowingly and revoking all previous wills. Following this information comes a statement that tells your **executor**—the person or persons who will administer your estate—to make sure your assets get distributed as you wish and to pay all your debts, taxes, and burial expenses promptly.

Most wills then provide for **specific bequests.** Perhaps you want to leave a friend an heirloom watch, a painting, or some other personal property. Or say you want to give a gift of cash or property to your favorite charity or to your alma mater. These gifts of personal property are called *specific bequests.*

You may also want to give items of sentimental value to one person you trust—your spouse, perhaps. Then you could list in a separate letter instructions on whom you want to receive these items. This type of letter is nonbinding, but that should be no problem as long as you choose someone on whom you can rely to distribute the gifts as you wish. Why not just give these items in your will? The problem is you might change your mind somewhere along the way, and, if you use a letter, you can change the nonbinding instructions as often as you like without rewriting your will.

Next in your will come **general bequests.** Perhaps you want to leave $5,000 to your first cousin. Joe Jones. So you say in your will, "I leave $5,000 to my first cousin, Joe Jones." Is that a specific or general bequest? You may think it's a specific bequest, but it's not. A specific bequest would be worded, "I leave to my first cousin, Joe Jones, the $5,000 I have in my money-market fund, number 01604444, at the ABC Financial Institution." A general bequest doesn't tell from what specific source of funds it comes.

Finally, the will states what happens to your **residual estate** (what remains of your assets after you subtract specific and general bequests). Again, an example may help. Say you tell your executor to make three general gifts—$10,000 to each of your sisters, for example. You ask that all remaining assets be split equally among your surviving spouse and your children. Your residual estate is these remaining assets.

Recipients of specific and general bequests have first claim on your estate and, as we saw, specific legacies are paid before general legacies. That means you need to be careful. Make sure you have enough remaining in your estate for your principal beneficiaries after all debts, expenses, taxes, and specific and general bequests are paid.

High-Tech Wills

Tip

If you want to prepare your own will and use a personal computer, several good software packages will make the process much easier. The following packages are available at software stores and are generally priced at $50 or lower:

- It's Legal (Parsons Technology).
- Personal Law Firm (BLOC Publishing).

- Willmaker (Nolo Press).
- Will Builder (Sybar Software).
- Home Lawyer (MECA).

We generally recommend that you use software to help you understand the questions that need to be asked and the documents that need to be drafted, but always have your estate planner review your final documents.

can pay a modest annual fee in exchange for basic legal services such as real estate closings, leases, and simple wills. For these relatively straightforward legal documents, joining a group legal plan can be a cost-effective alternative compared to having them prepared by a local attorney.

Depending on where you live, you may have heard of a statutory witnessed will, which is simply a printed form that comes with written instructions for filling in the blanks. These are often sold in stationery stores. Some computer software packages are also available. (See the accompanying Tip.) Many states accept these "do-it-yourself" documents as valid, but that doesn't mean you should always use them. They may be fine if your estate is quite modest (certainly under $600,000) and your bequests entirely straightforward, but we recommend that you take no chances. Plain and simple, most people should hire an attorney to prepare a will—it's well worth the modest cost. With an experienced, competent attorney preparing your will, you can be confident that your document is valid and contains the necessary clauses and provisions to accomplish your goals.

THE IMPORTANCE OF PROPERTY OWNERSHIP

For most people, the will is the means by which property is passed to heirs. But the will operates to pass only property that is *not* effectively passed using some other means. Often, property passes to heirs in other ways, such as through beneficiary designations or legal forms of property ownership. (This is commonly called *passing property outside the will*.) These alternative ways of passing property, particularly property ownership, can also greatly influence the cost of administering your estate and the amount of federal estate taxes your estate ultimately pays, as explained further in Chapters 23 and 24.

The way you own an asset, or what lawyers call the *form of ownership*, will determine *how much* of the asset will be included in your taxable estate and *who* will inherit your share of the asset. Lawyers refer to ownership of property as *titling*. (For example, the owner holds title to the property.) The property ownership table in Table 22–1 summarizes the different forms of ownership:

- Individual ownership.
- Joint tenancy.
- Tenancy in common.
- Community property.
- Trusts.
- Beneficiary designation—for example, in a retirement plan or life insurance policy.

Table 22–1   Property Ownership Table

How Asset Is Held	Includable in Estate	Who Gets Property	How It Is Transferred
Individually owned	100%	Beneficiary of choice	By will
Spousal joint tenancy with right of survivorship	50%	Spouse	By form of ownership
Other joint tenancy with right of survivorship	Up to 100%	Other joint tenant	By form of ownership
Tenancy in common	% owned	Beneficiary of choice	By will
Retirement plans	100%	Named beneficiary	By contract
Life insurance	100%, if deemed owner	Named beneficiary	By contract
Community property	50%	Beneficiary of choice	By will
Trusts	0–100%	Beneficiary of choice	By contract

These forms of ownership determine how much of the asset's fair market value is included in your estate for estate tax purposes and how your property legally passes to your heirs at death. We'll leave a detailed discussion of estate taxes to the next chapter. For now, let's focus on the many forms of property ownership and how they operate to pass your property to your heirs.

Individual Ownership

Individual ownership simply means you alone own and control the entire interest in a piece of property. For example, let's say you bought 100 shares of stock and own the shares *individually*; that is, only your name is on the stock certificate. On the day you die, whoever you name in your will gets the shares.

Joint Ownership

Joint ownership means that you own property with one or more other people; for example, instead of owning the stock individually, you can buy those shares with your spouse or another person as *joint tenants*. The stock certificate should indicate that you own it as joint tenants with some notation, such as "as joint tenants with right of survivorship" or "JTWROS." In this case, your spouse automatically inherits your shares, *regardless of what your will says*. The titling on the stock certificate will overrule your will because your joint tenant has a *right of survivorship*—that is, if she survives you, she will inherit your portion of the stock.

Tenancy in Common   Another way to own an asset jointly with someone is as *tenants in common*. Tenancy in common is somewhat similar to joint tenancy in that two or more people have an ownership interest in property. But unlike joint tenancy, tenants in common do not have *right of survivorship*; therefore, the other "tenants" do not inherit your share of the property. Instead, it is your will that determines who receives your share of the asset.

Community Property   The last form of joint ownership is community property. It does not depend on titling, but rather is a result of living in one of the nine community property states (Arizona, California, Idaho, Louisiana, Nevada, New Mexico, Texas, Washington, and Wisconsin). Generally, community property is all assets that you acquired during your marriage, except for gifts and inheritances, which are considered individually owned property. Under community property rules, the asset does not automatically pass to your spouse. Instead, it is your will that determines who receives the property. (Community property can be converted to separate property by legal agreement.)

Beneficiary Designations

A beneficiary designation isn't really a form of ownership. Rather, beneficiary designations control the disposition of property at death and are another way of passing property "outside of the will." They are most common with retirement plans and life insurance policies. Under a beneficiary designation, the beneficiary that you indicate for each individual plan or policy will receive the assets. That is, the person you named as beneficiary on the beneficiary designation for your 401(k), IRA, life insurance policy, and so on will overrule the person you named in your will.

Beneficiary designations are extremely important to the success of your overall estate plan, yet people often ignore them. Remember, the beneficiary designation overrides your will so make sure your retirement plan and life insurance beneficiary forms are current. One story we know of makes this point quite clearly: A person took out a sizable life insurance policy and made it payable to his spouse, but then was divorced. After he remarried, he never changed the beneficiary designation to reflect his new spouse. Upon his sudden death, his ex-spouse became quite wealthy, even though his properly drafted will gave all of his property to his new spouse, because the insurance company was forced to follow the beneficiary designation it had on file. The moral: Regardless of what your will says, always make certain that your beneficiary designations are up to date.

Trusts

A trust is another form of property ownership that is used quite commonly in estate planning. Trusts are arrangements under which you transfer title to property to a trustee (who can be yourself) with instructions on what to do with it, such as pay the income or principal to a beneficiary or accumulate the income for payment at some future

Figure 22–3

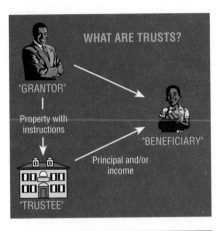

date. Trusts provide a great deal of flexibility in planning to manage estate taxes and pass property to your heirs.

Trusts come in two basic types: (1) irrevocable, meaning that you can't amend, revoke, or change the trust, and (2) revocable, meaning it can be amended or even revoked entirely. You might use an irrevocable trust to remove property and any future appreciation from an estate, but you must be willing to give up complete control of the property. If you retain certain powers in the trust, such as the trust income or a right to change a beneficiary, the trust property will be included in your estate because you didn't give up complete control of the trust assets. Also, keep in mind that because you give up control over the property you give to the trust, you have made a gift for which there may be gift tax consequences.

As we'll see in the next chapter, irrevocable trusts are commonly used to remove life insurance from the value of the gross estate since an insurance policy (especially a term insurance policy without cash value) doesn't do you much good during your life!

Table 22–2	Types of Trusts
Revocable	**Irrevocable**
Can be revoked/amended	Cannot be revoked
Frequently used to avoid probate on trust assets	Often used to remove insurance from both spouse's estates
During life, income taxed to grantor	
After death, income taxed to beneficiaries or trust	Income usually taxed to beneficiaries or trust
Trust assets included in grantor's estate	Usually excluded from grantor's estate
No gift tax	May be gift tax

The other main type of trust, the revocable trust, is also known as a living trust. This trust can be amended or revoked so you have the power to get back the assets you transfer to it. For most purposes, you retain control over the property: You've simply changed title to it from yourself to the trust.

Revocable trusts don't help remove assets from your estate since you retain control over the property you transfer to them. But they are valuable tools for avoiding probate since assets that pass under the trust agreement aren't controlled by your will and don't go through the probate process. As we'll see in Chapter 24, revocable living trusts are the most common planning tool for avoiding probate.

YOU'RE RETIRED—DO YOU NEED LIFE INSURANCE?

Your need for life insurance changes as you grow older. Sometimes you need sizable amounts of coverage, and sometimes you don't. Most people, if they work for someone else, receive life insurance from their employer. When they retire, however, their coverage ends or is reduced. If you want additional coverage—or coverage at all—you have to buy your own policy. So you need to rethink your life insurance needs when you retire.

When do you need life insurance? These are five situations when you might want to have it.

First, say you have a pension, which may be reduced when you die. In this case, your spouse will have less to live on than he has now. In addition, Social Security benefits may be less after your death. So you might want to buy enough life insurance to make up the amount your spouse will lose *if* your other assets cannot provide your spouse with enough income.

Figure 22–4

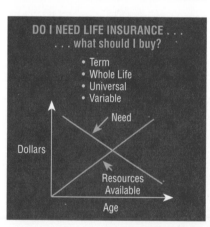

Second, you may need life insurance to cover your final expenses: medical bills, the cost of your funeral, and so on. You may want to look into a so-called burial policy that will cover the amount you need for these purposes.

The third instance in which you need life insurance is to provide your estate with liquidity. Say, for instance, you own a business, which is your primary asset. Since you want your family to keep the business after you die, you may need the proceeds from a life insurance policy to pay the estate taxes if all of your wealth is tied up in the business and you don't want to sell it. Or say that most of your assets are in real estate. Again, your survivors could use the proceeds from a life insurance policy to pay the estate taxes on your real estate holdings if they don't want to sell them.

Fourth, you may want to leave your spouse or children with a sizable estate, one that's larger than you've been able to amass in your lifetime. In this case, you can use the proceeds from a life insurance policy to make a "final gift" to your loved ones.

Finally, you may want to purchase a life insurance policy to pay off what you owe—the mortgage on the family home, say—when you die. That way, your survivors aren't burdened with debt after your death. Again, don't forget to see if you already have enough assets that could be used to leave your family debt-free.

If you do need—or want—to buy life insurance, what type of policy is right for you? You should know that life insurance comes in two general forms: term and whole life.

With term insurance, you buy only the so-called death benefit—the amount your beneficiaries receive when you die. Whole life, by contrast, has an investment component. Part of your premium pays for the insurance portion of the policy; the other part the insurance company invests on your behalf.

Term insurance is less expensive at first since you're buying *only* insurance. However, it does become increasingly expensive as you grow older. A whole life policy, by contrast, will initially cost considerably more than term insurance, but has the advantage of a fixed premium. You pay the same amount each year

Figure 22–5

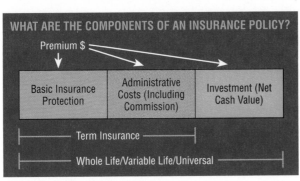

regardless of your health or age. The bottom line, then, is to shop around and compare before purchasing a life insurance policy.

Now that we have the basics down, we'll move to discussing the various ways of planning your estate to meet your personal objectives, starting with tax aspects of estate planning.

CHAPTER 23

MAKING SENSE OF ESTATE TAXES

In this chapter we discuss the federal estate tax system and ways to maximize the amounts passing to your heirs. Read on to understand:

- How the federal estate tax system works.
- What's included in your gross estate.
- The marital deduction for property passing to your spouse.
- The unified credit and why you should use it.
- How to remove property from your taxable estate.
- State estate and inheritance taxes.

We've taken a look at the nonfinancial aspects of estate planning and the documents you may need to implement an estate plan so let's move on to the financial considerations—starting with federal estate taxes.

FEDERAL ESTATE AND GIFT TAXES

Minimizing or eliminating federal estate and gift taxes is the main reason people do estate planning. In a nutshell, estate planning can ensure that your heirs, not the IRS, get the property you worked so hard to acquire.

Generally, the amount of your estate tax liability is directly tied to the size of your estate so that the lower the value of the estate, the lower the potential liability. Rates go as high as 55 percent. Obviously, failing to minimize estate taxes at your death can be a very expensive mistake.

OK, you might say, then the simplest estate plan is to give your property away during your lifetime so that there's nothing to tax at death. Unfortunately, the IRS is way ahead of you—there's also a gift tax on lifetime property transfers over certain levels to prevent you from avoiding estate taxes through lifetime transfers. The bottom line is to plan for both types of transfer taxes so that you minimize the amount of gift taxes during life and ensure that the value of your estate is as low as possible at death.

IS ESTATE PLANNING FOR THE WEALTHY ONLY?

There is a threshold you've probably heard about at which you will pay no estate or gift taxes at all—$600,000. Called the *unified credit equivalent*, it's the maximum amount of property that any one person can pass on free of estate taxes. The $600,000 threshold applies to lifetime gifts too, so you could give away up to $600,000 during your life (not including the $10,000 annual gift tax exclusion discussed later)

Figure 23–1

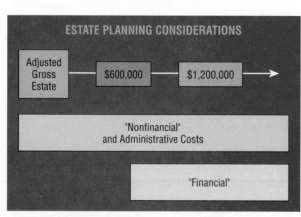

ESTATE PLANNING CONSIDERATIONS

Adjusted Gross Estate — $600,000 — $1,200,000 →

"Nonfinancial" and Administrative Costs

"Financial"

without incurring gift taxes, but you wouldn't have the $600,000 exclusion available for your estate.

The term *unified credit equivalent* means that the IRS gives each person a tax credit of $192,800, which is exactly the tax on $600,000. Subtracting the credit from the tax on $600,000 equals zero, which means the IRS collects no taxes from your estate. If you're married, each person gets one $600,000 exemption during life or at death so you and your spouse combined can pass up to $1,200,000 free of federal estate taxes.

Say, though, you have an estate that adds up to more than $600,000. Then estate taxes add up quickly. In fact, this is the highest tax rate system we have. As Table 23–1 shows, if you had left $700,000 instead of $600,000, Uncle Sam would have collected $37,000, or 37 percent of the $100,000 that topped $600,000. Take a look at the rate wealthy people with estates over $10 million pay!

While many people will never end up paying estate taxes because of the unified credit equivalent, don't think that you don't need any estate

Table 23–1   Federal Estate and Gift Taxes

If Your Taxable Estate Is between		You Owe	Plus	On Amount over
$ — and $	10,000	$ —	18%	$ —
10,000	20,000	1,800	20	10,000
20,000	40,000	3,800	22	20,000
40,000	60,000	8,200	24	40,000
60,000	80,000	13,000	26	60,000
80,000	100,000	18,200	28	80,000
100,000	150,000	23,800	30	100,000
150,000	250,000	38,800	32	150,000
250,000	500,000	70,800	34	250,000
500,000	750,000	155,800	37	500,000
750,000	1,000,000	248,300	39	750,000
1,000,000	1,250,000	345,800	41	1,000,000
1,250,000	1,500,000	448,300	43	1,250,000
1,500,000	2,000,000	555,800	45	1,500,000
2,000,000	2,500,000	780,800	49	2,000,000
2,500,000	3,000,000	1,025,800	53	2,500,000
3,000,000	10,000,000	1,290,800	55	3,000,000
10,000,000	21,040,000	5,140,800	60	10,000,000
21,040,000	—	11,764,800	55	21,040,000

planning where the combined assets of you and your spouse are currently less than $600,000. Chances are your assets will grow over time and you'll eventually be over the $600,000 mark. Planning techniques can save your estate from writing a big check to the IRS. For example, let's look at a couple who said they only wanted to maintain a level of purchasing power that equaled $500,000 in *today's dollars*. You would think that their estate planning would be quite simple. But don't forget what inflation will do! In 20 years, it will take over $1 million to maintain the purchasing power of $500,000 today. And with a home worth, say $200,000, some life insurance, and several hundred thousand in retirement assets, it isn't too difficult to get over these estate tax thresholds.

HOW MUCH OF YOUR ESTATE IS TAXED?

On the day you die, the fair market value of all the assets you own—your home, car, investments, retirement accounts, life insurance policies, and so on—is combined to determine the value of your gross estate. The value of your estate, in turn, will determine the amount that's taxable under federal estate tax laws.

The key word in that last paragraph is *own*—if you don't own the property at death, it isn't taxed. This concept, while seemingly simple, is the basis for many of the most common planning techniques that are used to reduce estate taxes. Let's take a closer look at how different property that you own at death can be included in your estate. Figure 23–2 shows what is included in the gross estate for estate tax purposes.

Individually Owned Property Any property you own individually and transfer by your will is included in your estate. For convenience, this property is often referred to as your probate estate. It can include real estate, personal property, stocks and bonds, and almost any other type of asset you own. As we discuss in the next chapter, however, even if

Figure 23-2

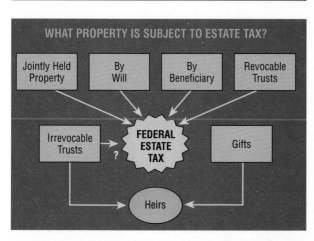

WHAT PROPERTY IS SUBJECT TO ESTATE TAX?

Jointly Held Property

By Will

By Beneficiary

Revocable Trusts

Irrevocable Trusts   ?

FEDERAL ESTATE TAX

Gifts

Heirs

you hold your assets in a revocable living trust to avoid the probate process, the trust assets are still included in your estate because you still are considered to own the trust property for estate tax purposes. Furthermore, assets passing under beneficiary designations, such as life insurance, are included in the gross estate even though they aren't transferred by will. To remove an asset from your estate, you must completely transfer ownership to someone else.

Jointly Held Property   As you will recall, property held in joint tenancy is not part of your probate estate because it doesn't pass under your will. If you own an asset in joint tenancy with your spouse, only half of the property is included in the calculation of your estate. Upon the surviving joint tenant's death, however, the entire value of the property will be taxed, assuming it is still held at her death.

If the joint tenants aren't married, however, the entire value of the property is included in the estate unless the other joint owner furnished all or part of the payment for it. As an example, let's look at what would happen if you bought some shares of stock with your brother. In this case, the full value of the stock is included in your estate unless your brother can prove that he contributed to the purchase of the stock. Regardless of how much is included in your estate, your brother automatically receives your shares. Again, the titling on the stock certificate overrules your will.

Life Insurance and Employee Benefits   Again, these assets do not go through probate because they are transferred under beneficiary designations, not under your will. However, the full value of these assets is still included in your estate because you owned them at death.

When to Value Property?

Tip

Your estate can be valued either at your date of death or six months later, by election of the executor. Your executor should determine which is better. For example, if the estate had depreciated in value since death, valuing the estate six months after death may produce a tax advantage. However, your executor can't pick and choose assets in valuing the estate. The six-months valuation election applies to all assets in the estate.

While you might not count them as assets for determining your net worth during your lifetime, your "estate" net worth includes them. Consequently your taxable estate could be much higher than you might think.

Community Property   If you live in a community property state, you are considered to own a one-half interest in all property acquired during the marriage, so half of the value is included in the estate. However, property acquired before the marriage or by gift or inheritance during the marriage is separate property and is included in full.

Trust Property   Inclusion of trust property in your estate depends on the type of trust. Recall from Chapter 22 that if you place assets in a revocable trust, you haven't really given up ownership, so the assets must be included in your estate. On the other hand, if you use an irrevocable trust, you may be able to exclude the value of trust assets from the estate if you do not retain any ownership rights. Later in this chapter we discuss using trusts to remove the value of assets from your estate.

DEDUCTIONS FROM YOUR ESTATE

We explained above how to calculate the value of your gross estate, that is, your share of the fair market value of all your assets. But, thankfully, that is not the amount that the government will tax. The following items can be deducted from your gross estate to obtain the amount that will be taxable:

- Your share of liabilities, such as mortgages or other enforceable debts on property included in the estate.

- Amounts spent on final expenses, including funeral and burial costs.

- Estate administration expenses, such as court costs, appraisal fees, and attorney, accountant, and executor fees. You can generally estimate these expenses at between 2 and 5 percent of the estate's gross value, although they could be less or more depending on the complexity and size of your estate, and whether or not your estate goes through the probate process.

- Charitable gifts contained in your estate documents.

- And last but certainly not least, the unlimited marital deduction for property passing to a spouse.

ESTATE PLANNING TECHNIQUES

The deductions shown above will reduce the value of your estate, but perhaps not below the $600,000 level, and that's where estate planning becomes critical. Good estate planning involves both structuring the ownership of your assets to remove as much value as possible from the estate, and maximizing all available estate tax deductions. Of the many techniques available, proper use of the estate and gift tax marital deductions is probably the most important. When it comes to estate taxes, it pays to be married!

Figure 23–3

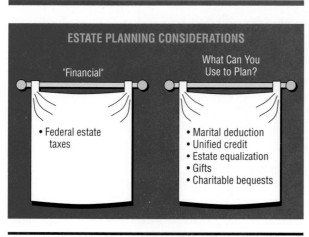

ESTATE PLANNING CONSIDERATIONS

"Financial"

What Can You Use to Plan?

- Federal estate taxes

- Marital deduction
- Unified credit
- Estate equalization
- Gifts
- Charitable bequests

Marital Deduction Planning

The unlimited marital deduction lets you pass your entire estate to your spouse free of tax, no matter how large. The marital deduction also applies to gifts between spouses so you can give

Watch Those Beneficiary Designations!

Tip

Remember, in order for the value of assets to qualify for the marital deduction, they must be **payable** to your spouse at death. A common problem we see is beneficiary designations on qualified retirement plans and life insurance proceeds that were originally payable to an estate and were never changed when the owner remarried. Check yours out. If the proceeds are payable to your estate, they will not qualify for the marital deduction, and your estate could be stuck with a hefty tax bill!

unlimited amounts of property to your spouse during your lifetime free of tax.

Unfortunately, the marital deduction does not eliminate estate tax; it only postpones it. The IRS does get its due eventually, but not until your spouse dies. Then the value of your estate and any additions that have been made to it will go to someone who is not a surviving spouse—a child or relative, for example. When that day comes, the marital deduction isn't available, and the IRS collects its due, but only if your spouse's estate is over $600,000.

What happens if you don't leave your entire estate to your spouse. In this case, you subtract the portion you gave to your spouse from your total estate. The remainder is your taxable estate and is

Figure 23–4   All Property to Spouse

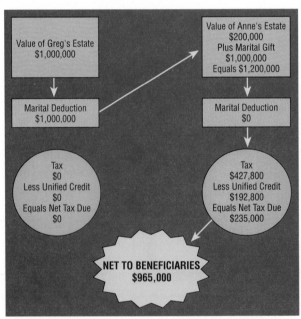

subject to estate taxes. However, as we explained above, all or a portion of this amount may not be taxed, thanks to the unified credit.

Your first order of business should be to try to use both the unified credit and marital deduction to minimize the total amount of estate taxes paid. As we saw, the rules let you give all of your assets to your spouse tax-free. However, it's not always a good idea to leave everything to your spouse outright. Many couples whose wills do exactly that end up paying far more than they should in estate taxes.

Here's an example. Say Greg dies in 1995 and has a will that leaves his entire estate worth $1 million to his wife Anne. (This is commonly called a *sweetheart will*—everything to your spouse, no strings attached!) Anne has other assets worth $200,000. Thanks to the marital deduction, no federal taxes are due on the $1 million she received from Greg. But then Anne dies four years later and gives the estate to the couple's two sons.

We'll assume the assets haven't grown, so Anne now has an estate of $1.2 million. The unified credit shelters only $600,000 from federal taxation. So the estate (more specifically, the children) must pay a hefty $235,000 on the remaining $600,000 even though they could have theo-

Figure 23–5   Using the Unified Credit

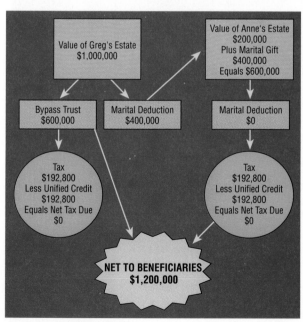

retically passed the full $1.2 million free of tax. The reason: instead of using his $600,000 unified credit, Greg gave all of his property to Anne, which qualified it for the marital deduction. This is commonly called *wasting the unified credit*, and in this case it was a $235,000 mistake.

Here's a strategy that will work better. Greg shouldn't leave the entire $1 million to Anne. Instead, he should divide the amount into two shares. His will leaves all but $600,000 in property to Anne. This $600,000 is the unified credit shelter share known in estate-planning jargon as the *bypass share*. It will go to the two children after Anne dies. Therefore, it will *bypass* Anne's estate.

Greg puts the bypass share in a trust known, appropriately enough, as a *bypass* or *credit shelter trust*. Anne can receive income from this trust as long as she lives, and get principal distributions for her health, welfare, and maintenance, **but she does not own the trust property outright!** (If she did, it would qualify for the marital deduction.) When she dies, any leftover principal goes to the couple's two children free of estate taxes.

This strategy has two advantages. First, Greg and Anne both take advantage of passing $600,000 of assets estate-tax–free. More importantly, they save $235,000 in estate taxes. That's because Greg left part of the estate to Anne, and that amount escapes taxation thanks to the marital deduction. The remaining $600,000 is in trust for Anne and the kids—and that amount isn't taxed because of Greg's unified credit. When Anne dies, her estate adds up to only $600,000 (the $400,000 received from Greg and her own $200,000) and, again, the unified credit keeps that sum out of Uncle Sam's pocket.

Planning for Children from a Prior Marriage

Tip

Consider the QTIP trust. QTIP stands for *qualified terminable interest property*. An election made with the estate tax return allows QTIP property to qualify for the marital deduction.

A QTIP trust lets you take advantage of the unlimited marital deduction and lets you decide who gets these assets after your spouse dies. In other words, a QTIP lets you keep control of your assets long after you've passed on.

Here's an example. Say you place all your stock holdings in a QTIP trust for your husband with the remainder to be left to your daughter from a first marriage after your husband passes away.

The result: your husband receives annual income from the stock—but only for his lifetime. Additionally, he may be able to sell the stock and use the funds, but only for his own use. The stock goes directly to your daughter after your husband passes away. Under a regular marital trust, your husband could leave the trust property to anyone; with a QTIP, he has no say in who receives the stock holdings.

You may have noticed that the QTIP trust and the bypass trust are quite similar. With both, the surviving spouse receives income from the trust, while the rest can go to your children (or whomever the trust designates) when your spouse dies. The major difference is the amount of direct control your spouse has over the principal.

REDUCING THE VALUE OF YOUR GROSS ESTATE

Because the amount of tax you ultimately pay is directly related to the size of your estate, other planning techniques are available to reduce the amount of property that will be in your estate at death. Three of the most common techniques are lifetime gifting, an irrevocable insurance trust, and charitable giving.

Lifetime Gifting

Making gifts to slash the size of your estate often makes sense. As you probably know, each year you may give up to $10,000 free of gift tax to each of your children—or to **anyone else** of your choosing, relative or not. Furthermore, if you're married and elect to "split" the gift with your spouse, you may give up to $20,000 annually to each recipient. So if you're married and have two children, you and your spouse may give away gift-tax–free up to $40,000; if both children are married, you could give them and their spouses $80,000 annually, and so on. Keep in mind that the recipient of a gift does not have to pay income tax on the amount of the gift.

What happens if you give someone more than the $10,000 annual limit, or give a married couple more than $20,000? If you give amounts that top the $10,000 annual exclusion, you use up part of your lifetime $600,000 exemption. This provision means you can give up to $600,000 ($1,200,000 for a married couple) more than the annual exclusion before you'll pay a gift tax. But the portion of your unified credit that you use while you're alive will reduce the amount you can use at the time of death. In choosing which assets you want to give to your children, it's best to include those that may be appreciating rapidly but produce little or no current income. Note, too, that you (not the recipient) pay the gift tax.

Is giving over the limit a good idea? It is if you feel comfortable financially and want to be exceptionally generous while you're still alive. It's also a good idea if you want to get appreciating assets out of your estate.

Irrevocable Insurance Trusts

You can also remove the proceeds of any life insurance from your estate. However, to remove it means you must give up all ownership privileges to the policy. You can relinquish your ownership in two ways. Either you can transfer ownership of the policy directly to another person or you can set up an irrevocable life insurance trust. Like the bypass trust, an irrevocable life insurance trust can provide income to your surviving spouse during his lifetime and pass the remaining value of your estate to your beneficiaries when your spouse dies.

There are two pitfalls you must watch out for when it comes to transferring policies. First, the annual insurance premiums will constitute gifts to the trust, and if your policy has cash value, you also make a gift of that value. (Most life insurance trusts have provisions called *Crummey provisions* that allow these transfers to qualify for the annual gift tax exclusion.) Second, if you give an existing policy, you must transfer it more than three years before your death. Otherwise, the law treats the transfer as if it never occurred, and the proceeds are automatically included in the value of your estate. However, a life insurance trust can acquire a new policy at any time, and the three-year rule would not apply.

Charitable Giving

Naturally, if you make charitable contributions while you're living, they are no longer part of your estate since what you gave away is no longer yours. But what about those charitable bequests in your will? Your estate can deduct these gifts for estate tax purposes so you can be as generous as you like with your charitable contributions.

PLANNING TECHNIQUES BY SIZE OF ESTATE

Estates Less Than $600,000

As far as federal taxes go, planning for this size estate is fairly easy. You have no taxes to worry about thanks to the marital deduction and the unified credit. But you may have to concern yourself with state and local taxes so try to structure your assets to avoid these taxes.

Regardless of whether you'll pay estate taxes, you still want to be sure that both you and your spouse have updated wills. Since you

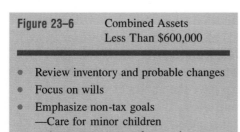

Figure 23–6   Combined Assets
Less Than $600,000

- Review inventory and probable changes
- Focus on wills
- Emphasize non-tax goals
  —Care for minor children
  —Asset management for survivor
  —Passage of property at second death
- Use marital deduction to avoid tax at first death
- Unified credit avoids tax at second death

probably want to provide for any children, you and your spouse might write wills bequeathing your estate to the surviving spouse—or to your children, if your spouse has predeceased you.

Don't forget about the non-tax issues you should address in your will: appointing guardians for your young children, selecting an executor, and making specific bequests (e.g., leaving your coin collection to your niece). These nonfinancial issues should be addressed no matter what size your estate is. We discuss wills in much greater detail in the next chapter.

Estates Between $600,000 and $1.2 Million

This size of an estate can be quite difficult to plan for. Here's why. You can often set in motion a strategy that may help you when it comes to taxes, but really isn't too practical. Here's an example.

Say you want to avoid estate taxes entirely so you arrange that neither you nor your spouse has more than $600,000 in assets while you both are alive. After you die, say you've arranged that your spouse be left with no more than $600,000.

But there are problems with this idea. From a practical point of view, the spouse who has more money usually hasn't enough in liquid assets

Figure 23–7   Combined Assets Between
$600,000 and $1.2 Million

- Consider using first-to-die's unified credit
- Consider using trust to facilitate marital and family distributions
- Consider a QTIP trust for special situations
- If estate is large due to life insurance, consider an irrevocable life insurance trust
- Consult estate/financial planner

to transfer funds to the spouse with less money. Moreover, the survivor, especially if she's young, might well feel more comfortable with access to more than $600,000.

What can you do if your estate is of this intermediate size? First, transfer enough liquid assets to bring the "poorer" spouse's wealth up to $600,000. In technical terms, it's called *estate equalizing.* Do so within the bounds of common sense, however. And keep in mind that you're relinquishing control over these assets.

Then, each spouse should leave his or her entire estate to the other spouse. But each spouse should also have the ability to "disclaim assets"—that is, choose not to inherit them. If he or she does disclaim them, they pass to a *bypass trust* (also called a *credit shelter trust*), thus taking advantage of passing up to $600,000 estate-tax–free.

If you take these steps, you'll have some flexibility if an estate tax problem crops up for the surviving spouse. In fact, as a surviving spouse you have three choices. You can remove assets from the estate by disclaiming them and placing them in the credit shelter trust (usually no more than $600,000); you can simply spend the money; or you can make tax-free gifts to members of your family, friends, or a favorite charity to reduce the estate.

Estates over $1.2 Million

The strategies are similar to those with combined estates of $600,000 to $1.2 million. Both of you should take advantage of passing the $600,000 estate-tax–free by having your wills provide for bypass trusts. Then the surviving spouse would receive the remainder of the estate either outright, in a "regular" marital trust, or in a QTIP trust.

With such a large amount of assets, a gifting program becomes even more appropriate as you probably have more money than you need. If you hold onto it, it is your beneficiaries who will suffer when they have to pay a very steep estate tax bill.

And if you have any charitable desires, now is the time to think about them. Not only do you get an *income tax deduction* when you make charitable contributions while you're still alive, you're also reducing your eventual estate. Depending on what and to whom you donate, you may get a tax deduction for somewhere between 20 and 50 percent of your adjusted gross income *each year.* And at the time of death, there is absolutely no limit on the amount you may give to charitable organizations.

Something else to think about is life insurance. If it's life insurance

Figure 23-8	Combined Assets Greater Than $1.2 Million

- Consider same techniques as medium-size estate
- Gifting program
- Charitable gifts or bequests
- Consult an estate/financial planner

proceeds that cause your estate to be so large, consider transferring the policy directly to a beneficiary (that is, making her the owner of the policy), or setting up an irrevocable life insurance trust that we discussed previously.

Here's another idea to consider: "second-to-die" life insurance policies. These policies pay off after your surviving spouse dies. Since assets from the first death can pass free of tax to the spouse because of the unlimited marital deduction, the payment of estate tax doesn't usually occur until the surviving spouse dies. The second-to-die policy then is intended to give your beneficiaries the necessary cash to pay the tax bill.

As the policy is insuring two lives, more premiums will be paid over a longer time period than under a policy insuring only one life. Because of this, the annual premiums on these policies are normally significantly lower than under a conventional single-life policy.

EXCESS RETIREMENT ACCUMULATIONS

Similar to the 15 percent excise tax we discussed earlier, an additional 15 percent excise tax is imposed on qualified plan and IRA retirement benefits that are included in your gross estate. The tax is imposed if the value of your accounts at death exceeds the hypothetical value of an annuity of $150,000 per year based on your remaining life expectancy immediately before death. Unfortunately, no credits, deductions, or exclusions apply against this tax.

Generally, the best way to avoid this tax in your estate is to have your spouse inherit all of your retirement accounts, and then make an election to defer application of the tax until *his* death. Making the election might eliminate the tax since your spouse has the chance to spend much of the excess accumulations before death.

WHAT IF YOU ARE SINGLE?

The good news? Estate planning is much simpler for a single person than for married individuals. The bad news? There are not as many techniques to keep Uncle Sam away. For instance, there's no unlimited marital deduction or bypass trust concept.

But the unified credit exists just as much for a single person as it does for old married folks. Therefore, a single person with an estate worth $600,000 or less will not have to share any of it with Uncle Sam.

Once it gets over that amount, then she should consider if she can afford to start gifting part of it away so the estate stays at the $600,000 level. The other alternative is to make charitable bequests at the time of death.

STATE TAXES

Most states impose some form of estate taxes and/or inheritance taxes. However, this isn't as bad as it seems because you get a credit for state death taxes paid against the federal estate tax. In fact, most states only impose a tax in an amount that equals the credit allowed for federal purposes; this is commonly called a *pickup tax*, and the net effect to you is zero.

Keep in mind, though, that some states impose their own estate taxes or inheritance taxes. Inheritance taxes differ from pickup taxes in that they are assessed against the recipients of your estate, not against the estate itself. Therefore, in states that have inheritance taxes, state death tax planning becomes much more important.

In this chapter, we focused on the most common ways of planning to preserve your estate by cutting estate taxes. One other area in which you can preserve assets is by avoiding the cost of probate, to which we now turn.

Table 23–2	States Imposing Estate or Inheritance Taxes
Connecticut	
Delaware	
Indiana	
Iowa	
Kansas	
Kentucky	
Louisiana	
Maryland	
Massachusetts	
Mississippi	
Nebraska	
New York	
North Carolina	
Ohio	
Oklahoma	
Pennsylvania	
South Dakota	
Tennessee	

CHAPTER 24

UNDERSTANDING ESTATE ADMINISTRATION AND PROBATE

In this chapter, we discuss probate and estate administration. Read on to understand:

- The probate process.
- What it takes to be an executor.
- Using living trusts to avoid probate.
- Appointing a guardian for your children.

Next to reducing estate taxes, minimizing probate costs is an important estate planning goal since estate administration can be time consuming and expensive. In this chapter, we discuss probate and how to plan your estate to minimize the costs of administering it.

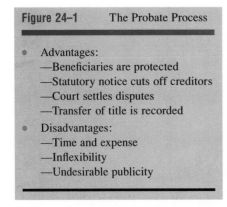

Figure 24–1   The Probate Process

- Advantages:
  - —Beneficiaries are protected
  - —Statutory notice cuts off creditors
  - —Court settles disputes
  - —Transfer of title is recorded
- Disadvantages:
  - —Time and expense
  - —Inflexibility
  - —Undesirable publicity

WHAT EXACTLY IS PROBATE?

Probate is a court process in which the executor of an estate accumulates probate assets, pays debts and taxes, and distributes assets to beneficiaries. During the probate process, your executor is responsible for submitting your will to the court, as well as preparing an inventory of your estate assets and liabilities. Tax elections and returns will be prepared and filed, and taxes will be paid. Debts and claims against the estate will also be settled. Once the will is approved, the probate process generally takes from six months to two years to complete.

There are some advantages to the probate process. For one, beneficiaries are protected because a court oversees the process and makes sure that the right person inherits the proper assets. Also, statutory notices are given that cut off creditors from presenting claims after a certain point (usually four to six months). Also, the court is available to interpret any ambiguous portions of your will and settle claims or disputes, such as will contests. Finally, the transfer of title will be properly recorded in the probate process.

In spite of these benefits, many people want to avoid probate because it is time consuming, cumbersome, and expensive. The cost of probate will be based on the amount of your property that actually passes under the will and thus goes through the

Figure 24–2

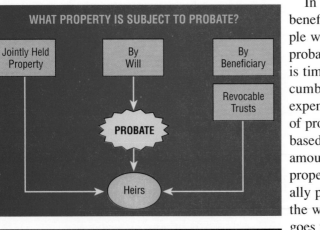

WHAT PROPERTY IS SUBJECT TO PROBATE?

Jointly Held Property

By Will

By Beneficiary

Revocable Trusts

PROBATE

Heirs

probate proceeding. Remember, the entire value of your estate will not necessarily go through probate. Assets that you own under joint tenancy, retirement accounts, life insurance proceeds, and assets held in trust don't go through probate.

So avoiding the probate process requires that you analyze the way your assets will pass and structure your estate so that everything passes outside of your will. The most common way to achieve this objective is the revocable living trust explained below.

LIVING TRUSTS

A living trust makes a lot of sense for people who live in a high–probate-fee state and have a fairly large probate estate (say, $500,000 or more). Also, if you have real estate in another state, a living trust will eliminate probate in that state as well as your home state. In addition to avoiding the expense and time delays of probate, living trusts (unlike wills) can also provide for the orderly management and distribution of your assets if you become incapacitated or incompetent.

There are a few disadvantages to setting up a living trust. For one, you must change the title on all real estate, securities, and other assets from your name to the name of your trust. This does take time, and there might be fees involved with real estate.

Remember, a living trust does not eliminate the need for a will. A will names a guardian for minor children and disposes of personal property. It should also have a "pour-over" provision to transfer any assets outside the trust to the living trust at your death; otherwise, those assets will end up in probate.

One disadvantage of

Figure 24–3	Living Trusts
Revocable	**Irrevocable**
Can be revoked/amended	Cannot be revoked
Frequently used to avoid probate on trust assets	Often used to remove insurance from both spouses' estates
During life, income taxed to grantor	
After death, income taxed to beneficiaries or trust	Income usually taxed to beneficiaries or trust
Trust assets included in grantor's estate	Usually excluded from grantor's estate
No gift tax	May be gift tax

living trusts is you will probably pay more for a living trust than a simple will. Whereas drafting a simple will usually costs $200 to $500, a living trust can costs around $750 to $1,000 and can go as high as $3,000 if you include a bypass trust, marital trust, pour-over will, and so on. However, the extra money you spend now can save your beneficiaries a fortune in probate fees in the future.

A living trust can also help avoid the costs of legal guardianship proceedings if you become incapacitated. Without a living trust or the durable power of attorney discussed in Chapter 22, the determination of whether you are incapacitated and who will handle your affairs would be left to a costly court proceeding.

THE ROLE OF THE EXECUTOR

Except for naming a guardian, which we'll discuss next, choosing your executor is probably the most significant decision you'll make when drafting a will. The executor is in charge of taking care of your estate until your assets are distributed. What many executors learn to their dismay is that it is a time-consuming, burdensome process for which they may not be qualified!

Being an executor requires good financial, organizational, and administrative skills. Also, very often good people skills are needed, especially when the heirs start calling with demands for their share of the property. But the most important thing to understand is that an executor is a fiduciary, meaning that there can be significant personal liability if the property is not managed and preserved in the best interest of the heirs. Because of the risks and responsibilities, many people simply hire a professional such as an attorney or bank trust department to help with the probate process.

Your executor is entitled to a fee or commission, which is determined by the laws in each state. Some states let the courts determine these fees, while others base them on the size or complexity of

Table 24–1	Executor's Duties

- Hiring competent professionals (attorneys, accountants)
- Filing the will
- Accounting for assets and liabilities
- Paying debts of the estate
- Making tax elections
- Filing federal and state tax returns
- In general, acting in the best interests of the heirs

your estate. As a rule, these fees come to about 1 to 3 percent of your gross estate. Should you name two people to act as coexecutors, the fees may double. So it's a good idea to ask your estate planning advisor about the rules in your state before you name more than one executor.

If your estate is simple—a home, some cash, and a little stock and insurance, say—it should take less than a year to settle, and your executor will probably encounter few difficulties. So there should be no problem if you choose a financially unsophisticated family member or friend as executor, provided the person is well organized, honest, and responsible. She can probably manage quite well with some help from your attorney or accountant. Many states have adopted simplified probate procedures for small estates, which reduce costs and lessen complexity.

On the other hand, if you think there may be family disagreements over your wishes, it makes sense to name your attorney or some other advisor you trust as co-executor. Moreover, if your estate is large and complex, you should name a professional—a trust company officer or a bank—to act as executor. Then you can add a trusted family member or friend as coexecutor.

It's general practice in writing wills to list a first, second, and third choice for executors. The third choice is usually an institution, such as a bank or trust company. The reason? You choose a third option just in case your first two choices aren't able to fulfill these responsibilities or decline them.

NAMING A GUARDIAN

If you're the parent of minor children, it's critical to name a guardian in your will. Doing so guarantees that your children would have a guardian of your choosing if you and your spouse die simultaneously. It's important, of course, to thoroughly talk over the matter with potential guardians before you finally settle on one. You want someone who's not only able to handle this important responsibility but is also completely willing. If you're unable to decide on a guardian, you may want to designate someone in your will—your executor, perhaps—to name a guardian.

You should also know that if you're divorced, the courts won't honor your choice of guardian as long as you're survived by a former spouse who is the natural parent. That rule holds true even if you have full custody. If you die, your child automatically goes to your former spouse. But what if your spouse predeceases you. In this case, you can make sure that your children have the guardian of your choice—not the court's—by naming that person in your will.

ESTATE PLANNING IS NOT A DO-IT-YOURSELF JOB!

Estate planning can be difficult for several reasons. For one, it's hard for most people to talk about death. And the concepts and terms involved in estate planning are complicated. That's why we highly recommend that you carefully select your trustees, executors, and especially your attorney. Be sure your attorney is someone who specializes in estate planning and someone you can trust. Remember, it's your beneficiaries who benefit from good estate planning so the sooner you start the process, the more they stand to gain.

NOT ALL RETIREMENT PLANS ARE CREATED EQUAL

In planning for retirement, many people enlist the help of accountants, brokers, and other professional advisors to perform retirement income calculations. Also, for the do-it-yourselfers, PC software is available from many organizations (including Price Waterhouse) to help you do retirement calculations and develop your own retirement plan. Retirement planning is one of the hot financial issues of the 1990s, and the marketplace is becoming flooded with retirement planning toolkits, brochures, and other information designed to help you get the job done.

One of this book's goals has been to make it clear that retirement planning is not a one-dimensional activity. Many variables can affect your retirement sufficiency calculation. Some are within your control and some aren't, but be aware that they'll all affect your ultimate retirement position. It is the interplay of savings, investment returns, spending patterns, and many other factors that really determines your ability to meet your goal, not just saving a lot of money and investing it well. Unfortunately, many analyses we see only deal with one or two of these factors—for example, "here is what you should save" or "here is what happens if you invest your money (with me!) and we earn 10 percent." With this point in mind, we offer a some thoughts on what to look for in an analysis prepared by a financial advisor or in some of the retirement planning tools that are so popular these days.

DETERMINING LIFE EXPECTANCY

Many analyses use actuarial tables to project your life expectancy. Keep in mind that these tables are based on historical life expectancies of broad population groups, and thus may be inaccurate when used to project future life expectancies. For example, a commonly used life expectancy table is based on statistics through 1980 so it's already 15 years out of date. Given the medical improvements and greater awareness of health issues we've seen over the past 15 years, it is likely you will outlive the life expectancies shown in that table.

Also, remember that these tables don't recognize the unique circumstances of individuals, including family history and medical conditions. Using these tables may give you a false sense that you have sufficient retirement assets because they show life expectancies in the early 80s, for example. In reality, particularly if you're below age 50, you might easily outlive current life expectancy tables and have insufficient retirement assets in later years because your plan was based on these assumptions. Our recommendation? Regardless of what the tables say, use a life expectancy of at least age 90 in your projections.

INVESTMENT RETURN

Remember that the investment return used in your analysis should vary with changes in your asset allocation based on your time horizon before and after retirement. For example, as you approach retirement, your return expectations should decrease to reflect the rebalancing of your portfolio into lower-risk investments. Many analyses we see are limited to one investment return over both the accumulation and distribution phases of retirement, which can give a false sense of savings accumulation since your investment return is likely to be quite a bit lower after your retirement. This will result in overestimating your retirement assets.

Also, the relationship between investment returns and inflation in your calculation is critical. Your analysis shouldn't overstate the historical relationships between investment returns and long-term inflation rates. Remember that historical returns of 4 to 6 percent over inflation rates have been achievable over the long term if there is a reasonable weighting of investments in equities. Anything higher than this probably means the illustration assumes an overly risky portfolio.

VARIABLE SAVINGS RATE

Your analysis should also recognize that your annual savings amounts may change over time. Many people expect to save more "later"; that is, they think that the closer they get to retirement, the more they can afford to save. Your analysis should take into account variable savings rates in different retirement saving vehicles, like 401(k), IRA, and profit sharing plans.

On the flip side, if your strategy calls for saving more later as you approach retirement, you should challenge the effect this may have on your overall accumulation plan. Often, saving more the last five to seven years before retirement is not enough.

GOAL-BASED PLANNING

Your analysis should have some way of tying your retirement assets to a retirement income goal. Many plans that we see aren't goal-based; they merely show you what future income you can have from your present saving and investment strategies or, worse yet, only what balances you will have in your retirement plans. By establishing a retirement income goal, you can determine whether you may have shortfalls or surpluses.

Perhaps equally important, when you establish a goal, make sure that you consider your current lifestyle as a benchmark. It's unlikely that your retirement income goal will be less than 70 percent of your current income.

Also, if your analysis is goal-based, make sure that you consider the effect a changing goal level may have throughout retirement. Use of a single, level goal is generally inappropriate, as the effect is to often overstate the retirement savings needed. We recommend that you consider a variable goal to reflect the fact that you aren't likely to spend money at the same rate throughout your entire retirement. If your income needs fall in later years of retirement, not using a variable goal will result in overstating the retirement resources needed. If the variable goal increases (say for long-term care), then the retirement resources required will be underestimated.

POST RETIREMENT INCOME OR EXPENSES

Many analyses we see also tend to ignore the fact that you may continue to work in some capacity well into your retirement years, inherit money, or have significant one-time expenses (a retirement home, major purchases, etc.). Not recognizing these in your analysis may lead you to overstate or understate required resources as the case may be.

PRESENT VERSUS FUTURE DOLLARS

Many analyses, particularly in retirement planning software, show all calculations in future dollars without taking into account inflation. As we saw in Chapter 4, we recommend analyzing your retirement in inflation-adjusted dollars so that you can relate it to what you're spending today. Otherwise, you can get a false sense of security because your achievable retirement income will be a large number, perhaps even more than you're spending today!

Also, be careful that your analysis shows pension calculations in today's dollars. It's not uncommon to see future dollar pension illustrations that project pensions of more than a person's current salary!

CONSUMPTION OF PRINCIPAL

Your analysis should also show the effect of different approaches to spending your principal. For example, your retirement plan will look much different if you live off of your income only (passing on the principal to your heirs) than if you plan to die broke after spending all of your resources. Or, what happens if you set aside a reserve (say, 50 percent of your assets) for your heirs and spend the rest? Your analysis should take into account these variables. Many analyses we see do not.

Not coincidentally, the Price Waterhouse Retirement Planning System incorporates all of the above factors and gives you the flexibility to change them and analyze the impact such changes will have on your retirement sufficiency calculation. But this isn't just a commercial. Remember that while some of these aspects are more advanced concepts in understanding retirement needs, they can have a significant effect on your saving and investment strategy. (Recall Chapters 4 through 6 of this book.) So ask your financial advisor to help you model the effects of these different variables, or choose retirement planning tools that have these capabilities. Your retirement plan will be better for it, and so will your peace of mind.

A FINAL THOUGHT

As we bring this book to a close it is fitting that we tie everything together. In our daily reading a recent article by the noted personal finance columnist Humberto Cruz caught our attention. In it he took Stephen Covey's widely acknowledged book *The Seven Habits of Highly Effective People,* adapted the key principles and formed an article entitled *"Habits of Highly Effective Savers."* The following are some of the relevant excerpts from his article which similarly captures some of the essence of our book. We basically have two resources available to us: one is time and the other is money, . . . and the seven habits apply to both. So here is my version of "The Seven Habits of Highly Effective Savers."

- **Begin with the end in mind.** The end, or goal, could be a dream vacation, your first home, a college education for your children, a comfortable retirement for you and your spouse. Whatever it is, know clearly what you want before you draw up your financial plan.
- **Put first things first.** Concentrate on the important, not the urgent. Pay yourself first, by saving something out of every paycheck. Ignore the urgent and often seductive pleas of advertisers intent on selling you instant gratification at the expense of long-term goals.
- **Be proactive.** This means you take charge and assume responsibility for what you do. You choose your response, and do not blame circumstances or other people for your behavior. So you wouldn't say: "I can't save because I need money for new clothes." You would have to say: "I choose to use my money to buy new clothes instead of saving it."

- **Sharpen the saw.** That means taking time out to renew yourself physically, spiritually, mentally, and socially. It also means you do not obsess over money, do not squeeze pennies or any other coins. You enjoy the security money can bring you, but you do not spend every waking moment working, or figuring out ways to add to your worth. Instead, you take time out to enjoy family and friends, to exercise your body and mind, to learn new things, to worship.

If you want the remaining parts of Mr. Cruz's article you can reach him at his e-mail address:HCruz5040aol.com.

Source: Humberto Cruz, "Habits of Highly Effective Savers: These Seven Principles Can Help You Take Control of Your Financial Life," *Chicago Tribune,* Your Money Section, September 15, 1995. Reprinted by permission: Tribune Media Services.

RETIREMENT PLANNING WORKSHEETS

SECTION I
GATHERING THE BASIC INFORMATION

	Husband	Wife
1. Current age	_____	_____
2. Retirement age	_____	_____
3. Life expectancy	_____	_____
4. Years until retirement	_____	_____
5. Years in retirement	_____	_____
6. Current annual income	_____	_____
7. Retirement income replacement ratio	_____	_____
8. Annual retirement income goal (today's $)	_____	_____
9. Estimated Social Security benefits (today's $)	_____	_____
10. Estimated pension income (today's $)	_____	_____
11. Value of investments available to fund retirement	_____	_____

SECTION II
CALCULATING HOW MUCH YOU NEED TO SAVE EACH YEAR
TO MEET YOUR RETIREMENT GOAL

	Husband	**Wife**
1. Annual retirement income goal (today's $)	_____	_____
2. Estimated Social Security benefits (today's $)	_____	_____
3. Estimated pension income (today's $)	_____	_____
4. Income needed from investments (today's $) (Line 1 − Line 2 − Line 3)	_____	_____
5. Income needed from investments at retirement (Line 4 × factor from Table A–1) Factor: _____	_____	_____
6. Capital needed to fund income from investments (Line 5 × factor from Table A–2) Factor: _____	_____	_____
7. Income needed to maintain purchasing power of pension (Line 3 × factor from Table A–1) Factor: _____	_____	_____
8. Capital needed to fund income to maintain purchasing power of pension (Line 7 × factor from Table A–3) Factor: _____	_____	_____

	Husband	**Wife**

9. Total capital required at start of
   retirement (future $)   _____   _____
   (Line 6 + Line 8)

10. Value (in today's $) of investments
    available to fund retirement (401(k),
    IRA, profit sharing, deferred
    compensation, and personal
    investments)   _____   _____

11. Value of investments at retirement
    (future $)   _____   _____
    (Line 10 × factor from Table A–4)
    Factor: _____

12. Write in amount from Line 9.   _____   _____
    If Line 11 is greater than Line 12, you do not need to save any
    more for retirement. If Line 12 is greater than Line 11, enter the
    difference between the two on Line 13.

13. Additional capital needed at
    retirement (future $)   _____   _____
    (Line 12 − Line 11)

14. Additional capital needed at
    retirement (today's $)   _____   _____
    (Line 13 divided by factor from Table A–4)
    Factor: _____

15. Required annual savings (today's $)   _____   _____
    (Line 14 × factor from Table A–6)
    Factor: _____
    Each year, to maintain the constant purchasing power of the
    amount you save, this should be increased by 4 percent.

16. Required annual savings next year   _____   _____
    (Line 15 × 1.04)

Table A–1   Inflation Factor

Years to Retirement	Factor
1	1.04
2	1.08
3	1.12
4	1.17
5	1.22
6	1.27
7	1.32
8	1.37
9	1.42
10	1.48
11	1.54
12	1.60
13	1.67
14	1.73
15	1.80
16	1.87
17	1.95
18	2.03
19	2.11
20	2.19
21	2.28
22	2.37
23	2.46
24	2.56
25	2.67
26	2.77
27	2.88
28	3.00
29	3.12
30	3.24

Table A–2

Retirement Period	Investment Return		
	6%	**8%**	**10%**
20 years	16.79	14.31	12.38
25 years	20.08	16.49	13.82
30 years	23.07	18.30	14.93
35 years	25.79	19.79	15.76
40 years	28.26	21.03	16.39

Table A–3

Retirement Period	Investment Return		
	6%	**8%**	**10%**
20 years	4.63	3.70	3.00
25 years	6.53	4.96	3.84
30 years	8.48	6.14	4.56
35 years	10.42	7.21	5.15
40 years	12.31	8.15	5.63

Table A–4

Years to Retire-ment	Investment Return Factor		
	6%	8%	10%
1	1.06	1.08	1.10
2	1.12	1.17	1.21
3	1.19	1.26	1.33
4	1.26	1.36	1.46
5	1.34	1.47	1.61
6	1.42	1.59	1.77
7	1.50	1.71	1.95
8	1.59	1.85	2.14
9	1.69	2.00	2.36
10	1.79	2.16	2.59
11	1.90	2.33	2.85
12	2.01	2.52	3.14
13	2.13	2.72	3.45
14	2.26	2.94	3.80
15	2.40	3.17	4.18
16	2.54	3.43	4.59
17	2.69	3.70	5.05
18	2.85	4.00	5.56
19	3.03	4.32	6.12
20	3.21	4.66	6.73
21	3.40	5.03	7.40
22	3.60	5.44	8.14
23	3.82	5.87	8.95
24	4.05	6.34	9.85
25	4.29	6.85	10.83
26	4.55	7.40	11.92
27	4.82	7.99	13.11
28	5.11	8.63	14.42
29	5.42	9.32	15.86
30	5.74	10.06	17.45

Table A–5

Years to Retire-ment	Present Value Factor		
	6%	8%	10%
1	1.000	1.000	1.000
2	0.535	0.550	0.565
3	0.360	0.374	0.387
4	0.273	0.285	0.299
5	0.220	0.233	0.245
6	0.185	0.197	0.210
7	0.160	0.172	0.185
8	0.142	0.153	0.166
9	0.127	0.139	0.151
10	0.115	0.127	0.140
11	0.106	0.118	0.130
12	0.098	0.110	0.122
13	0.091	0.103	0.116
14	0.085	0.097	0.110
15	0.080	0.092	0.105
16	0.076	0.088	0.101
17	0.072	0.084	0.098
18	0.067	0.081	0.094
19	0.066	0.078	0.092
20	0.063	0.075	0.089
21	0.061	0.073	0.087
22	0.058	0.071	0.085
23	0.056	0.069	0.083
24	0.054	0.067	0.081
25	0.053	0.065	0.080
26	0.051	0.064	0.078
27	0.050	0.063	0.077
28	0.048	0.061	0.076
29	0.047	0.060	0.075
30	0.046	0.059	0.074

Reflects 4 percent annual increase to keep pace with inflation.

INDEX

A

Aging
  healthy behaviors and, 21-29
  theories of, 24
American Association of Homes for the Aging
  (AAHA), 282
American Association of Retired Persons (AARP),
  16, 38, 39, 271, 280
American depository receipts (ADRs), 181
American Health Care Association, 274
American Stock Exchange (AMEX), 179
American Telephone & Telegraph, 178
Annuities, 50, 69, 71
  See also Insurance
  distributions from, 231-237
  joint-and-survivor (J&S), 99, 231
  single-life, 99, 231
  as a tax-deferred option, 123-124
  tax-sheltered, 105
Apple Computer, 38
Asset allocation, 187-188, 216
  the concept of suballocation in, 192-195
  defining, 190
  and diversification, 150-151
  model, 192
  rebalancing in, 195
  strategic, 188-190
  what determines the appropriate, 190-191
Asset allocation funds, 204
Atchley, Robert, 12

B

Back-end loads, 207-208
Bailard, Biehl & Kaiser (B,B&K), 150

Balanced funds, 204
Bequests, general and specific, 292
Binder, 234
Bird, Caroline, 16, 19, 38
BLOC Publishing, 293
Bolles, Richard Nelson, 36, 39
Bond funds, 203-204
Bond laddering, 164
Bonds. *See* Fixed-income investments
Buck Consultants, 226
Business and Health, 264
Business Week, 206

C

Capital gains, 126-127, 129-132
Capital sufficiency analysis, 6
Career average plan, 98
Cash and cash equivalent investments, 144, 150,
  155-160
Caterpillar Tractor, 181
CDA/Wiesenberger, 206
Certificates of deposit (CDs), 158-159
Chapman, Elwood, 19, 38
Citicorp, 181
Coca-Cola, 178, 181
Columbia Retirement Handbook, 33
Company retirement plans, 95-96
  contributions to, *See* Contributions
  defined benefit, *See* Defined benefit plans
  defined contribution, *See* Defined contribution
    plans
  employee stock ownership, *See* Employee stock
    ownership plans (ESOPs)
  401(k), *See* 401(k) plans

Company retirement plans—*Cont.*
  403(b), *See* 403(b) plans
  money purchase, *See* Money purchase plans
  pensions and, *See* Pensions
  profit-sharing, *See* Profit-sharing plans
  savings for, *See* Savings
Compaq, 179
Conner, J. Robert, 37, 38
Consolidated Omnibus Budget Reconciliation Act
    (COBRA), 226, 227
Consumer Information Center, 289
Continuing care retirement communities (CCRCs),
    280-282
Contributions
  calculating employer, 104
  deducting IRA, 116-119
  IRS caps on, to defined contribution plans, 105
  limits on, to 401(k) plans, 114-115
  the value of matching, 112-114
Contributory plans, 96
Convertible bonds, 172
Corporate bonds, 169-170
Cost-of-living adjustments (COLAs), 71
  pension plans and, 101-102
  Social Security and, 88
Coupon rate, 160
Crummey provisions, 312

D

Deferred compensation, 114
Defined benefit plans, 96-97
  versus defined contribution plans, 102
  how pension formulas work in, 98-99
Defined contribution plans, 103
  versus defined benefit plans, 102
  IRS caps on, 105
  why, are so popular, 106-107
Dennis, Helen, 11n, 21n, 31n
Determinants of Portfolio Performance II, 189
de Vries, Herbert A., 27
DFA Small Company 9/10 US Index, 194
Distributions
  annuity, 231-237
  individual retirement account (IRA), 249
    excise taxes on, 255-256, 315
    income taxes on, 250
    penalty taxes on, 250-255
    state taxes on, 256
    tax payments on, 257-259
  introduction to evaluating pension, 229-230
  lump sum, *See* Lump sum distribution
Diversification, 201
  asset allocation and, 150-151
  three levels of, 152-153
Double tax-exempt funds, 203
Dow Chemical, 178

Drexel Burnham Lambert, 170
Drucker, Peter, 32
Du Pont, 178

E

Efficient frontier, 191
Elderhostel, 17
Employee stock ownership plans (ESOPs), 103, 105
Employee thrift plans, 103
Employment. See Work
Equities
  characteristics of, 145, 174-175
  risks of investing in, 175-177
  the role of, in a portfolio, 173-174
  types of, 144, 150, 177-182
Estate administration. *See also* Estate planning
  introduction to, and probate, 317-319
  living trusts and, 319-320
  naming a guardian as part of, 321-322
  the role of executor in, 320-321
Estate planning. *See also* Estate administration
  anatomical gifts and, 289-290
  beneficiary designations in, 296, 308
  determining personal objectives in, 286-288
  introduction to the fundamentals of, 285-286
  life insurance and, 298-300
  living wills and, 288-289
  and Medicaid, 276
  power of attorney in, 289, 290
  property ownership and, 293-298
  reducing the value of an estate through, 311-312
  for a single person, 315-316
  software packages for preparing wills in, 293
  taxes and, 301, 304-306
    calculating, 306-307
    excise, 315
    federal estate and gift, 302
    state, 316
  techniques for, 307-315
  trusts in, *See* Trusts
  who should consider, 302-304
  wills and why they are necessary in, 290-293
Executor, 292, 320-321
Exxon, 181

F

Factor, defining a pension formula, 98
Fannie Mae, 167, 168
Federal Deposit Insurance Corporation (FDIC), 120,
    157, 158
Federal Home Loan Mortgage Corporation
    (FHLMC), 167, 168
Federal Housing Administration (FHA), 167, 168
Federal National Mortgage Association (FNMA),
    167, 168
Federal Reserve Bank, 159, 166, 171

Fees, mutual fund, 206-210
Final average plan, 98
Financial Analysts Journal, 189
Financial goals. *See also* Retirement
  the importance of understanding your, 55
  investing and, *See* Investments
  key elements to reaching retirement, 54
  planning and, *See* Financial planning
  setting, 57
    and assessing when to retire, 63
    by determining how spending in retirement will
      change, 62-63
    by determining retirement spending, 59-62
    and estimating life expectancy, 64
    and the impact of inflation, 58-59
Financial planning. *See also* Asset allocation; Estate
  planning; Retirement
  and the cost of retirement, 46-49
  financial goals and, *See* Financial goals
  income for, *See* Income
  introduction to the process of, 43-45
  investing and, *See* Investments
  a philosophy for, 53-54
  savings and, *See* Savings
  using the concept of variable goal in, 60, 61, 63
  weaknesses in conventional retirement analysis
    and, 46
Fixed-income investments, 155-156
  characteristics of, 145
  risk and, 162-166
  the role of, in a retirement portfolio, 160-162
  types of, 144, 150, 166-172
Forbes, 179, 206
Forty Plus, 39
Forward averaging, 242-243
401(k) plans, 103, 104, 111
  borrowing from, 113
  limits on contributions to, 114-115
  reasons to participate in, 112-115
403(b) plans, 105
Frank Russell NCREIF Index, 194
Freddie Mac, 167, 168
Front-end loads, 207, 208

G

General Electric, 178
General Mills, 178
General obligation bonds, 169
Gillette, 181
Ginnie Mae, 167, 168
Government agency securities, 167
Government National Mortgage Association
  (GNMA), 167, 168
Guide to Health Insurance for People with Medicare,
  270

H

Hard assets, 144, 145, 150, 182-185
Harty, Karen Kerstra, 19, 38
Health Care Financing Administration, 280
Healthcare proxy, 289
Health Insurance Association of America, 275
Hedging, 182
Hewitt Associates LLC, 101
High-yield bonds, 170

I

Income
  converting investment balances into annual, 75-77
  example of analyzing sources of, 49-53
  investing, *See* Investments
  key elements to achieving retirement, 54
  relationship between current, and retirement, 59
  saving, *See* Savings
  sources of retirement, 65-66
    employment. *See* Work
    inheritance, 73-74, 136-137
    insurance. *See* Insurance
    other, 125
    retirement plans. *See* Company retirement plans;
      Pensions
    reverse mortgage, 134-135
    sale of home, 74-75, 126-127, 129-134
    Social Security benefits. *See* Social Security
Individual retirement account (IRA), 111
  the allowable types of transfers for an, 121
  borrowing from an, 122
  deducting contributions to an, 116-119
  determining whether to invest in an, 115-116
  distributions from an, *See* Distributions
  investment vehicles for an, 120-121
  putting an, in perspective, 122-123
  setting up more than one, 119-120
  switching from one investment to another in an,
    121-122
Inflation, 58-59, 101-102
  See also Cost-of-living adjustments (COLAs)
Inheritance, 73-74, 136-137
Insurance. *See also* Annuities
  life,
    and employee benefits, 305-306
    and estate planning, 298-300
    as a source of retirement income, 135-136
    removing the proceeds of, from an estate, 312
    second-to-die, 315
    using benefits from, during your lifetime, 281
  long-term care, 276-280
Intel, 179
International funds, 204-205
Intestate, 290
Investment Company Act of 1940, 200
Investment life cycle, 143, 192

Investments. *See also* Company retirement plans
  asset allocation of, *See* Asset allocation
  cash and cash equivalent, 144, 150, 155-160
  diversification of, *See* Diversification
  the effect of the time horizon on, 147-149
  equity, *See* Equities
  fixed-income, *See* Fixed-income investments
  four broad categories of, 144-145
  hard assets as, 144, 145, 150, 182-185
  implementing strategies for, 197-198
  the importance of making sound, 141-144
  income and, *See* Income
  mutual fund, *See* Mutual funds
  risks that affect, *See* Risk
  savings for, *See* Savings
  understanding the volatility of, 145-147
  withdrawals from, *See* Distributions
IRA. *See* Individual retirement account (IRA)
ITT, 178

J

Junk bond, 170

L

Lehman Brothers 1—3-year Short-Term Government
  Bond Index, 194
Levine, Mark, 33
Life insurance. *See* Insurance
Long-term care
  cost of, 274-275
  insurance for, 276-280
  introduction to, 273-274
  Medicaid and, 275-276
  other options for, 280-282
Low-load funds, 207
Lump sum distribution, 69-70, 71, 230, 239
  choosing an annuity versus a, 235-237
  determining which option to elect for a, 244-248
  and the excess distribution tax, 248
  flexibility of a, 240
  paying taxes on a, 240-241, 242-244
  using the rollover IRA option in a, 241-242

M

Market timers, 176
MECA, 293
Medicaid, 275-276
Medicaid Qualifying Trust (MQT), 276
Medicare, 82, 269, 274
  applying for, 266-267
  coverage under, 266, 267
  doctors and, 268
  waiting to enroll in, 270
  where to learn more about, 270-271
Medicare Handbook, The, 268

*Medicare Participating Physicians/Suppliers
  Directory,* 268
Medigap, 269-270
Menchin, Robert S., 39
Merck, 178
Merrill, Fred, 38
Merrill Lynch, 5
Microsoft, 179
Midwest Exchange, 179
Modern capital market theory, 188-189
Modern Maturity, 16
Modified endowment contract (MEC), 136
Money, 206
Money managers, 213-216
Money market accounts, 157-158
Money market funds, 157-158, 202-203
Money purchase plans, 103, 104-105
Moody's Investor Services, 165, 166, 203
Morgan Stanley Europe, Australia, Far East Index,
  194
Morningstar, 206
Morningstar, Inc., 208, 212-213
Morningstar Mutual Funds, 212
Mortality experience, 100
Mortgage-backed securities, 168
  See also Government agency securities
Municipal bonds, 168-169
Mutual Fund Report, 206
Mutual funds
  advantages of, 200-202
  defining closed-end, 199, 200
  defining open-end, 199-200
  evaluating individual, 205-206
  fees of, 206-210
  index funds as an option in, 210-213
  introduction to investing with, 198-200
  as part of a fund family, 210
  types of, 202-205
  utilizing money managers of, 213-216

N

National Association of Insurance Commissioners,
  269, 280
National Association of Security Dealers Automated
  Quotation (NASDAQ), 179
National Council on the Aging, 39
Net asset value per share, 200
New York Stock Exchange (NYSE), 179
New York Times, 36
Nike, 17
No-load funds, 208-209
Nolo Press, 293

O

Oil and gas, investing in, 184-185
Operation ABLE, 39

Oppenheimer Funds, 126
Over-the-counter (OTC) market, 179

P

Pacific Exchange, 179
Parsons Technology, 293
Par value, 162
Patient Self-Determination Act of 1990, 288
Pension Benefit Guaranty Corporation (PBGC), 97
Pension indexing, 70-71
Pension maximization strategy (pension max), 233-234
Pensions. *See also* Company retirement plans
    early retirement reductions from, 99-100
    estimates of benefits from, 101
    how formulas for, work, 98-99
    income choices from, 68-71
    indexing, for inflation, 101-102
    and life expectancy, 100
    the problem of underfunded, 97
    types of, *See* Company retirement plans
    withdrawals from, *See* Distributions
Philadelphia Exchange, 179
Pollan, Stephan M., 33
Power of attorney
    durable, for healthcare, 289
    general, 290
Precious metals, investing in, 185
PREP, 18
Price Waterhouse Retirement Planning System (RPS), 77
Probate. *See* Estate administration
Profit-sharing plans, 103-104

R

Real estate, 183-184
Real estate investment trusts (REITs), 184
Rebalancing, 149, 195
Residual estate, 292
Retirement. *See also* Company retirement plans;
        Estate administration; Estate planning
    change as part of the process of, 12-13
    the changing face of, 32-33
    determining the right age for, 63
    evaluating offers for early, 221-227
    financial goals for, *See* Financial goals
    financial planning for, *See* Financial planning
    health during, *See* Aging
    how long to plan for, 64
    income sources for, *See* Income
    introduction to planning for, 1-8
    investing for, *See* Investments
    long-term care and paying for it in, *See* Long-term care
    medical coverage during, 263-271
    personal identity and relationships in, 15-20

preparing for, 11-12
relocation issues and, 127, 129
saving for, *See* Savings
three broad phases of, 62-63
work and, *See* Work
Retirement Planning for Women, 18
Return
    historical, 194
    real rate of, 149-150
    the relationship of risk and, 145-147
    variable rates of, 149 Revenue bonds, 169
Reverse mortgages, 134-135
Rider, 234
Risk
    business, 177
    credit, 165-166, 177
    currency, 182, 205
    interest-rate, 162-165
    life expectancy, 100, 106-107
    market, 175-177
    political, 205
    prepayment, 167
    purchasing power, 149-150
    reducing, 151-152, 163-165
    the relationship of, and return, 145-147
    types of, 151
Russell 2000 Index, 211

S

Savings, 52, 77
    See also Company retirement plans; Income;
        Investment(s)
    benefits of tax-deferred, 110-111
    determining how much to put into, 77
    financial planning and, *See* Financial planning
    in a 401(k) plan. *See* 401(k) plans
    introduction to tax-deferred, 109-110
    investing, in annuities. *See* Annuities
    in an IRA. *See* Individual retirement account
        (IRA)
    rate of, needed to achieve goals for retirement, 5-6
    types of qualified or tax-favored plans for, 118
    where to invest, 111-112
Secondary payor, 270
Securities and Exchange Commission (SEC), 158,
        200, 210, 215
Sharpe, William F., 190
Social Security, 50, 66-68
    additional information about, 92-93
    applying for benefits from, 88, 89
    calculating how long to recoup taxes from, 83-84
    causes of the problems with, 82
    collecting benefits from, 88-89
    cost-of-living adjustments to, 88
    determining what you will receive from, 86-87
    early retirement and, 92

Social Security—*Cont.*
  earnings and benefits from, 85-86
  earnings limitations and, 90-92, 93
  overview of, 81-83
  proposals for resolving pending deficits with, 82
  taxes and, 91
Social Security Act of 1935, 81
Social Security Administration, 85, 92-93, 266
Standard & Poor's, 165, 203
Standard & Poor's 500 (S&P 500) composite index,
  150, 151, 176, 177, 178, 201, 211
Standard deviation, 146, 194
Stock bonus plans, 103
Stock funds, 204
Stocks. *See also* Equities
  aggressive growth, 179
  blue chip, 178
  common, 174-175
  growth, 178-179
  growth and income, 178
  income, 178
  international, 180182
  risks of investing in, 175-177
  widow-and-orphan, 178
Summary Plan Description (SPD), 100
Sweetheart will, 309
Sybar Software, 293

T

Tax(es). *See also under specific investment or
    specific retirement plan*
  distributions and, *See* Distributions
  estate planning and, *See* Estate planning
  head, 97
  pick-up, 316
  relocation issues and, 127, 129
  and the sale of a principal residence, 126-127,
    129-134
  savings and, *See* Savings
  and Social Security, 91
Tax Reform Act of 1986, 184
Term certain option, 232
Testator, 292
Time horizon, 147-149, 191, 216
Towers Perrin, 5
Treasury bills (T-bills), 156, 159-160
Treasury securities, 166
Trusts, 296
  bypass, 310, 311, 314
  credit shelter, 310, 314

  irrevocable insurance, 312
  living, 319-320
  qualified terminable interest property (QTIP), 310,
    311, 314
  real estate investment, (REITs), 184
  types of, 297-298

U

Unified credit equivalent, 302, 303
U.S. Department of Agriculture, 28
U.S. Department of Health and Human Services
    (HHS), 28, 266
U.S. Department of Labor, 115
U.S. savings bonds, 171
U.S. Treasury bills (T-bills), 156, 159-160
U.S. Treasury securities, 166
University of Michigan, 32
University of Southern California, 27

V

Vanguard Index Extended Market Portfolio, 213
Vanguard Index Trust 500 Portfolio, 212
Vesting schedule, 113-114
Veterans Administration (VA), 167, 168
Volatility, understanding investment, 145-147

W

What Color Is Your Parachute, 36
Wills. *See* Estate planning
Wilshire 5000 Index, 211
Wilshire 4500 Index, 213
Wilshire MidCap 750 Index, 194
Work
  assessing what kind of, to do in retirement, 35-38
  choosing to, in retirement, 31-33
  the marginal value of continuing to, 223-224
  reasons to, in retirement, 33-35
  as a source of income in retirement, 71-73, 126
  transition from, to retirement, 13-15
Wrap accounts, 214-216
Wyatt survey, 264
Wyman, Jack, 39

Y

Yield, current, 162
Yield curve, inverted, 164-165
Yield to maturity, 162

Z

Zero-coupon bonds (zeros), 170-172

SECURE YOUR future

Do you have a financial plan?

If so, is it up-to-date?

Don't reach for the aspirin. Financial planning does not have to be a headache, and you don't have to have a lot of money to have a plan.

The process just got easier with financial planning tools from Price Waterhouse.

All of our goals are different. We need personalized planning from someone who is unbiased and objective. Price Waterhouse does not sell investments, and is not affiliated with anyone that does. Financial planning is provided to help you determine, clarify, and reach your financial goals. All information is kept strictly confidential and is not released to anyone else for any reason.

Our tools are designed to help you answer what most consider to be the three most important questions in financial planning: What do I want? What do I have? What do I need to do?

We will tell you where you are in relation to your goals; but, more important, we will provide you with strategies and recommendations to help you achieve your goals. Unbiased, objective guidance from experienced financial and investment advisers.

A suite of financial planning products that address **your** goals and **your** situation...

Personal Financial Analysis

Designed for all ages, this analysis gives you a comprehensive look at your overall financial picture. If you have a variety of financial concerns and are in need of a broad financial plan with recommendations, this may be the analysis of choice. This analysis examines your family's goals and resources relating to: Retirement Funding, Investment Strategies, Social Security, Education Planning, Disability and Life Insurance Needs, and Estate Planning.

The *Personal Financial Analysis* is a 50-60 page, easy-to-read report. This personalized analysis addresses your goals and provides you with an action plan to achieve them. The analysis comes complete with reference material and is available for $275.

Too comprehensive? Perhaps your interests are more focused on education or retirement. Not to worry! We also have more targeted, single-topic analyses available.

Education Funding Analysis

For those who wish to focus strictly on education funding (and have no need of the comprehensive analysis), we have developed the *Education Funding Analysis*. This 10-12 page, easy-to-read, color report examines your education goals and resources. The analyses comes complete with reference material and provides you with savings and investment strategies for meeting education goals. The *Education Funding Analysis* is available for $60.

Retirement Planning Analysis

The *Retirement Planning Analysis* is designed for those within 10 years of retirement. It contains an analysis of your situation and recommendations of important issues related to retirement planning, including: Retirement Funding and Distributions, Social Security, Investment Strategies, and Estate Planning.

This 35-40 page personalized analysis is easy-to-read and comes complete with strategies and recommendations to help you reach your retirement goals. The *Retirement Planning Analysis* is available for $185.

Retirement Funding Analysis

If you are more than 10 years from retirement and would like to focus only on your retirement goals, the *Retirement Funding Analysis* is designed for you. This 10-12 page color report examines your current retirement resources, what they may be worth when you plan to retire, and provides you with savings and investment strategies to achieve your retirement objectives. The *Retirement Funding Analysis* is available for $60.

Our financial planning tools are not limited to paper based reports. Price Waterhouse also makes it possible for you to modify your analysis with interactive software. Play what-if scenarios with a software package that allows you to instantly see the implications of even the smallest modification to your financial plan.

Education Planner: The Education Funding System

The *Education Funding System* (EFS) makes it easy for you to focus on your children's college expenses and start planning with specific goals in mind. EFS enables you to set up separate funds for up to five children or create a special family fund. Then, you can see at a glance how you can improve your saving and investment strategy to achieve your education funding goals. Available in Windows or DOS, the Education Planner is $45.

Retire Secure: The Retirement Planning System

If you're wondering whether your current savings will be enough to support your retirement lifestyle, the *Retirement Planning System* (RPS) can answer your questions quickly and easily. RPS helps you set clear retirement goals and then lets you understand the simple, yet significant, implications of variable goals, savings and investment returns, inflation, life expectancy, and much more. Available in Windows or DOS, Retire Secure is $45.

Survivor Secure: The Survivor Income Planning System

The *Survivor Income Planning System* allows you, with little understanding of the complexities of survivor income planning, to: set goals, understand the value of available resources, and develop strategies to ensure the financial security for those financially dependent upon you. Available in Windows, Survivor Secure is $45.

The decision is yours. The first step to securing your future is having a plan. It's within your reach. Sign-up for the option(s) of your choice and allow the professionals at Price Waterhouse to guide you through the process. If you need assistance in selecting the right option, completing the questionnaire, understanding the results, or operating the software, Price Waterhouse representatives are waiting to take your call.

1-800-752-6234

Monday through Friday
8:30 a.m. - 5:30 p.m. central time

Price Waterhouse LLP

Retirement and Financial Education Group